CW01022450

RESPONSES TO TERR

Why do responses to terrorist attacks often perpetuate cycles of deadly violence? Can an understanding of the psychology of these cycles help us to break them?

Drawing on clinical experience of the care of people and communities affected by violence and disasters and on advances in cognitive and dynamic psychology, attachment theory, group psychology and thanatology, this ground-breaking work by a prominent and varied array of contributors casts light on the causes of terrorism, the reasons why responses to deadly attacks easily give rise to or maintain cycles of violence, and some ways to prevent and interrupt these cycles.

Using the violence in Northern Ireland and Rwanda as case studies throughout, Part I, The context of terrorism, looks at the psychological and social influences behind extremism, terrorism and conflict. Part II, Reponses to a terrorist attack, examines the responses that can feed a cycle of violence and assesses a range of approaches for their success in ending violence. Part III, Breaking the cycle, looks in depth at specific environments, influences and changes that can affect how violence can be prevented or mitigated, including the role of schools and the media and an examination of how peace processes were carried out in Northern Ireland and Rwanda. The book works to demonstrate how psychological responses to a terror attack can trigger unstable emotional responses and override judgement and to identify the five key points in a cycle of violence where change, for better or for worse, is possible.

Of special interest to politicians, diplomats, military, media, psychiatrists, thanatologists, palliative care and bereavement staff as well as anyone with an interest in terrorism and its causes, this is a thought-provoking and accessible work on a highly topical subject.

Colin Murray Parkes, OBE, pioneered development of psychological support for families facing the death of a family member. His recent work has focused on traumatic bereavements with special reference to violent deaths, armed conflict and the cycle of violence. He is the author of two previous books: *Bereavement: Studies of grief in adult life* and *Love and Loss: The roots of grief and its complications*.

RESPONSES TO TERRORISM

Can psychosocial approaches break
the cycle of violence?

Edited by
Colin Murray Parkes

The Clemens Nathan Research Centre

Routledge
Taylor & Francis Group

LONDON AND NEW YORK

First published 2014
by Routledge
27 Church Road, Hove, East Sussex, BN3 2FA

and by Routledge
711 Third Avenue, New York, NY 10017

Routledge is an imprint of the Taylor & Francis Group, an informa business

British Library Cataloguing in Publication Data
A catalogue record for this book is available from the British Library

Library of Congress Cataloging in Publication Data
Responses to terrorism : can psychosocial approaches break the cycle
of violence? / edited by Colin Murray Parkes.
pages cm
1. Terrorism. 2. Terrorism–Psychological aspects. 3. Terrorism–Prevention.
4. Disasters–Psychological aspects. 5. Post-traumatic stress disorder. I. Parkes,
Colin Murray.
HV6431.R468 2014
363.325'17–dc23
2013030916

ISBN: 978-0-415-68855-0 (hbk)
ISBN: 978-0-415-70624-7 (pbk)
ISBN: 978-1-315-87983-3 (ebk)

Typeset in Times New Roman
by Cenveo Publisher Services

MIX
Paper from
responsible sources
FSC
www.fsc.org   FSC® C013604

Printed and bound by CPI Group (UK) Ltd, Croydon, CR0 4YY

In memory of the late Professor Hugh Freeman,
FRCPsych., FFPHH, former Professor of Psychiatry,
Honorary Visiting Fellow, Green College, Oxford University,
an active member of the Clemens Nathan Research Centre,
and past Editor of the *British Journal of Psychiatry.*

He originated the idea of this research project and chaired
the planning group which culminated in this publication.
His death, shortly after the plan was approved for publication
by Routledge, was a great loss to us all.

CONTENTS

CONTENTS

CONTRIBUTORS

David Abrahamson, MBE, FRCPsych, Consultant Psychiatrist.

John, Lord Alderdice, MB, BCh, FRCPsych, Retired Consultant Psychiatrist; former Senior Lecturer, Queen's University, Belfast; former Leader of the Alliance Party, Member (MLA) and Speaker of the Northern Ireland Assembly; and former Commissioner of the Independent Monitoring Commission (IMC, Northern Ireland). Currently Convenor (Chair) of the Liberal Democrat Parliamentary Party in the House of Lords and Senior Research Fellow, Harris Manchester College, University of Oxford.

Berthold P.R. Gersons, MD, PhD, Professor of Psychiatry, Academic Medical Centre, University of Amsterdam. President of European Society for Traumatic Stress Studies. Adviser on counter-terrorism to the Dutch government.

Anthony Glees, MA, MPhil, DPhil, Director of Centre for Security and Intelligence Studies (BUCSIS), Buckingham University.

Nora Gribbin, MB, BCh, BAO, MRCPsych, DipCBT (Oxf), Consultant Psychiatrist and Medical Psychotherapist, London. Born in Northern Ireland, Roman Catholic. Author of the paper 'Historical Reflections on the Northern Ireland Conflict' delivered at the international conference 'Conflict mental health and making the peace', 12 and 13 May 2008, hosted by Institute of Psychiatry.

Pater Hall, MB, BS, MRCPI, DGM, Chair of Doctors for Human Rights. Led a team into Rwanda after the genocidal massacres.

Clemens M. Nathan, First Chairman, Clemens Nathan Research Centre for the Study of Human Rights with particular reference to genocide.

Mirjam J. Nijdam, MSc, Post-doctoral Research Psychologist, Centre for Psychological Trauma, University of Amsterdam.

Colin Murray Parkes, OBE, MD, FRCPsych, LLD. Consultant Psychiatrist Emeritus to St Christopher's Hospice, Life President of Cruse Bereavement Care, researcher and author of books and articles on bereavement, attachments and disasters. Consultant to the Trauma Recovery Programme in Rwanda.

Jenny Parkes, PhD, Educational Psychologist, Reader, Institute of Education, London University. Researcher and author of papers on the magnet of violence in childhood. Editor of forthcoming *Gender Violence in Poverty Contexts: The educational challenge*.

Brian Rowan, journalist, author and broadcaster. Four times a category winner in the Northern Ireland journalist-of-the-year awards. Formerly BBC Security Editor in Belfast and now contributes regularly to the *Belfast Telegraph* and *UTV live*. Author of *How the Peace was Won*.

Rodney Turtle, BSc (Hons), MBA, MIMechE, CEng, MCIM, President of BEAMA the trade association for the UK's electro technical industry. Born in Northern Ireland, Protestant. Partner to Nora Gribbin.

FOREWORD

Clemens M. Nathan

From the very earliest times of the Biblical zealots to the Kamikaze suicide bombers, people have been manipulating others (including children) to carry out acts of terrorism. The range of examples is incredibly large and includes some who maintain that they were 'freedom fighters'.

MI5 stated some time ago that they were monitoring over 2000 potential terrorists and 200 organisations in the United Kingdom, and they found that these organisations had very little in common. There is no actual definition of a terrorist which has been universally accepted, but perhaps some individual cultural and psychological factors can help us to understand this better. There are so many layers and cross-currents with which one is confronted that this is not at all easy. The 9/11 disaster brought home the need for some form of disengagement from terrorism, if possible, and generated a great number of studies, a few of which focussed on psychological issues. The Clemens Nathan Research Centre holds many public meetings on human rights and related subjects, and Professor Hugh Freeman was an enthusiastic supporter. He approached me after one meeting on Terrorism & Human Rights at which Lord Guthrie (former Chief of the Defence Staff) was the keynote speaker, among other outstanding people. Freeman proposed that he chair a small group of eminent psychiatrists and others to discuss the psychological aspects of terrorism. I was enthusiastic, knowing that he was an outstanding psychiatrist, having been a past editor of the *British Journal of Psychiatry*.

The group was set up at Professor Freeman's home, and many people presented papers examining different root causes of terrorism and studies of its psychological consequences. We found that there could be no simple answers from a psychological point of view, but an outline of a possible book emerged that might clarify some of the issues.

The group identified a list of possible contributors, most of them psychiatrists, with a special interest in this field, and organised a weekend meeting at Ditchley Park at which seven of the contributors presented outlines for discussion (in addition there were written contributions from two who were not able to attend). They appointed Freeman and Parkes to firm up the plan for the book.

We hope that this volume will enable people to become aware of some of the complexities which have confronted us all for a long time and maybe clarify a few of the important attitudes of the terrorists and those who have suffered at their hands.

The Clemens Nathan Research Centre was established as the research arm of the Consultative Council of Jewish Organisations. The eminent human rights pioneer, the late René Cassin – a Nobel Prize lawyer and a principal drafter of the UN Declaration of Human Rights, was its first chairman. The writer is the joint chairman, with Professor A. Steg, of this organisation, which is now a non-governmental organisation accredited to the United Nations. Since its establishment, the centre has initiated a number of projects in association with other organisations, and alone, including a long-term research project on collaboration with the International Bar Association and the Raoul Wallenberg Institute at the University of Lund, Sweden, to formulate rules of conduct for human rights fact-finding missions. It has also held major conferences on 'Does God Believe in Human Rights?', 'Racism & Human Rights', 'Terrorism & Human Rights', 'Foreign Policy & Human Rights' (CNRC, 2007), 'International Development & Foreign Policy' (CNRC, 2008), 'Reparations for Victims of Human Rights Abuses and Prosthetic Services' (CNRC, 2009a), 'Media & Human Rights' (CNRC, 2009b), and 'Health & Human Rights'. The CNRC also organises the René Cassin Memorial Lectures.

The aim of all these proceedings has been to publish them so that the fruits of our labour are available to a wider audience and to propagate the late René Cassin's spirit to help make people more aware of what needs to be done in the field of human rights.

It is with deep sadness that we report that Professor Hugh Freeman died before the completion of this work, and we have all agreed that this book should be dedicated to his memory. We are also extremely grateful to Dr Colin Murray Parkes, who took over the editing of the book and to all the outstanding people who have worked hard to make it a reality, and we wish to thank them most sincerely for all their efforts.

ACKNOWLEDGEMENTS

History is full of the exploits of warriors whose heroism and self-sacrifice have made us proud. They have deserved our praise. But there is another kind of hero no less deserving of esteem, the men and women of all ages who 'saw the thick planks of peace'. They include the countless witnesses, UN observers, members of non-governmental organisations (NGOs), politicians, civil servants, family liaison officers, counsellors and victims who have striven to bring something good out of the bad consequences of terrorism and the desperate circumstances out of which it arises.

We have met many of them in the course of preparing this book and have been impressed by the selfless devotion with which they quietly get on with the business of clearing the ruins, healing the wounds, cherishing the bereaved, recording the facts, mediating, negotiating, healing, and loving to life those who are dying or trapped in cycles of deadly violence. We met them in Rwanda after the genocide, in Belfast during the Troubles, in New York after 9/11, and in the psychiatric clinics and other caring services where we work.

In particular, we acknowledge the help of the many survivors of the Rwandan genocide who told us their stories; they include Eugenie Mukanohele, Albert Najambe, and the other staff of UNICEF's Trauma Recovery Programme; the staff of the several NGOs in Kigali to whom they introduced us; the staff of the Rwandese Genocide Memorial Museum; and Jean Hatzfeld, along with those who contributed to his three books of verbatim records (2000, 2003, 2007), that ensure that the suffering that took place is recorded and preserved in the hope that it will help us to understand the circumstances wherein an entire ethnic community turned upon, and killed, 800,000 of its fellow citizens.

The chapters on Northern Ireland were facilitated by the full reports of the Saville Enquiry, whose witnesses add much to our understanding of the roots and consequences of terrorism along with numerous other contacts and conversations over many years. John, Lord Alderdice, in addition to contributing two chapters to the book, also gave valuable information and advice about the peace process in Ireland, as well as his address to the General Assembly of the United Nations that is quoted in the concluding chapter.

We have been assisted by the members of the planning committee, notably John Cox, Matthew Polden, Nathaniel Minton, Cesare Sacerdoti, Elizabeth Sydney and Graham Howes. Fleur Sandler prepared a valuable transcript and report of the Ditchley Conference.

Thanks, also to the *Belfast Telegraph* for permission to quote, on pages, 172 & 183, from their article published on 20 April, 1972, and to Telegraph Media Group Limited for permission to quote, on pages 210, 361–3 and 368, from 'Rwanda's Redeemer or Ruthless Dictator' by Richard Grant, published in *The Telegraph* on 22 July, 2010.

Finally, we are grateful to Clemens Nathan and the late Hugh Freeman without whom this work would never have come about. Clemens initiated the research centre and funded the Ditchley Conference which brought us together, and Hugh set up and chaired the planning committee in the hospitality of his home and helped us to hammer out the structure and authorship of the book.

INTRODUCTION

Colin Murray Parkes

Terrorism is a tactic of the weak aimed at exploiting chinks in the armor of the more powerful.

(Cronin 2009, p. 198)

An action of violence is labelled 'terrorist' when the psychological effects are out of proportion to its purely physical result.

(Aron, 1966)

These brief statements contain the nub of the matter. Terrorism is, in essence, a form of psychological warfare. Its consequences depend upon its psychological impact and the responses that it evokes in political and military leaders, the media through whose eyes it is seen and the public on all sides of the conflict. Sadly, these responses often aggravate the situation and create, or perpetuate, cycles of deadly violence. In this book, we examine these psychological effects and explore their implications for making or breaking cycles of violence.

Most books on 'terrorism' have devoted much space to defining what it means. The very word is unsatisfactory since the term is often misused by one side to condemn justifiable expressions of anger, protest or verbal abuse in another. The very term alienates us from those it describes; as Rowan puts it on page 151, the '"terrorists" are meant to be the "monsters" and "psychopaths" ... with their involvement in killing often presented as some kind of unthinking and uncaring bloodlust'.

One thing is clear, 'terrorism' is an attribution by one side in a conflict, and here we do not imply anything more than that. Our role is not to judge or to exculpate but simply to understand the psychological nature and causes of such attributions. We have been unable to find an alternative term in common usage and hope that this book will help to add depth to a term that can have many meanings.

Here, we shall confine our attention to acts leading to one or more deaths of non-combatants, and conducted by actors on behalf of an organisation or group. Thus, we shall not be concerned with non-fatal acts of aggression, nor shall we focus on individual terrorists acting on their own initiative who are unlikely to trigger cycles of violence. We do include assassinations and acts by military groups acting without legal authority. Within these limits, each contributor has his or her own take on the meaning of terrorism.

The meaning of terrorism is not the only issue on which our contributors vary; each has his or her own view of the psychological and philosophical issues that explain terrorism and its consequences. The reader should not, therefore, expect to find us speaking with a single voice. My role as editor has not been to produce uniformity; it is to recognise, and even to highlight, the value of a frame of reference that allows for more than one way of construing the working of that complex mechanism, the human mind, acting, as it does, both as an individual and in society. In this book, we shall cross many boundaries, between theories of mind, theories of society, ethics and even style. For psychology is the study of the brain by the brain, and this is reflected in the writer's style and the reader's understanding. All I would ask of the reader is to tolerate these differences in the hope that what will emerge is new insight into and empathy for us all in our struggle to make sense of a world that often seems senseless.

Clemens Nathan took the initiative in setting up a study group to examine the possibility of breaking the cycle of terrorist violence, and I am grateful to him for providing us with this opportunity to come to grips with a problem that will surely escalate as the impact of global warming and other environmental threats increases discontent in weaker nations and cultural groups. Clement Nathan's study group decided that such a book would be valuable and appointed Hugh Freeman and Colin Parkes as editors. Sad to say, Hugh Freeman was to die shortly after our proposals had been accepted for publication by Routledge. Without his leadership, the book would not have come about, and we owe him a deep debt of gratitude.

Given the number of psychiatrists among the contributors, the reader may well ask: 'What has terrorism to do with psychiatry?' If we think of psychiatry as being solely concerned with mental illness, the answer must be 'very little'. Any contribution that we can make to this problem derives from our understanding of the roots of the less rational elements in human thought and behaviour, in both the terrorists and the victims of their attacks and on our ability to help people to understand their own irrationality and to empower them to make more rational choices.

Diagnostic labels may help to explain irrational behaviour, but it is just as important is to understand the person's point of view and to adjust our responses accordingly. To do that, it helps to have theories that help us to focus attention on the interaction between people, to look at the context in which problems arise and the many ways in which they are perceived by the various affected parties.

Desmond Pond, late president of the Royal College of Psychiatrists, used to say 'Paranoia is always justified'. What he meant was that, if we could see the world through the eyes of our patients we would understand why they behaved as they did. I recall a ward round at St Christopher's Hospice, where a patient had become violent and thrown a bucket of enema solution over a nurse. I had been asked to diagnose her mental condition. It did not take long to find out that she was suffering from a confusional state brought about by a lesion in her brain. How did that explain her violence? I asked the nurses to tell me how she saw the world. One nurse said, 'She thinks this place is a hotel', another said, 'Although she has been here a week she still does not recognise me, she says "Who are you?" every time I come into the room'. With this evidence of memory loss, I only had to ask one further question to clarify the problem: 'Suppose a complete stranger came into your hotel bedroom and tried to give you an enema, how would you respond?'

This example also illustrates how psychiatry can play a part in hospice care (or 'palliative care' as it is better termed), the body of knowledge that has revolution-ised the care of patients and families confronting life-threatening illness. Does this have something to teach people in communities confronting life-threatening terrorism?

The plan of this book rests on four areas of current study that have developed in recent years: *attachment theory*, which explains the roots of insecure attach-ment to people, places and God; *cognitive psychology*, which explains the roots of prejudice and deeply held assumptions about the world; *transition theory*, which explains resistance to change at times of crisis and the means by which change can be achieved; and *group dynamics*, which explains the powerful psychological influence of group interaction on human behaviour.

Although these areas of study are not inherently incompatible (the human mind is sufficiently complex to allow of many interpretations), it is in our nature to overvalue most the schools of thought in which we invest. As a result, competition and rivalry between them arises and gives rise to the very tensions and hostility that are our main object of study in this book! Furthermore, these schools of thought offer different viewpoints from the current academic fields of political science and international studies, which focus on issues such as power, ethnicity, gender, security and conflict resolution. It is our intention to set aside our differ-ences and to draw on all of these areas of scholarship in the hope of achieving some mutual benefit. The task is a hard one and will require a measure of toler-ance from us all as we 'change gear' from chapter to chapter.

In this volume, we examine how the insights emerging from this work can help us to understand both the roots of terrorism and the response to terrorist attacks. They also suggest ways in which the risk of terrorism can be reduced and cycles of violence broken.

The book is divided into three parts. In each, we start by examining theoretical models and move on to explore the links between theory and practice in two coun-tries in which cycles of terrorist conflict have been broken: Northern Ireland and Rwanda.

Part I is mainly concerned with the history and psychological context in which terrorism arises.

In chapter 1, Colin Parkes shows how patterns of secure and insecure attach-ment to parents and others, during childhood, eventually come to include attach-ments to authority figures and even to God. Likewise, attachments to homes as secure or insecure places feed later assumptions about homelands and territories. Because insecure attachments may become extremely powerful and override other relationships, they can give rise to extremism and illogical responses when under threat.

This is followed, in chapter 2, by David Abrahamson's analysis of how these illogical responses come about. He focuses on the various ways in which thought processes take place outside consciousness, particularly in times of danger or threat. Emotions influence thinking and vice versa, and can lead to distorted perceptions and the dehumanisation of others.

In chapter 3, John, Lord Alderdice sees young people drawn into terrorism more as a feature of group phenomena than of particular individual psychopathology. He draws on psychodynamic models for an understanding of the ways in which young persons, who see themselves as shamed and deprived of their rights, can be drawn into groups dominated by primitive modes of thinking and retaliation that is deadly to others and ultimately self-defeating.

Many of the psychological factors that have emerged from these three chapters throw light on the roots of the long-standing terrorist conflicts in Northern Ireland and in Rwanda. Northern Ireland is reported by a Catholic, Nora Gribbin, and her Protestant partner, Rodney Turtle; and Rwanda by Peter Hall and Colin Parkes, who have been involved observers. These two countries have been chosen because they have been well researched and illustrate the issues considered in all three parts of the book. In chapters 4 and 5, we examine the roots of terrorism in each country.

They set the scene for Part II, which focuses on the factors likely to initiate or perpetuate a cycle of violence following a terrorist attack.

Colin Parkes, in chapter 6, examines six factors, starting with the nature of the attack itself, the perception of the attack as influenced by the media of communication, the likely immediate public response, the response and actions taken by leaders, the polarisation that can then take place, and the retaliation that results. He suggests that each of these influences can contribute to the establishment of cycles of deadly violence that are then examined in more detail in relation to Northern Ireland (ch. 7), where the focus is on responses to an event when British troops killed 14 unarmed protesters (Bloody Sunday), and in Rwanda (ch. 8), where terrorists employed a ground-to-air missile to destroy an aircraft and its passengers, who included the presidents of Rwanda and Burundi. This, in itself, is controversial as there will be some who have no difficulty in accepting both as involving terrorism, while others will say 'But *that's* not terrorism'. All we ask, at this point, is for our readers to withhold judgement and, like the comparative anatomist who finds in the wings of a bird the same bones that make up the arms of a human being, to see what each can teach about the other. In both examples, it was soldiers acting without state authority who could be seen as 'terrorists' and, while the British soldiers were not criminals, that's how they were seen by some. In both cases, their actions triggered a response that aggravated an existing conflict.

Part III examines possible ways of preventing or breaking the cycles of violence that were described in the preceding parts.

In chapter 9, Jenny Parkes describes ongoing work aimed at helping schoolchildren in areas of high and often deadly violence and terrorism in Africa and the United Kingdom. Her aim is to enable them to develop strategies for coping that reduce that risk. Anthony Glees (ch. 10) challenges us to consider the failure of teaching staff to recognise and counteract the emergence of terrorist cells in British universities. Another challenge is described in chapter 11, where Brian Rowan, who reported the Northern Ireland conflict for the BBC, describes the dilemmas faced by journalists in providing impartial information about both sides and suggests solutions to this problem. We then direct our attention to the problems of leadership at times of terrorist attacks. In chapter 12, John, Lord Alderdice draws on his own experience as a politician and psychiatrist to tackle the inherent difficulties of leaders in a divided country beset with terrorism. While he worked with others to develop a new political language based on relationships and carefully calibrated 'to convey an exquisitely delicate process' *from within* the political system, Berthold Gersons and Mirjam J. Nijdam, in the Netherlands, were called upon to provide psychological support *from outside* the political system, to politicians who had themselves been the subject of terrorist threats (see chapter 13).

Chapters 14 and 15 conclude this part with two accounts of the responses to terrorism that may well have broken the cycles of violence in Northern Ireland and Rwanda. In chapter 16, Colin Parkes draws conclusions from the preceding chapters and suggests that, just as peace processes flourish when people open their minds to new ways of thinking, so do conflicts between academic models resolve when new models of thought make possible the decommissioning of the old.

Part I

THE CONTEXT OF TERRORISM

1

ON THE PSYCHOLOGY OF EXTREMISM

Colin Murray Parkes

Everyone, without exception, believes his own native customs, and
the religion he was brought up in, to be the best, and that being so,
it is unlikely that anyone but a madman would mock at such things.
Herodotus, *Histories* 3.38, c. 420 BCE

Introduction

While terrorist attacks are, by their very nature, acts of extreme violence, it is
naive to assume that they are only carried out by extremists. Given the right circumstances and training, we are probably all capable of terrorism, just as we are
of fighting wars. Nor are all religious, nationalistic or ethnic extremists potential
terrorists, though they may be dangerous for other reasons.

Even so, religious beliefs play a large part in many terrorist movements. When
Nasra Hassan (Reported in Merari 2010, pp. 83–102) interviewed the parents of
36 suicide bombers following their death, she found that the bombers all came
from 'very religious' Muslim families within which 56% of them were seen as
'more religious than the rest of the family'.

Nationalism and ethnic extremism also play a large part in other terrorism as
epitomised in the Baader-Meinhof gang and the Tamil Tigers. Most dangerous of
all is a combination of religious, nationalistic and ethnic motivation, as exists at
the present time in Palestine. Thus, although Hassan found that religious extremism may have played a part in providing a socially acceptable excuse for suicide
in the course of murder in the eyes of Allah and his followers, the decision to carry
out a suicide bombing was also fed by extremely powerful feelings of national
and ethnic obligation, and was usually rewarded by popular esteem and the promise of glorious martyrdom.

In this chapter, we explore the roots of these issues of faith in the light of recent
research into the nature of human attachments. Why are we repeatedly faced with
assumptions that my God is better than your God, that my nation or race trumps
yours, and that my survival and the survival of all the objects of my attachments
are sacrosanct while yours are not?

We may be tempted to argue such assumptions out of existence, by an appeal to reason; yet these beliefs refuse to go away. It seems that, like dreams, beliefs about spiritual and national matters have a logic of their own; or, like the love we bear for our parents and children, they exist with little regard to their objective merits. Indeed many people love God(s) and love their nation in much the same way that they love their parents. We denigrate the objects of their attachment at our peril.

Attachment and religious extremism

Case study

Mohammed Atta, who piloted the first plane to impact the World Trade Center on 9/11, was a committed Muslim extremist who became increasingly convinced of the need for violence and who underwent training by al-Qaeda.

The following account, recounted by Stein, is based on a letter which he addressed to a group of his peers, and left in his car at Logan airport before the attack:

> This was no diatribe of hatred against the people whom he was about to kill, rather it was an expression of devotion to God and an opportunity to purify himself by a sacred act of submission to His will. The slaughter he is about to commit is a sacrifice through which he will achieve transcendence. Life is a veil of sin, a transient aberration from which he has the privilege to escape to a 'marriage' with God, (and the holy virgins, who are described, not as overtly sexual objects, but as pure maids clad in white)
>
> (Stein, 2003).

The people he is about to kill are referred to as 'animals' to be cared for: 'You must not discomfort your animal during the slaughter.'

> Mohammed Atta seems more intent on submitting himself to God than on saving mankind. His faith enables him to deny death in favour of merger with God. In the end, his love of God outweighs his love of any other person, and his obedience to what he believes is God's Will transcends any other duty
>
> (Stein, 2003).

Religious extremism can give rise to cruelty, bigotry, intolerance, discrimination against women, neglect of parental and societal duties, self-mutilation, the mutilation of others, and terrorism. In an age of nuclear weapons, it constitutes a threat to mankind. But its consequences are not all and necessarily bad; it can also give rise to heroism, selflessness and obedience. To combat its harmful consequences, we need to understand its origins and nature.

In order to do this we need to look more closely at the ways by which we become attached to God. This is a topic that we approach with apprehension for reasons that will become clear. Let it be said at the outset that the fact that some people's attachment to God can have evil consequences is as irrelevant to any argument about the existence, nature or goodness of God, as the fact that some attachments to parents have disastrous consequences is an argument against the existence, nature or value of parents.

The nature of attachments

In recent years, the ways in which the attachments of children to parents, parents to children, peers to peers and adults to other adults come about and are maintained throughout life has been closely studied. A body of knowledge, loosely known as attachment theory, has been developed and is supported by evidence from copious research. Attachment theory now has its own journal, *Attachment and Human Development*, and its own academic body, the International Attachment Network (for a review of the field, see Cassidy & Shaver, 1999).

This work has taught us much about the ways in which our inborn tendencies to become attached (i.e., to love) are influenced by our experience of the parenting and other relationships in which we are involved. Not all relationships are attachments; attachments are characterised by being unique (not transferable) sources of security that give rise to a specific set of feelings and attachment behaviours, some of which are maintained by closeness to the object of the attachment (e.g., smiling, hugging and clinging) and others triggered by any perceived threatened or actual separation (e.g., searching, crying and following) (Bowlby, 1969). They have the function of increasing the probability of the survival of our genes by promoting and maintaining protection, when needed, but also by providing safe opportunities for exploration and play that enable the child eventually to achieve autonomy.

Thus, security and freedom, affiliation and autonomy, are in a delicate balance. The children of parents who manage to get the balance right grow up with a reasonable degree of trust in themselves and others. They feel, and usually are, secure, and this pattern of attachment has been termed *secure attachment*.

Patterns of attachment made to parents, and other primary caregivers in childhood, have proved highly predictive, not only of subsequent attachments, but of the ways in which people view themselves and their worlds (Sroufe, 2005). These patterns are a source of much happiness and fulfilment, but they can also, at times, give rise to serious problems in social behaviour and mental health.

Two main patterns of insecure attachment have become clear; these reflect the needs of some parents who are intolerant of closeness, and of other parents who are fearful of distance from their child (Ainsworth, Blehar, Waters & Wall, 1978).

In the first case, the children of parents who are intolerant of closeness learn to inhibit their attachment behaviour and keep a safe distance from the parents. This avoidance of closeness may not *feel* satisfactory, but enables them to stay near enough to survive. At a deep and barely conscious level, they long for a closer relationship but, out of necessity, they learn to stand on their own two feet from an early age.

Likewise, those children whose parents see the world as a dangerous place in which the children must stay close and obedient if they are to survive tend to become dependent and clinging. They accept the need for closeness but are aware of their unsatisfied needs for freedom and autonomy; hence, they feel intruded upon, and their relationship is one of anxious ambivalence. In both of these patterns, the balance between affiliation and autonomy is out of kilter, and the attachment is said to be insecure.

Unsurprisingly, the strategies that enabled each child to survive in infancy set the pattern for their later attachments. Children brought up to keep their distance from parents have learned that too much closeness is dangerous, and they tend to avoid closeness with everyone; but their independence is more apparent than real, and their felt need for closeness, while impossible to fulfil, leads to much ambivalence, distrust and, often, attempts to control others from a distance. This is evident after bereavements, when they blame themselves for their failure to express love or grief (Parkes CM, 2006, ch. 5). Conversely, those who have learned to inhibit their needs for freedom tend to cling to others, but they then discover that their excessive demands for closeness may not be reciprocated. Again, the delicate balance between affiliation and autonomy is out of kilter, and a measure of distrust sneaks into all relationships.

In adolescence and young adult life, attachments to parents diminish, and the dawning of sexuality facilitates new attachments. Attachments to peers, leaders and/or God often arise or become more powerful at this time. Such attachments make adolescents and young adults more vulnerable to exploitation by irresponsible leaders, and they can be more easily recruited into terrorist causes (see on p. 76 how Hutu youths in Rwanda have been recruited in this way).

Attachment to God

Kirkpatrick (1999) points out that 'perceived relationships with God meet all of the defining criteria of attachment relationships and function psychologically as true attachments'. This is evident in proximity seeking (going to church, prayer, meditation, household shrines and the sense of presence or closeness to God that results from our search), turning to God in times of danger or sickness, perception of God as providing a secure base or 'rock', and seeing separation from God as the ultimate punishment, for example, in excommunication. People who leave cults may mourn for their loss. Both attachments to parents and attachment to God are sources of security, and they tend to grow stronger when we feel insecure.

It is well recognised that people in love tend to read into the loved person virtues and characteristics that may have little to do with the actual person. Love is indeed blind. Of course, it is not entirely blind and, while we may be biased in favour of those we love and forgive them their faults, some relationships founder when the discrepancy between the person loved and the actual person becomes too obvious.

Falling in love with God

Although there are many arguments for belief in God, the relationship between man and God is more a love relationship than a logical relationship. We become attached to God by much the same means as we form other love relationships.

Research shows how people's view of God is much influenced by the attachments that they have made to their parents during their childhood. These attachment patterns persist into adult life and influence their attachments to other people. It appears that we often perceive God in the model of our parents and assume that he or she has the same characteristics.

Using a self-report measure, Kirkpatrick and Shaver (1990) found that people who classed their attachments to their parents as 'secure' were more likely than those who classed them as 'avoidant' to see God as loving. The 'secure' were also more likely to see themselves as having a personal relationship with God and to be evangelicals, while the insecure saw God as distant. Those who were 'avoidant' were more often agnostic, and the 'ambivalent' were most likely to see God as punitive.

In recent years, psychologists have debated the ways in which small children gradually develop ideas. Small children cannot love God because they have no perception of God to which they can get attached. But the time comes when it becomes possible to get attached to invisible objects, including God. Grandqvist, Ljungdahl and Dickie (2007) place this change between five and seven years of age or, as the Jesuist proverb says, 'Give me a child until he is seven years of age, and I will give you the man'. Religious education starts with stories about gods as persons, usually in human form or with human characteristics. These gods are made real by means of rituals of communication, prayers, offerings, pleas, sacrifices, acts of worship, contrition and submission. Like relations with parents, relations with God are governed by rules. 'Good' behaviour will be rewarded, 'bad' behaviour punished. Thus, a set of coping strategies becomes a set of moral imperatives.

The rules are a complex mixture of dogma and selective interpretation. They serve psychological functions, which may or may not fit the current situation. Thus, dietary rules may have had survival value at one time but may be irrelevant today. This said, they continue to serve secondary functions by cementing family or cultural identity. Not eating pork (declared by God to be 'impure') identifies the believer as a Jew or Muslim. Likewise, sexual rules may have been developed to reduce the chance of unwise pregnancies, but persist, despite the existence of contraceptives, as tests of loyalty to the tribe, self-control, purity and superior worth.

Attachment to God is mediated through His (or Her) representatives on earth, the clergy and priests. The clergy are aware of the extent to which they too become the objects of the love of their 'flock', which sometimes becomes embarrassingly sexual. More often, however, the love relationship approximates more to a parent/child attachment. Indeed, both priest and God are 'father' or, in some faiths, 'mother', and some faiths involve both male and female gods or demigods.

Attachments to God eventually come to include attachment to places of worship, prayers, songs and other rituals by which we express our love, for God is more plastic than man.

The plasticity of our relationship with God is both a blessing and a problem. On the one hand, each person's view of God is unique to them, as we tend to mould our beliefs to fit our ideal of what God ought to be; on the other hand, most assume that there is only one, or a few gods, referred to as 'mine'. Differences between such possessive assumptions have been a major problem within and between societies from time immemorial.

Religious denominations vary in the ways in which they deal with this problem. Some (such as orthodox Islam and Roman Catholicism) adopt a rigid dogma, a set of assumptions/beliefs about God, to which their members *must* adhere; these are recorded in holy writ and studied to ensure conformity. Such sects value obedience and 'faith' while abhorring heresy and non-conformity. Others (such as some Hindus and most Unitarians) tolerate differences and may even recognise and value each person's personal and unique relationship with God. Neither 'solution' is entirely satisfactory; the former because freedom of thought is discouraged and different sects rely on different dogmas, the latter because they lack the uniformity, clarity and cohesion that come from sharing a common faith.

Between the dogmatic and the free thinkers there is a wide variety of understandings of God allowing elements of individual emphasis.

The roots of extremism

All kinds of attachment vary greatly in their intensity, security, ambivalence, endurance and object; some are extremely strong, and grow stronger in the face of separation, whereas others are easily severed. Research has shown that insecure attachments to parents are often stronger than secure attachments and that intense, insecure attachments cause many problems later in life (Ainsworth, Blehar, Waters & Wall, 1978).

In the course of my studies of dysfunctional reactions to bereavement, I have shown that these are often preceded by extremely powerful and insecure attachments to parents (Parkes, CM, 2006). These insecure attachments are usually evident in childhood. As we have seen, they may cause children to become intolerant of any separation from a parent (usually mother) or home. In an extreme form, this problem has been identified as *separation anxiety disorder*, a pervasive and excessive need to be taken care of that leads to submissive and clinging behaviour and fears of separation (American Psychiatrc Association, 2013).

My own studies (*v.s.*) and those of Vanderwerker, Jacobs, Parkes and Prigerson (2006) showed that bereaved people seeking psychiatric help for prolonged grief disorder, that is to say, extreme grief that is so intense, protracted and obsessive that it interferes with other mental functions and goals, are more likely to have experienced intense separation anxiety in childhood than other bereaved psychiatric patients.

Can our understanding of extreme forms of attachment shed light on religious extremism?

The characteristics of religious extremism are as follows:

1. *Powerful attachment* to God and His/Her representatives on earth, overriding all other attachments.
2. Blind, unquestioning *faith* in the literal truth of all doctrine, laws and other assumptions (including faith in the value of rituals) believed to emanate from God.
3. *Fear of punishment* by God should one fail to carry out these rituals, obey God's commands, or live up to idealised expectations.
4. *Fear of separation from or rejection by God.*
5. *Obsessive repetition* of rituals and other acts of worship that are expected to bring one closer to God and promise rewards (e.g., of eternal bliss).
6. *Extreme distress* in the face of any perceived threat, insult or challenge to God, God's representatives or the symbols of God (including God's holy writ).
7. *Intolerance* of and outright hostility to heretics or those who contradict or ridicule any aspect of God's assumed laws, dogma or representatives.
8. *Willingness to go to extremes;* behave in ways normally seen as improper, anti-social, or immoral; to sacrifice others or oneself; and to kill or to die in order to defend or maintain this rigid, strict set of assumptions about God and his or her representatives.
9. *Apocalyptic thinking.* The most dangerous consequence of this willingness is the belief that, since the next world promises to be better than the present, for the faithful, it would be better to destroy the world than to compromise with the enemy.

Compare these extreme attachments to God with the problems of attachment to parents described earlier:

- Both are powerful, exclusive and obsessive.
- Both involve fear of separation.
- Aggressive responses to anybody seen as threatening to bring this separation about.
- Both involve idealisation of the parent/God, whom they see as all powerful.
- Both are very obedient to the parent/God.
- Both tend to misperceive and exaggerate danger from others.

- Similar misperceptions are also held by and communicated to the person by the parent or priest.
- Both will defy social expectations if these are seen as separating the person from the parent or God.
- Both are particularly likely to arise in the face of trauma, bereavement and persecution.
- Extreme religious and familial attachments may be fostered by the family and society. Love of God/parents is regularly seen as a virtue and a blessing.

Differences exist in the use of ritual, religious symbols and repetition of prayers, which are ways to maintain attachment to an invisible, untouchable and unresponsive God; parents, however, are visible, touchable and responsive. But what if the parents are absent, intolerant of touching and unresponsive? At such times, the children may engage in compulsive rocking to and fro, cling to dolls or alternative symbols of a person and obsessively mutter the same phrases over and over.

Extremism and violence

While religious extremists are not uncommon, most are not violent, and many deplore violence. Indeed, they often bring hope to the hopeless, and may set an example of virtue and charity.

What factors incline religious extremists to violence? Again, we can find some clues in the factors that incline children to violence in their relationship with each other. It is established that many adults who abuse their children were themselves abused in their own childhood (Dutton & Hart, 1992; Taft, Schumm, Marshall, Panuzio & Holtzworth-Munroe, 2008). To abused children, their parents are experienced, paradoxically, as both a danger and their sole source of security. They have no choice but to submit and, like most children, to adopt their parent's view of the world. Thus, children whose parents see others as hostile and aggression as the only reasonable way of controlling them learn to see others in the same way. Anna Freud refered to this as 'identification with the aggressor' (Freud A, 1946).

I know of no consistent evidence that most religious terrorists were abused as children, but there is evidence that 60% of suicide bombers, who are not typical terrorists but are much more dangerous, have anxious/dependent personalities typical of the avoidant and/or dependent patterns of attachment described above. Merari has carried out a study of 15 would-be suicide bombers who were arrested on suspicion, or whose bombs failed to explode, and compared them to a control group of non-suicidal terrorists (Merari, 2010). He describes them as 'shy, socially marginal followers' (as opposed to leaders) who 'harboured feelings of having disappointed their parent'. This study revealed suicidal tendencies in 6 out of 15 (40%) would-be suicide bombers. In a society in which suicide is strictly forbidden by Allah and man, the provision of a method of self-destruction that was not only approved, but glorified, was a powerful inducement.

Parents are not the only sources of oppression. Juergensmeyer observes that 'perpetrating acts of terrorism is one of several ways to symbolically express power over oppressive forces and regain some nobility in the perpetrator's personal life'. In situations of deprivation and perceived danger, people may become attached to charismatic and militant religious leaders, whom they see as a source of security, and who teach a set of rules and behaviours by which they can attain security in this world or the next.

As Alderdice shows in chapter 3 (pp. 43–45, they may be drawn into what Moghaddam terms the *staircase to terrorism* [my extrapolations in square brackets]:

1. Membership of a proud (e.g., previously dominant) group seeing itself as unjustly deprived [of its established sources of security].
2. Legitimate ways of [regaining security by] achieving justice and redressing wrongs had been blocked.
3. Recruitment to a 'parallel' organisation that sanctions and even sees moral value in illegal acts that outsiders see as immoral.
4. Indoctrination into a small secret group with strong charismatic leaders [demigods] who reward conformity and insist on absolute obedience and unity.
5. Distancing, both psychological and physical, from the 'enemy' (who include civilians). This counteracts normal inhibition of taboos on killing or extreme violence (Moghaddam 2007, pp. 69–77).

Are terrorists religious extremists?

Although we tend to assume that terrorists are the epitome of religious extremism, this is often not the case. Several of the 9/11 terrorists were not conscientious in their religious observance; they met in Las Vegas and are said to have hired a stripper. Indeed, they seem much closer to the keen young recruits who volunteer for army training than to the religious bigots who train and lead them. Their attachment was to their leaders and their peer group rather than to God. Perhaps we should not be surprised when we remember the enthusiasm of other young soldiers who are prepared to die for other causes in times of war.

As with other attachments, we take our leaders and friends for granted until we feel threatened. Thus, attachments to officers and peers become very strong in battle. At other times of threat, the image of national leaders to whom one becomes attached is perceived through the mediation of propaganda, the media, our own needs for security, etc.

Societies and child-rearing practices with high levels of uncertainty that emphasise the superiority of the adult/leader, the weakness/inferiority of the masses/children, and the need for obedience rather than autonomy tend to have high levels of anxiety and a powerful attachment dynamic. A Hutu woman attempted to explain the genocide that followed the assassination of President Habiyarimana: 'The truth is the Hutus loved their president too much.'

17

On the other hand, many terrorists, such as Mohamed Atta, are undoubtedly religious extremists, and others are attached to God *and* to charismatic leaders who are seen to represent God.

Conclusions

It is clear that there is more to terrorism than religious extremism alone, and in this book we spell out what some of the other influences may be. It seems, from this analysis, that religious extremism is a type of powerful attachment that could, in some circumstances, be regarded as an attachment disorder. The circumstances that would justify such an attribution would be if people experiencing this condition were, as a result, suffering or causing suffering to others, and that they were unable to carry out their domestic, occupational or other functions in life. However – and this is an important qualification – if the condition falls within cultural norms of belief or behaviour, it is not regarded as a mental disorder. Regardless of this issue, there are important implications of attachment theory for understanding religious extremism.

Problems arising from attachment to homes and territories

In the preceding section, I argued that religious extremism can be seen as a complicated form of attachment to God, a love relationship similar, in many ways, to complicated types of attachment to parents and others. Here, I shall compare problems in attachment to people with problems arising from attachment to homes and territory. Can these be viewed in a similar light, and if so, what implications do they carry for solving the problems that arise?

The primary function of all attachments is to provide security and ensure genetic survival. Thus, parent/child attachments increase the chances that the child will survive by motivating parental protection and support. In discussing child–parent attachments, Bowlby referred to the mother as having 'home valency' (Bowlby, 1988). By this he meant that she is the person to whom the child turns when it feels fearful or insecure. The same, of course, applies to all homes, which are defined in the *Concise Oxford Dictionary* as '5. A place, region, or state, to which one properly belongs, in which one's affections centre, or where one finds rest, refuge or satisfaction'. Such places are a source of security and a safe place in which adults can rest and the developing child can gradually learn to become independent. They are identified as 'mine' (even though they may be owned by others).

The nature of attachments to places

Although the developing child's attachment to a parent (usually the mother) is generally accepted as the primary attachment, and more essential to survival than attachment to a place, children soon become aware that some places are safer than others and can serve as a refuge. By contrast, strange places are sources of fear, and it is no coincidence that Ainsworth's studies of parental attachment were all carried out in a 'Strange Situation', an unfamiliar room in which the child's attachment to its parent was stimulated and accessible to systematic study (Ainsworth et al., 1978).

In other words, the child's attachment to its parents is closely bound up with its attachment to its home and, as we shall see, separation from either or both gives rise to similar distress.

Many other animal species make homes or nests. These are places of relative safety to which they return when threatened and in which they rear their young. Such homes are often located in the centre of an area of family territory which is defended against potential rivals, enemies or predators. A tribe or living group will often include a much wider tribal territory within which many home territories are located. Much of the social organisation of the living group is concerned with the establishment and maintenance of such territories. Thus, the boundaries of the territory are often controlled by males, while that of the home is controlled by females. As with all animal behaviour, the instinctual roots of such behaviour are modified by learned experience from the moment of their first inception. What results is great variation from one individual to another, from one family to another, and from one flock or other living group to another in the intensity, flexibility and duration of attachment to places.

Aggression, submission and territoriality

Since the function of a home is to provide security, any threat of loss of a home or experience of separation from home is likely to undermine security and evoke fear. Fear and anger are closely related. Both are responses to perceived danger and may occur together. Anger may be expressed as aggression if the individual anticipates a successful outcome or if escape routes are blocked and no alternative is available.

Whereas attachments to human beings are clearly defined by the physical identity of a person bounded by skin, the boundary around a territory is often unclear. This opens the door to a major source of dispute. It is easy to understand the importance of attachment to territory and home for the survival of the occupants, and it is not unreasonable to suppose that many wars and other bloody conflicts are attributable to perceived threats to territorial boundaries and dictated by genetic evolution. In non-human species, conflicts for territory seldom lead to anything more bloody than a scratched nose. Despite all the trumpeting, breast-beating and ritual battles that go on, particularly when young males are seeking to establish their own territories, the main function of such display is to intimidate (to terrorise), and it only continues until one side submits or runs away. Within communities, such interactions lead to the establishment of social hierarchies in which each individual knows his or her place (Lorenz, 1966).

Despite a copious literature on the psychology of aggression, little attention has been paid to the importance of its counterpart, submission; yet, in most societies, human beings (and other animals) live in peace most of the time. Once they have found their place in the social hierarchy, they submit to rules and assumptions about possessions, territory, home and access to food and other resources. It seems that, just as attachments within families reduce the risk of conflict within the family, so lasting attachments to possessions and places reduce the risk of conflict within the home or territory. And because families occupy homes, the attachment to family is often conflated with attachment to home. Mothers do indeed have home valence, and homes have mother valence.

Do people grieve for loss of a home?

Just as separation from those we love causes the distinctive reaction of grief, so does separation from home. Stroebe et al. (2002), who studied the homesickness of college students in the Netherlands and the United Kingdom, conclude that 'the results supported the conceptualization of homesickness as a "mini-grief", to be viewed from theoretical perspectives in the field of loss and bereavement'. They point to the wide variation in the intensity and duration of this reaction.

Fried describes similar reactions among slum dwellers to compulsory relocation:

> While there are wide variations in the success of post-relocation adjust-ment and considerable variability in the depth and quality of the loss experience, it seems quite precise to refer to the reactions of the majority as grief: These are manifest in the feelings of painful loss, the continued longing, the general depressive tone, frequent symptoms of psychological or social or dramatic distress, the active work required in adapting to the altered situation, the sense of helplessness, the occasional expressions of both direct and displaced anger, and tendencies to idealize the lost place … 46% gave evidence of a fairly severe grief reaction or worse.
>
> (Fried 1962)

Causes of grief after separation from or loss of a home

Given this variation, it is reasonable to ask why some individuals make the transi-tion from one place to another with little or no expression of grief, while others suffer greatly. In their studies of homesickness, Brewin, Furnham and Howes (1989) and Stroebe, Vliet, Hewstone and Willis (2002) found that securely attached students and those with good relationships with their families adjust to their transition to college with less homesickness than insecurely attached ones. These factors had an impact on ruminations about home and loneliness, and were associated with depression and difficulties with concentration on college work. Women were more prone to homesickness than men.

Likewise, in each of 31 cases, Liotti (1991) claimed that 'early patterns of inse-cure, anxious attachment were the starting point of the development of agorapho-bia' (of which, more later).

When Fried's slum dwellers were re-interviewed after relocation, he found that those who had expessed a commitment to people, places or both showed much more grief than those who had valued the neighbourhood for its accessibility or financial aspects or those who had expressed no commitment at all (Fried 1962).

These observations begin to point the way towards an understanding of the causes and consequences of extreme reactions to loss of places.

Given the importance of territory and home to our survival, we should not be surprised if territorial threats and losses give rise to severe reactions. To be regarded as 'pathological', however, these reactions would have to be out of proportion to the actual threat and/or give rise to emotions and behaviours that are dysfunctional rather than appropriate responses to unjust territorial incursions; they should also be out of keeping with cultural norms.

Possible causes of problems arising from attachment to places

We saw in section I, Context, that some children suffer separation anxiety disorder in childhood, one of the features of which is severe homesickness. Some children will refuse to go to school or to leave their home, even when accompanied by a parent. It seems likely that the extreme homesickness reported by Stroebe, Vliet, Hewstone and Willis (2002) in some college students is a continuation of the separation anxiety that arose during childhood. Likewise, in the common psychiatric condition of agoraphobia, it is fear of separation from home that is the diagnostic symptom. In these cases, it is not a person whom the patient is afraid to leave, but a home. The condition is disabling because it prevents people from working outside the home, shopping, or performing other extramural activities.

There are, of course, many possible causes for the increased rates of mental ill-health commonly found among new immigrants (see, for instance, Carta, Bernal, Hardoy & Haro-Abad 2005), but one thing they all have in common is the loss of a 'homeland'. In addition to a home, the immigrant has lost a territory or a community and, often-times, the culture that goes with them.

As we saw earlier, my own studies of the determinants of reactions to bereavement indicate the following:

1. Severe, prolonged grief most often follows the experience of frequent separations from parents and homes during childhood, or parenting that reflects fear on the part of parents that the child will not survive unless it stays close.
2. Inhibited grief is most likely to follow the experience of parents who are intolerant of closeness or who reject or punish the child for clinging or crying. In boys, it is aggravated during adolescence by the inculcation of macho expectations.

Fried's assessments of the health and psychosocial adjustment of his respondents revealed two patterns of reaction that were associated with a high incidence of dysfunction. There were some individuals who overreacted to relocation; although they did not seem to be strongly committed to the neighbourhood before reloca- tion, they showed severe grief afterwards and required a great deal of help from social and legal agencies. There were others who seemed strongly committed to the neighbourhood prior to relocation but who showed minimal grief afterwards; they were found to have a disproportionate frequency of physical and psychoso- matic problems (Fried, 1962). It seems quite likely that these two patterns of 'overreaction' and 'denial' correspond to the 'severe' and 'inhibited' forms of grief that have been found following bereavement.

Although, in all of these studies, the emphasis has been on the fear and grief to which these problems give rise, anger is also evident and may be expressed towards the supposed authors of the separation.

Aggressive responses to loss are most likely when:

- There is a threat of loss rather than an established loss.
- The individual is male, young, and/or trained to violence.
- There is assumed to be a good chance of preventing or reversing the loss.
- The individual can see no alternative, for example, he or she feels trapped.
- Social pressures favouring aggression are strong.

Compare problematic attachments to people (attachment disorders) with these problematic attachments to places:

- Both are particularly likely to arise in the face of trauma, bereavement and persecution.
- Both are powerful, exclusive and obsessive.
- Both involve fear of separation.
- Both involve aggressive responses to anybody seen as threatening to bring this about.
- Both involve idealisation of the value of the parent or place.
- Both tend to misperceive and exaggerate danger from others.
- Similar misperceptions are often also held by and communicated to the person by the parent or community leaders.
- Both will defy social and moral expectations if these are seen as separating the person from the parent, home or territory.
- Extreme familial, domestic, territorial and national attachments may be fostered by family and society. Love of parents, home and country are all seen as a virtue and a blessing.

Differences exist between attachments to people and places because of our limited ability to interact with or influence places. This does not mean that we may not attempt to do just that; homes and territories are part of the earth, sources of secu- rity, food, drink and much else. It comes as no surprise that many peoples worship household or national gods who will protect and succour them. Harvest festivals are some of the oldest forms of worship and only lost significance when we stopped living off our own land.

Home, homeland and culture

Our attachment to our home soon becomes part of an attachment to all that we associate with home – our homeland and its assumed unique characteristics (Read, 1996). This extension of attachment theory from attachment to home to attachment to homeland becomes apparent in adolescence. Studying Jewish adolescents born in Russia, Walsh and Tartakovsky have shown significant correlations between attachments to mothers and attachments to the country in both resident Jewish youngsters in Russia and young immigrants to Israel (2012). In the latter, who have been brought up to think of Israel as their rightful homeland, it is Israel rather than Russia, their country of birth, to which they are most powerfully attached.

My country includes my language (English), my government (British), my history and its assumed blessings (British civilisation), and my way of life (British). At this point, the overlap between the objects of attachment become blurred. Attachments to home are often conflated with attachments to people (e.g., my neighbours or employees), to leaders (my monarch or prime minister) and to God (e.g., Britain is a predominantly Christian country). In this way, attachments to places become very much more than attachment to a particular location; they become attachments to a nation or state that includes God, priests, people, leaders and football teams. Any or all of these can come under threat. Just as we take pride in our families, our attachment to our country or nation becomes a source of national pride.

Just as individuals extend their range of attachments beyond their own families, to include allies and friends who can be trusted to give support when it is needed, so attachments to places can be broadened to include other familiar places and people; and just as attachments to God include the ethics, values and religious ideology associated with God, so our body of attachments come to include attachments to the whole culture associated with our assumptive world, indeed, *everything that I call mine.*

While it is unquestionable that all people have a right and duty to obtain and protect territory that is justly theirs, this does not mean that violence is a just way of resolving competing claims. This holds true whether we are speaking of armed incursions into another person's territory or attacks on the possessions, symbols, ideas and systems that they hold dear. The conflicts between people who are attached to political systems such as Marxism and Fascism can rival religious conflicts in their bitterness and intransigence.

Adolf Hitler was a leader who fostered, exploited and betrayed the attachment of his followers; his plan (*Mein Kampf*) comprised an ideology that promised to lead the German nation out of the shame and misery that followed their defeat in World War I and the retaliation that followed. In return he expected, and obtained, widespread devotion, blind obedience, and the right to ruthlessly disregard human rights and ethical behaviour.

Do cultural differences reflect patterns of attachment?

It would seem, as we have seen, that all attachments reflect our need for security. Children, and some adults, find their security in their attachments to their families, some adults in their attachments to God and God's representatives on earth, and others to powerful nations and political leaders. When these patterns of difference are shared by large numbers of people, they influence social organisation and cultural values.

Hence, we have some cultures where the family, or larger extensions of the family (or dynasty), remain the main source of security throughout life. In such families, loyalty to the family is the predominant value, higher than loyalty to the state or to God; other cultures are theocentric, God being the ultimate source of security; and in others, it is the state or a charismatic leader who is seen as keeping us safe and who receives our loyalty.

Each of these patterns of attachment gives rise to different values. When people from state-centred cultures (which include most Western cultures) meet people from family-centred cultures (which include many African cultures), we may be shocked to find that the family-centred are likely to distrust the law and government, and see nepotism as a virtue; we may dismiss them as 'corrupt'. On the other hand, people from family-centred cultures are likely to see those who are state-centred as dependent on the impersonal mechanisms of a cruel or indifferent state. Likewise, state-centred people see theocentrics (which include Islamic cultures) as bigots whose religious laws and customs conflict with their own justice and right thinking. And the family-centred see theocentrics as being enslaved to alien gods. Finally, those from theocentric cultures may see the rest of the world as sinful and ignorant of 'the truth'.

Of course, there are many among us who hedge our bets. We spread our investment of love across more than one source of security and ignore any inconsistencies or conflicts to which this gives rise. Alternatively, having learned to distrust all attachments, we convince ourselves that we can stand on our own two feet, remaining smugly confident that we shall always have a leg to stand on.

Territory and terrorism

Terrorism is usually an example of asymmetrical conflict, the weak against the strong. Even state terrorism often reflects a weak state faced by a threat perceived by its leaders as emanating from a more numerous and dangerous populace. Disadvantaged ethnic minorities may be drawn to terrorism in the hope of persuading governments to grant them independence (e.g., ETA separatists in the Basque area of Spain and the Kurdish Worker's Party (EKK) in Turkey). Similarly disadvantaged majorities in colonial countries or under the power of another ethnic group (e.g., the African National Congress (ANC) in South Africa and the Chechens in Chechnya) may also be drawn to terrorism.

Such conflicts do not necessarily involve extremism although it may take the actions of a few extremists to take a lead. Sadly, the powerful emotions stirred up by the conflict may cause people to select leaders for their aggressive territoriality rather than their political wisdom. The leaders will tend to gather around them like-minded individuals who share their misperceptions. Once established, the leaders develop their own mutual attachments, which may cause them to give priority to their own survival over that of the population their group was created to serve (Crenshaw, 1989).

Intervention

In tackling any problems to which extreme attachments may give rise, we should not assume that the *traditional means of problem solving* or negotiation will bear fruit. Appeals to reason, dismissal of beliefs and behaviour that appear contradictory or ridiculous, punishment, persecution, or denigration are seldom successful. Indeed, they may increase the insecurity that lies at the root of much extreme attachment and evoke extreme anxiety and anger. Polarisation and cohesion to followers of the cult or creed in question may then increase.

Would-be religious leaders who feed insecurity are a menace, but so are the opponents whose use of disproportionate violence to contain or eliminate them increases the feelings in the affected community of injustice, disempowerment and persecution. It is on such feelings that the terrorists rely.

Does our knowledge of attachments suggest other alternatives? As we have seen, the function of all attachments is to provide sufficient security to give people the confidence to explore, play and try out new ways of thinking and behaving, both alone and with others.

Insecure attachments undermine the trust in oneself and others that facilitates such exploration. A prerequisite to intervention would therefore seem to be the creation of safe places and trusting relationships in which people will feel safe enough to begin to explore the painful reality of threats, losses and their implications. This, as we shall see, is one of the factors making for successful peace processes.

Attachment theory suggests two types of action that might reduce the risks of terrorism: prevention and postvention. Prevention includes actions to reduce the incidence of extreme or insecure attachments to people, places and possessions. It necessitates recognition of the ways in which powerful and insecure attachments can destroy the potential for other attachments, undermine human kindness, feed alienation and brutality, and induct children and adults into 'the magnet of violence'. Action is needed to create safe and supportive settings (such as schools and youth clubs) in which individuals and groups at risk of being seduced by extreme groups can consider the alternatives available to them and find creative solutions to their problems (this will be examined in more detail in chapters 8 and 9).

Postvention is aimed at those who have already made extreme, insecure attachments; it includes attempts to facilitate communication and open the door to insight and consideration of alternatives. Since terrorism cannot thrive without the support of substantial numbers of sympathisers, action also needs to be taken to influence those in less extreme populations who may be less resistant to change. These measures are most likely to succeed if carried out by individuals or groups who are from the same place, state or religion, and able to understand their attachment patterns and values; to form relationships of trust, and to propose alternative strategies without violating core assumptions. This will be discussed on page 39 and elsewhere in chapters 14 and 15.

Most people who are in love are not entirely blind to the weaknesses of the object of their attachment. At times they may even disagree with them or move back and forth between incompatible models of the world. This *ability to split* the assumptive world is illustrated by married persons who may have an affair while, at other times, remaining a good husband or wife to their spouse. As long as the two worlds do not meet, he or she can move back and forth between them with relative peace of mind.

It is interesting to find that most suicide bombers concealed their intentions from their own families (Merari 2010, p. 92). Their religious world and their family life were kept strictly separate. Several made commitments and attachments to women, planned for a future together and, in several instances, impregnated their wives. This separation of religious and secular life is fostered by some religious sects, perhaps because they recognise that ties to family can easily conflict with ties to God.

Psychological splitting will be discussed on pages 48–50. It makes it easier for the would-be suicide bomber to avoid both the internal and external conflicts that would emerge if he chose, or was forced to face up to the implications for himself and his family, of killing himself and others. Hassan's interviews with families of suicide bombers showed that while they saw their dead child as 'martyrs', nearly all of them would have done their best to dissuade them from the act of suicide had they known about it. Their attachment to their child outweighed other considerations (Hassan's interviews as reported by Merari 2010, pp. 84–95).

One object of marital and family therapy is to help people to *bridge the gaps* between the various objects of their love; to repair the split in their assumptive worlds. Such splits may be more apparent than real, and there may well be a middle ground. For instance, it may be possible for a person to discover that it is possible remain a good Muslim without becoming a suicide bomber. Family and friends who share the same fundamental faith may, therefore, have more influence on jihadists than Christian 'soldiers'.

On the other hand, spouses and other family members who share extreme attachments may foster, and even reinforce, the drive to violence and 'martyrdom'.

Indeed, it is not unknown for the spouse of a suicide bomber to follow in the partner's footsteps.

If polarisation of extremes is facilitated by training and indoctrination, *re-training and re-education* may move people closer to the middle ground. We shall see on pp. 220–221. how laws against discrimination and tribalism have proved effective in Rwanda in virtually eliminating tribal conflicts.

While it is difficult to influence extremists, it may be possible to reduce their influence and to prevent polarisation. It also implies that we isolate the extremists by *identifying and countering the pressures that are pushing people out of the middle ground*. These pressures include extreme stress, feelings of helplessness, disempowerment, privation and the absence of perceived alternatives as well as political and social pressures.

It follows that removing or discrediting the leaders should reduce their following. In Cronin's analysis of the way terrorism ends, she was surprised to find that 'unexpectedly, the reaction of key audiences to a leader's removal, rather than the structure of a group or the availability of a successor, is the most important influence on the long-term outcome ... A clear finding is that arresting [itself humiliating] a leader damages a campaign more than killing him' (Cronin, 2009). In the latter case, the killing creates a martyr and may aid recruitment rather than undermining it. Because it is difficult to find a replacement, the loss of a charismatic leader may also affect the surviving leadership, causing splits and exposing ideological weaknesses.

In the end, it takes attachments to solve the problems of attachment. Given that extreme attachments often reflect attempts to find security in a world that feels chaotic, indifferent or even hostile, the essential prerequisite for successful communication must be to establish what Bowlby (1988) called a *secure base*. By this he meant a *relationship of trust* and a *safe place* where the affected person can begin to feel *safe enough* to review and revise their assumptions about the world. To people of faith, this will often be a church or temple within a religious community.

Empathy is the ability to see the world through the eyes of another person, to understand their point of view. This *does not mean* that we agree with it or take sides with the person against another. Indeed, empathy can be a valuable means of recognising misperceptions of the world and may be the first step to correcting them.

Representatives of the media are often in a position to do just this, as we shall see in chapter 11, where Rowan describes how he was able to develop relationships of trust with both sides in the conflict of Northern Ireland during the Troubles. His impartial reporting helped to pave the way for the peace process that followed.

Our attachments are our greatest source of pleasure and pain. If we accept that we cannot have one without risking the other, we shall be better prepared for the pain when it comes. While it would be going too far to expect us all to love those who cause us pain, we may at least take the time and trouble to understand them and to use that knowledge to plan rational responses, including the possibility of working with, instead of against them. In the words of a former terrorist:

> To make peace with an enemy, you must work with that enemy, and that enemy becomes your partner
>
> (Mandela, 1994, p. 735).

2

COGNITIVE PSYCHOLOGY, TERRORISM AND CYCLES OF VIOLENCE

David Abrahamson

The relevance of individual psychology to terrorism continues to be debated in the light of disputed evidence that some terrorists have abnormal personalities (Horgan, 2003; Rogers, *et al.* 2007). A widely accepted conclusion is that terrorism is better regarded as a 'tool' than a 'syndrome' (Kruglanski & Fishman, 2006), that is, a means used by rational actors to maximise the chance of achieving their ends rather than an expression of psychological disorder (Crenshaw, 1998). Silke (1998) argues that the only possible conclusion from the evidence is that terrorists are normal people, and he objects strongly to what he considers a trend to taint them with a 'pathology aura', with claims that they possess the traits of abnormal personalities despite not having 'the actual clinical disorders'. However, there is considerable expert support for the view that personality disorders are derived from traits continuous with those found in the general population so that, rather than being discrete clinical disorders, they shade into normality (Ghaemi, 2007; Trull, Tragesser, Solhan & Schwartz-Mette, 2007).

The tool and the syndrome approaches both identify irrationality with mental abnormality and normality with rationality, differing in which category they place those who carry out terrorist acts. But this dichotomy has long been unsustainable as even the most normal persons do not have full awareness and command of their thinking and judgement. Much thought and decision making inevitably occur automatically, outside consciousness and subject to influences of which the individual is also unaware (Hassin, Uleman & Bargh, 2005).

By 'automatic' is meant primarily that, once begun, the train of thought runs to completion without conscious attention or awareness. In most cases the process is triggered by environmental or internal cues but in some it may be started deliberately.

Automatic processing 'feels' as though it arises from a different cognitive mechanism than deliberate, analytical reasoning. Sometimes conclusions simply appear at some level of awareness ... and sometimes coming to a conclusion requires doing the work yourself, making an effort to construct a chain of reasoning.

(Sloman, 2002, pp. 379–380)

How do our minds deal, under pressure, with large amounts of information from the external world and from memory?

Automatic thought is essential for dealing with the enormous amount of information involved in even the most mundane activities, and draws on the huge resources of long-term memory. In contrast, the flexible thought involved in activities such as comprehension, reasoning and language is a *scarce resource* that involves a complex cognitive system termed *working memory*.

Working memory incorporates a mechanism to regulate the flow of information within itself and with other parts of the cognitive apparatus, including long-term memory; specialist components for language and visuo-spatial information; and a buffer between short-term and long-term memory that integrates information into units such as a story or scenario (Baddeley, 2007).

A key postulate of cognitive psychology is that the capacity of working memory is intrinsically limited because it operates with short-term memory traces that decay within seconds or tens of seconds, in contrast to the years or decades that long-term memories may last. Capacity may be further reduced by time pressures and multiple demands and by negative emotions such as anger and fear, which are typical of conflict situations (Evans & Over, 1996; Power & Dalgleish, 1997).

The term *heuristic*, from the Greek for 'find' or 'discover', is used in this context for mental shortcuts and rules of thumb that play an important part in compensating for the limited capacity of conscious thought – at the price of potentially biasing judgements. They normally operate automatically but can also be used as deliberate strategies. A large number have been described, and several are particularly relevant to the present subject (Kahneman, Slovic & Tversky, 1982; Kahneman, 2010).

If it looks like a duck, swims like a duck, and quacks like a duck, then it probably is a duck

The *representativeness heuristic* is based on how representative or typical of a particular category an entity appears to be. Typicality is judged by similarity to one or more remembered examples or to a more comprehensive mental model termed a *prototype*. For example, the contrasting 'tool' and 'syndrome' views of terrorism both draw on inaccurate prototypes of, on the one hand, mental illness as violent unreason and, on the other, normality as controlled rationality.

Reliance on prototypes may lead to the *conjunction fallacy*, the idea that the combination of several eventualities could be more likely than any one of them alone (Tversky & Koehler, 1994).

In a study during the first week of the 2003 Iraq War, estimates of the risk of at least one terrorist attack in the following six months was higher when either the possibility that they would be plotted by al-Qaeda or not was mentioned, compared to the omission of any reference to a possible perpetrator, which led to lower assessments of risk (Mandel, 2005).

Likewise, Pinker (2011, p. 369) provided 15 scenarios of violent events in a number of countries to 177 Internet users. About half estimated the risk that 'a nuclear bomb will be set off in the USA or Israel by a terrorist group that obtained it from Iran' as being more likely than that 'a nuclear bomb will be set off in a war or act of terrorism'.

Springing to mind

The aim of terrorist groups to create a climate of fear in the target population, and an impression of strength among their followers, potential allies and rivals, is facilitated by another mental shortcut, termed *the availability heuristic,* and the associated *accessibility bias*. These depend on the greater availability in long-term memory of recent, novel, conspicuous or disturbing events, including fictitious and imagined ones, and the consequent ease with which they are recalled into consciousness. Such events are thus likely to be assumed to be more probable than their actual rates of occurrence, and potentially more significant. Accessibility bias is increased by the culture of news reporting; indeed, novelty almost defines its practice, and by some 'sound bites' from political leaders. We shall find good examples of these in the analysis of the public responses of leaders and the media to terrorist attacks in chapter 6 (p. 86 and pp. 92–93).

The related *simulation heuristic* refers to the accessibility of explanatory models or scenarios, rather than of events; these may also bias estimates of likelihood because links that facilitate an anticipated outcome tend to be readily available to consciousness.

Tetlock describes multiple errors in a database of forecasts about an array of world events:

> Almost as many experts as not thought that the Soviet Communist Party would remain firmly in … power in 1993, that Canada was doomed by 1997, that neo-fascism would prevail in Pretoria by 1994, that the EMU [Economic and Monetary Union] would collapse by 1997, that Bush would be re-elected in 1992, and that the Persian Gulf crisis would be resolved peacefully.
>
> (Tetlock, 2002, pp. 752–753)

It was possible subsequently to question more than three-quarters of the experts about their original forecasts, and in most cases, erroneous predictions contrasted with their authors' high level of confidence in them at the time they were made: '… expertise thus may not translate into predictive accuracy but it does translate into the ability to generate explanations for predictions that experts themselves find so compelling that the result is massive overconfidence'.

The term *counterfactual* literally means contrary to the facts and refers to imagined, alternative scenarios to events ranging from missing a train to major cataclysms. With hindsight, the experts frequently emphasised counterfactual events that would have resulted in their forecasts becoming true, such as the overthrow of President Gorbachev in relation to the first prediction. 'Near-miss' and 'close-call' scenarios are readily accessible to consciousness as they require minimal change in the sequence of events, and may become automatic: missing a train by minutes more often provokes recurrent, intense 'if only' thoughts than doing so by hours.

Near-miss scenarios may plague relatives of those killed in terrorist attacks and also profoundly affect survivors; indeed, some of those who fortuitously escaped being killed on 9/11 were still haunted by their near miss ten years later (Park, 2011).

Controversies about counterterrorism policies illustrate how difficult it is psychologically to separate estimates of the *probability* of an event and of the *direness of its effects* were it to happen, which in a different context is illustrated by the *warning bias* towards detecting dangerous illnesses operated by clinicians, who need to maintain these readily available to consciousness while at the same time paying due attention to the traditional clinical maxim that 'common diseases are commonest' (Wallsten, 1981).

... Or unnoticed

Thought is not only unduly influenced by novel, dramatic information but at the opposite pole may be affected by unobtrusive, disguised or hidden material, which enters memory despite remaining below the threshold of conscious awareness. The early examples of this process, termed *psychological priming*, came mainly from word recognition experiments; for example, following exposure to terms only indirectly related to food, an individual is more likely to complete the word fragment so-p as soup, to recognise it when spoken in a whisper or printed indistinctly (i.e., subliminally), and similarly to recognise other indirectly related food terms. If words related to washing are used instead, 'soap' and other cleanliness associations show the effect.

Studies have since been extended to the *priming of moods, beliefs, judgements and motivation*, and it has been established that after priming of assumptions related to aggression, subjects both perceive ambiguous actions as aggressive and tend to act more aggressively themselves:

> Subjects who were primed by subliminal exposure to words that are part of a prejudiced African-American stereotype, such as 'ghetto', 'jazz', 'lazy' and 'minority', without being directly related to aggression or hostility, judged persons who performed ambiguously aggressive behaviours as more aggressive than did non-primed participants (Todorov & Bargh,

2002). Activating the same African-American stereotype by showing a series of pictures of black youths promoted subsequent hostile behaviour by the viewers.

(Devine, 1989)

Priming manipulations involving filling out a form that included words related to aggression in scrambled sentences led to participants administering 'stronger' dummy electric shocks in a reward and punishment situation similar to the well-known Milgram experiments (Carver et al., 1983).

Objects may also act as *primes for aggression*: US and Swedish subjects who were provoked behaved more angrily when a gun, rather than a neutral object such as a tennis racquet, was present in the room, although the studies were designed so that they had no reason to relate either object to the situation (Berkowitz & LePage, 1967; Frodi, 1975).

The penchant of authoritarian rulers for wearing military uniforms, and sometimes for carrying guns, may reinforce their followers' preference for military solutions to conflicts, and it is possible that 'photo-opportunities' that juxtapose democratic leaders with tanks and planes may have similar effects.

A key word?

It is unclear to what extent the word *terrorism* may by itself have priming effects: comparison of the responses of 176 subjects to reading eight different articles found that inclusion of the term alone did not affect worry, risk judgement or dread, but dread was provoked if reference was also made to nuclear devices, and reference to Islamic extremism accentuated all three dimensions. The effect of the word alone may have been obscured because it was implied even in those articles that did not actually contain it (Woods, 2011). Reactions to threats may be different from those anticipated by planners or perpetrators: official expectations that mass panic would be provoked by air raids in World War I were not realised, but nonetheless profoundly influenced both Royal Air Force and Luftwaffe policies in World War II:

> The Germans in raiding England expect to create a panic amongst the working classes. This has not been the case and their supposition is evidently based on the fact that they consider the psychology of the British working man as being the same as that of the German – hence it may be assumed that the ordinary working German is liable to panic.
>
> (Freedman, 2005, p. 167)

Us and them

Antagonism towards other individuals and groups is fuelled by *the fundamental attribution error*, an unconscious bias towards assuming that the actions of others are due to their personal dispositions, nationality or religion, while ours are responses to the demands imposed by the situation. This may be partially explained by greater subjective awareness of the pressures on and around oneself, and the advice not to judge others without first 'walking in their shoes', i.e., consider events from their perspective, is a well-known tenet of folk psychology.

Consideration of the perspective of others has been found to be more effective than empathy (connecting with them emotionally) in promoting agreement in simulated conflict situations (Galinsky, Maddux, Gilin & White, 2008). It is likely to be impaired when groups are separated from one another physically, educationally and socially, as in Northern Ireland. However, genocidal hatred and violence have easily been fanned by inflammatory propaganda in countries where the opposed groups lived closely together, including Rwanda (see p. 118 so that other factors are clearly also important).

Fixed prejudices

One such factor is a mental shortcut termed *psychological essentialism,* which involves the automatic categorising of groups in terms of a hidden underlying nature or essence. The essence is assumed to generate negative characteristics that persist even through major changes in dress, language, lifestyle and other overt behaviour. This is exemplified by the persistence of anti-Semitism through centuries of profound changes and variations in Jewish ways of life. In general, the effect of psychological essentialism is to 'deepen social divides, making differences appear large, unbridgeable, inevitable, unchangeable and ordained by nature' (Haslam, 2011). It has been claimed as a candidate for a universal human characteristic, though varying in degree, on the basis of evidence from groups as diverse as middle-class adults and children in the United States, Native Americans, residents of impoverished neighbourhoods in Brazil, and pastoral herdsmen (Norenzayan & Heine, 2005).

Emotion and reason: No longer emotion versus reason

Emotion has increasingly become a focus of cognitive psychology as the discipline has moved beyond earlier computer-based analogies. Traditionally separated from reason, or even regarded as antagonistic to it as in 'heart' against 'head', it is now recognised to be intimately involved in both conscious and unconscious thought (Davidson, Scherer & Goldsmith, 2009; Fox, 2008; Williams, Watts, MacLeod & Matthews, 1997).

The concept of a limited set of primary emotions was first put forward by Descartes and further elaborated by Darwin (1872: the most parsimonious estimate is five – happiness, sadness, anger, fear and disgust – but there are a number of other candidates, including compassion and contempt. Combinations are common, such as anger with sadness in depression, and even if they are not accepted as primary emotions, compassion is considered to blend sadness and love and contempt to combine anger and disgust (Eppel, 2009; Goetz, Keltner & Simon-Thomas, 2010).

How we think influences how we feel

A complex cognitive assessment termed *appraisal* is postulated to determine which emotion is experienced in particular circumstances: happiness is associated with the appraisal of movement towards a valued goal or role; sadness with assumptions of loss or failure; anger with an appraisal of frustration of a role or goal through a perceived agent; fear with a physical or social threat; and disgust with repulsive experiences or ideas. The process is not static, and reappraisal may lead to additional emotions, either congruent with the initial appraisal, such as further depression about being depressed, or in conflict, as when happiness at someone's downfall is followed by disgust at oneself.

Power and Dalgleish (1997) propose a model of the appraisal process with three functional levels:

- *An automatic level* that draws on associations built up in long-term memory by events, thoughts and emotions occurring together, probably also influenced by innate predispositions, and exemplified by phobias.
- A level that involves beliefs, ideas and concepts, and the relations between them, in the form of *propositions* that can be captured in language, such as that the world is safe or the world is dangerous. This level has no direct route to emotion but feeds into either the automatic or schematic systems.
- The most inclusive, the *schematic level*, which incorporates higher-order ideas that cannot readily be expressed in language, including models of the self, the world and others. For example, a schematic model of the world as a safe or a dangerous place is more complex than can be captured by the propositional-level statements above as it incorporates all aspects of what safety means to the person.

In phobic reactions, such as to spiders, open spaces or heights, the affected individual may be profoundly disturbed by automatic, associative appraisals of threat, although at the schematic level they are aware that these are irrational, The term *phobia* is also increasingly applied to complex sets of attitudes, including *Christianophobia* and *Islamophobia*, which in contrast are regarded as rational and justified by those subject to them (Ghanea, 2007). Exploring differences in the cognitive processes involved might throw light on such prejudices.

How we feel influences how we think

Following the terrorist attacks of 11 September, 2001 (9/11), Sadler Lineberger, Correll and Park (2005) investigated US citizens' emotional reactions, beliefs about their cause, and policy recommendations. Those whose reactions were dominated by anger attributed them to the fanaticism of the terrorists and poor US security, endorsed an aggressive military response and rejected humanitarian efforts abroad; those whose reactions were dominated by sadness disclaimed fanaticism and security lapses as causes, and both sad and fearful participants expressed doubts about a strong military reaction.

An individual's predominant emotion over a period is termed their *mood or affect*. *Positive mood* acts as a signal that the current situation is safe; happy individuals tend to employ more automatic processes, reach decisions more quickly, and be more confident about them; sometimes, they become overconfident. In contrast, negative mood signals problematic situations and evokes vigilant, effortful processing.

However, individuals in happy moods have also been reported to adopt more open and inclusive thinking styles, and it has been suggested that both positive and negative affect tend to reduce cognitive capacity; those experiencing the former may minimise the reduction by avoiding processing ideas that might interfere with their happy feelings, while unhappy or depressed individuals reduce it by struggling to achieve a more positive mood (Forgas, 2009).

Both the formation and the recall of memories tend to be congruent with the predominant affect, and the selective recall of negative memories is thought to play an important part in clinical depression. Sad memories may also be recalled during a happy mood as the cognitive system may unsuccessfully attempt to reinterpret past negative experiences in a better light. These complex processes may be critical to the emotional processing that occurs naturally following traumas and in psychotherapy (Beck, 1976; Teasdale & Barnard, 1993).

Disgust and contamination

The influence of the emotion of *disgust* extends well beyond taste or gustation, from which the term was originally derived. Its capacity to promote violence is easier to overlook than more obvious triggers such as anger but, especially in combination with contempt, it contributes to the dehumanisation of others that is a feature of mass atrocities (Goldhagen, 2009; Snyder, 2011).

Disgust is relevant to issues of contamination and impurity, which are prominent in many religions and much secular self-cleansing and its commercial exploitation is not directly related to actual physical dirt or infection (Smith, 2008). Contamination has a mysterious quality in its capacity to spread to places and persons without direct contact. Moreover, physical and mental contamination are closely related, and individuals may feel the need to wash after moral transgressions and even after being induced to read material that conflicts with strongly held principles (Fairbrother, Newth & Rachman 2005; Rachman, 2006). Similarly, automatic intrusive thoughts, images and urges may produce a sense of self-contamination that provokes thought suppression or repetitive washing, or both, in obsessive-compulsive disorders (Rassin, 2005; Rachman, 2006).

The ready availability to consciousness of the notion of contamination, even when inappropriate and unwanted, is illustrated by the widespread use of the term *ethnic cleansing*. This was introduced in the 1990s for enforced population change in the context of conflict in the former Yugoslavia, but the practice goes back centuries and featured in Nazi and other attempted genocides. Reference to 'cleansing' in this context risks priming the idea of the victims being in some way contaminated and undermining the intended condemnation of the perpetrators.

It is possible that, in some cases, religious practices in part serve to limit the mysterious power of intuitive feelings of contamination. According to Jewish dietary rules, food remains kosher if contamination is accidental and less than 1/60 in quantity, but Nemeroff and Rozin (1992) found that many Orthodox Jews found food offensive that was within this definition. The most orthodox were the most willing to consume it, and they concluded that deep commitment to religious rules may set limits on subjective feelings of contagion.

... And purity

Purity is often considered to be, not merely the absence of contamination, but a special state of physical and spiritual perfection, akin to holiness, and has long had links with ideas of sacrifice and martyrdom:

> Splendid and holy causes are served by men who are themselves splendid and holy ... Life springs from death: and from the graves of patriot men and women spring living nations....
>
> (Pearse, 1915)

There is often a striking symmetry in the use made by opposed groups of values considered sacred, such as honour and justice, to justify violence towards each other, and the enshrinement of holiness in territory, history, individuals and objects involves cognitive processes such as representativeness and essentialism.

The concept of *sacred or protected values* has been drawn on in relation to negotiation strategies in conflict situations. A situation that pits worldly considerations against a sacred or protected value, such as financial considerations against human life, is termed a *taboo trade-off; tragic trade-offs* involve two protected values contending against each other, as in losses of life on opposing sides, and *routine trade-offs* pit two secular values against each other. Atran (2010) claims, on the basis of interviews and simulated negotiations in the Middle East, Iran, India and Indonesia, that opposition to compromises over issues considered sacred increases when material incentives are offered but decreases when an adversary makes symbolic gestures that show recognition of their special character.

Moral heuristics

There is evidence that heuristics are as important in the moral sphere as in other decision-making processes. This contests the traditional view that moral preferences are formed by weighing up rights, fairness and potential harm, and suggests that they may also lead to mistaken judgements (Sunstein, 2005). The moral foundations theory proposes that particular cultural environments foreground particular innate, automatic moral intuitions and neglect others, and the five fundamental sets of values that result are described as follows.

Care/harm, which is related to attachment and underlies the virtues of kindness, gentleness and nurturance; *fairness/cheating*, which generates ideas of justice, rights and autonomy; *loyalty/betrayal,* related to patriotism and self-sacrifice for the group; *authority/subversion*, which underlies virtues of leadership and followership (sic), including deference to legitimate authority and respect for traditions, and *sanctity/degradation*, which is shaped by the psychology of disgust and contamination (Haidt, 2001). It is argued that

> '... the current American culture war' arises from 'liberals' trying to create a morality relying almost exclusively on the harm/care and fairness/reciprocity (moral) foundations; whereas 'conservatives', especially religious conservatives, use all five foundations, including in-group loyalty, authority/respect, and purity/sanctity.
>
> (Haidt, 2001)

A sixth foundation is proposed, *liberty/constraint*, to include both positive or lifestyle liberty, which is considered to appeal to liberals, and negative liberty, 'the freedom to be left alone by government', more often upheld by conservatives (Haidt, 2012, pp. 155–180). This appears to relate primarily to the current political situation in the United States, and it is difficult to regard the sixth foundation as based on moral considerations. It is also the case that the so-called 'wisdom of repugnance' or 'yuck factor', in which disgust is regarded as evidence of deep wisdom, is predominantly espoused by conservatives (Kass, 2002).

Reciprocity in some form appears to be a virtually universal value, exemplified by the golden rule to treat others as one would wish to be treated, which features in many religions, including Judaism, Christianity, Islam, Buddhism, Hinduism and Zoroastrianism, as well as in Confucianism and in ancient Greco-Roman philosophy (Neusner and Chilton, 2008). However, it is crucial to recognise the distinction between bonding reciprocity, which involves only in-group members, and bridging reciprocity between different groups:

> ... A group might direct the greatest care toward the honour of its poorest members, whilst simultaneously neglecting, abusing, or even killing unbelieving women and children ... 'the same SS men who took pleasure in throwing Jewish babies in the air and catching them with their bayonets ... distribute(d) fresh bread to poor Aryan women and children.
> ... The gravest danger to human psychology is not sadism, but selective sadism, not unqualified hate, but hate beyond the boundaries of one's moral universe.
>
> (Gopin, 2002, pp. 106; 243)

Not of one mind

The term *theological incorrectness* was coined by Slone (2007) in the context of a naturalistic approach to religion that emphasises the importance of cognitive processes (Boyer, 1994). It draws attention to the frequency with which members of religious groups hold personal beliefs at odds with the official teachings that they publicly espouse, usually sincerely, ranging from superstitions to reversals of important tenets.

In Judaism, shared practice is regarded as more important for belonging than beliefs, whereas in Christianity the reverse may be the case (Kellner, 1999; MacCulloch, 2009), but Solomon notes that:

> ... a conference of Christians and Jews might open with Jews on one side of the table and Christians on the other ... two or three days later ... several people had changed places so that you ended up with modernists/ liberals, whether Jewish or Christian on one side and traditionalists/fun- damentalists, whether Jewish or Christian, on the other.
>
> (Solomon, 2012, p. 13)

Similar disparities have been found in other domains, and the concept of *cognitive polyphasia* originated from studies of popular representations of psychoanalysis that indicated individuals may think simultaneously about an issue in different and even contradictory ways (Moscovici, 1976). Private or public efforts to rec- oncile discrepancies may be provoked, in some cases, as predicted by *cognitive dissonance theory*, which postulates a drive to reduce discrepancies by altering existing cognitions, adding new ones or reducing the importance of dissonant ele- ments (Festinger, 1957). For instance, as we shall see on p. 26, the families of would-be suicide bombers often do their best to dissuade them before the act, while expressing full approval after it has been carried out.

In other cases, there may be little or no attempt to resolve apparent disparities, and s*ocial representation theory* proposes that belief systems are not necessarily consistent as they are based on representational terms that dominate in one field while playing a minor role in others. Some may be more appropriate in families or other social groups, and others for particular religious, economic or scientific purposes (Wagner, Duveen, Verma, and Themel, 2000). A Christian priest whose daughter married an atheist was heard to remark to a colleague that his son-in-law was '... a good Christian at heart'.

Attempts directly to suppress specific thoughts are likely to be unsuccessful or counterproductive, as the metacognition or thought about a thought, 'I should not think about ...' necessarily refers back to the original, as in the well-known experi- ments in which participants instructed not to think of white bears, or some other unu- sual topic, find that such thoughts becomes more than usually intrusive (Rassin, 2005; Wegner, 1989). This process may provoke increasingly self-defeating attempts to con- trol the uncontrollable, as in obsessive-compulsive disorders (Salkovskis, 1996).

Discussion

The complexities of conscious and unconscious thought and emotion, and of their interactions, may contribute to the disjunction between intentions and outcomes that is a frequent feature of terrorism and cycles of violence. A detailed analysis of the 42 policy objectives of 28 terrorist groups estimated an overall success rate of only seven percent (the Sri Lankan Tamil Tigers were included among the successful groups, but their subsequent fate has been tragic failure.). Target selection was the key variable for accomplishing the intended goals: groups whose attacks were predominantly on civilian rather than military targets consistently failed to achieve their policy objectives (Abrahams, 2006). As described earlier, the mass bombing of civilians in wartime also failed to achieve the expected panic and capitulation (Freedman, 2005).

Enlightenment reverence for conscious thought as the hallmark of humanity was shaken by Freudian concepts of primitive unconscious forces, and was subsequently further called into question by developments in cognitive psychology that drew attention to the biases potentially induced by cognitive processes outside conscious control. The hope was that growing awareness of this aspect would increase the transparency and fairness of public discourse, but knowledge of such biases can also be used to manipulate opinion in the service of sectarian political, commercial and other interests, and it is doubtful how far the hope has been realised. The development and widening availability of new electronic media provides an opportunity to go further, although the above caveat applies here also.

The emphasis in both academic and popular thought is increasingly shifting from unconscious mental processes as sources of error to the positive role of fast, automatic thought and decision making, evidenced by the burgeoning of popular psychology and self-help books with this theme in fields ranging from sport, gambling and investment to personal relationships and politics (Gigerenzer 2008; Gladwell, 2005; Lehrer, 2009). However, it is important that the pendulum does not swing too far in any one direction.

A recent authoritative overview concludes that the evidence for conscious causation of behaviour is extensive and empirically strong, although this is often indirect and delayed and depends on interplay with unconscious processes:

> Nothing ... we have reviewed would prove that any behavior emerged from exclusively conscious processes. Likewise, ostensible evidence of unconscious causation is typically compromised by extensive reliance on conscious processes too, such as for giving instructions and focusing attention.
>
> (Baumeister, Mascampo & Vohs, 2011, p. 354)

Conscious, reflective thought is essential for considering past, present and future events within the same framework, for allowing behaviour to be informed by social and cultural factors, and in situations that present multiple alternative possibilities in which perspective taking, negotiating and accountability may be particularly important.

There is currently also a trend to import evolving ideas from neuroscience into popular psychology and other fields, including theatre and fiction: references to supposedly genetically determined, 'hard-wired' thinking and behaviour are becoming ubiquitous (Dar-Nimrod and Heine, 2011; Tallis, 2011). However, it is arguable that the complexities and interactions of conscious and automatic reasoning and emotions are more appropriately related to diversity and adaptability. Cognitive polyphasia, disparate social representations, theological incorrectness, and ironic mental processes are among mental processes that promote multilayered thinking.

It is essential that cognitive psychological research itself becomes more diverse: all but a fraction of psychological testing carried out between 2003 and 2007 was on subjects from countries with only 12% of the world population, characterised as Western, educated, industrialised, rich and democratic (WEIRD); 70% of the subjects were from the United States alone (Henrich, Heine & Norenzayan 2010). Research that has so far been carried out on other populations indicates that participants from Asian backgrounds are more likely than Americans to believe that behaviour is controlled by the situation and that individual traits do not describe a person as well as roles or duties. This calls into question the universality of the fundamental attribution error in its usual form (Miyamoto & Kitayama, 2002; Norenzayan, Choi & Nisbett, 2002; Church Katigbak, Del Prado, Ortiz, Mastor, Harumi, Tanaka- Matsumi et al., 2006).

It is also imperative that cognitive psychology draws attention to the importance of intense individual experiences. The most profound and enduring memories are autobiographical, tied to particular events, at particular times, in particular places and often formed in circumstances causing fear, anger and depression in which conscious reflection is immensely difficult.

Trakakis refers to:

> the almost exclusively *theoretical* character of the enterprise: the machinery of deductive and probabilistic logic plays an important role in the formulation of arguments, the debates are often couched in a highly abstract, technical and ahistorical language, and little attention is given to the concrete, emotional and practical problems that the occurrence of evil brings in its wake.
>
> (Trakakis, 2008, p. 183)

His comments are addressed to attempts to encompass evil and suffering within theological and philosophical systems but may serve as a warning for psychological disciplines.

3

GROUP IDENTITY AND THE ROOTS OF TERRORISM

John, Lord Alderdice

Violent acts are used to induce states of terror in various contexts, and the term *terrorism* is currently applied to many of them. Some involve authoritarian state forces in violent oppression of opposition activists. In other circumstances, the whole structure of a state and society breaks down, and long-standing divisions between communal groups are expressed in chaotic violence which may descend rapidly into what can, on occasions, only be described as butchery (as is demonstrated in situations described in chapters 5 and 8). In other cases, the failing institutions of a state may result in the gradual breakdown of law and order, and primitive violence and terror becomes the *modus vivendi* in that society. However, when it comes to research and the process of trying to increase understanding of the phenomena, the term 'terrorism' is probably best used to denote a rather specific tactic of asymmetric warfare, and I will follow that practice in this chapter.

A terrorist act is usually understood to be a violent, politically motivated attack undertaken not merely to kill or injure the victim of the attack, but with the purpose of putting a whole target population in fear of their lives by undermining the protective power of a government or authority. In this sense, it is a triangular tactic where the real target of the terrorist is not the poor victim who is injured or killed but the responsible government whose authority is undermined. While such acts are, of course, criminal, the purpose is generally the promotion of what the terrorist regards as a 'higher cause' than mere personal benefit or reward of the individuals who bring it about. The sense of terror in the target community is increased by the realisation that those who engage in the acts of terror have no regard for the well being of those who are injured or killed and are likely to attack again without warning. It is more frightening still when groups engage in suicide attacks, showing no regard for their own lives.

Normal, stable, people find it difficult to empathise with those who try to kill and maim innocent men, women and children and terrify whole populations in this way with no regard for normal human sympathy. The experience of global terrorism has made the term a universally, morally loaded one, and so it is difficult to discuss the roots of terrorism in a dispassionate, academic way. In the case of suicide bombers, the lack of concern for their own lives stretches beyond the understanding of most people. When we do not understand why people behave as they do, it is usually believed that they are either bad or mad, and so it is assumed that those who become terrorists must be either entirely evil individuals or at least psychologically very disturbed people. Such assumptions are not an unreasonable place to start in undertaking the challenging work of research into terrorism – trying to find evidence of whether the personal disturbance of individual people is being manifested in violent terrorist behaviour.

Relatively few individuals who are directly involved in terrorism come along for psychological treatment, and those who do tend to appear at the clinic when they are no longer actively involved. Some suffer from post-traumatic stress disorder, which is by definition a set of symptoms that developed as a result of violent experiences rather than a predisposing factor to involvement. It is also more common for former terrorists to present after the terrorist campaign is over when the esprit de corps and other group supports have faded away. Some of those who have been involved in terrorism and decide to come for treatment are indeed neurotic or internally conflicted people whose earlier difficulties were expressed through their violent behaviour. When, later in life they present for treatment, they are often suffering from anxiety or depressive disorders, alcohol and drug abuse and other psychiatric disorders. There are very few individuals with psychosis. Such vulnerable people are excluded by terrorist organisations since they create a high risk for the organisation.

It is hardly surprising that some who get involved in terrorism would conform to the diagnostic criteria for sociopathic personality disorder. Such people often become impossible for their organisations to handle and cause violent internal feuds, sometimes splitting off to form dissident groups.

However, as I have described elsewhere (Alderdice, 2003, 2005), it has become clear to me that many – almost certainly the majority of those who become involved in terrorism – are not psychiatrically ill or disordered personalities, and when the political issues that concern them are addressed, some go on to live upright and even distinguished public lives. The fact that whole communities of people may lead quite civilised lives and then at some point break down into terror and violence, returning again at some point to ordered and peaceful living, strongly suggests that all of those who get involved in such actions are not essentially 'evil' people, even though the actions that they engage in, and their effects, can properly be described in that way. It also seems clear that the dynamic which drew these people (usually young men) into terrorist activity was more a feature of group phenomena, than particular individual psychopathology (Alderdice, 2007).

In some communities the tradition of using physical force to address political problems has a long history. Young men grow up hearing about the exploits of fathers and grandfathers honoured for their participation in a historic struggle. When these young men get involved in terrorism, they are identifying with these significant figures as part of the normal process of growing up.

Some others get involved in terrorist groups as a result of traumatic experiences where friends or family members were killed or injured in violent episodes, and they feel that the official institutions – the police, the army and the justice system – failed to protect them, or even in some cases instigated the violence against them or their community. Joining a terrorist group is consciously seen by them as a way of protecting their community and of satisfying the wish for revenge for the death or injury of their loved one. At another level, it is also an expression of the shame-rage response engendered by narcissistic injury.

As Scott Atran (2010) has shown, many young men get involved in terrorist groups as others team up for football or in urban gangs. Their network of developing relationships takes them into this way of behaving as they search for models that inspire them and imbue their lives with an intense sense of meaning and purpose. It is not necessarily the case that such young people have to be indoctrinated or even recruited. They identify with someone or with a group that they admire, or they may respond violently to loss, injury or a situation they regard as deeply unjust, and they 'enlist' either virtually or in reality. In the work that Scott Atran undertook, he and his colleagues directly interviewed young people in the Arab street and in other parts of the world; however, many young people now develop their network of relationships not only amongst those with whom they play football or physically 'hang out', but on social networking sites and otherwise through the Internet. This means that some young people who otherwise appear as isolated individuals, do not regard themselves as such, but rather as part of a virtual community linked on the Internet. An example of this appears to be the young Norwegian, Anders Breivik, who on 22 July, 2011, bombed government buildings in Oslo, resulting in eight deaths, and then carried out a mass shooting at an island political camp of the youth wing of the Labour Party, where he killed 69 people, mostly teenagers. Although he appeared to have acted alone, he saw himself as part of a network with whom he communicated on the Internet, and he believed himself to be acting on behalf of his community. This new way of functioning in relationships through the Internet is also challenging because the way people function psychologically in cyberspace is not quite the same as in direct face-to-face social relationships.

At the Second Worldwide Cybersecurity Summit at The Queen Elizabeth II Conference Centre in London, in 2011, Misha Glenny (a former BBC journalist whose most recent book, *Dark Market* (2011), focuses on the world of cybercrime) pointed out that although that conference, like others, was replete with a multitude of papers, presentations and discussions on the hardware and software of cybersecurity, there was very little research being reported on the psychology of cyberspace. This is a major gap in the field because of the differences in the way people function, as individuals and as groups and networks in cyberspace; however, there is reason to believe that when they do engage in terrorist activities, they regard themselves as being part of a group.

Of course, there are those who join in terrorism of a more traditional type with the primary intention of benefiting from the culture of organised crime through which terrorist organisations survive and exert control in their own communities. This largely criminal element does seek to gain personally from extortion, racketeering, drugs and illegal businesses such as the sale of stolen tobacco, alcohol or laundered fuel. Such operations are necessary to raise the substantial funds to run a major terrorist campaign. However, the more committed terrorists have a political cause for which they may well have given up family and financial security and risked their lives, and they tend to resent and despise those who abuse the 'sacred' cause for crude personal material gain. In the later years of a terrorist campaign, some individuals justify slipping into this position with claims that these are the 'spoils of war'. One ageing terrorist wryly remarked to me that the IRA did not have a pension plan for their volunteers.

In summary, there is no one terrorist profile that describes the personality of the individual who engages in terrorism. Some terrorists were psychologically disturbed prior to their involvement, and others become disturbed as a result of involvement; some model themselves on people they admire; some identify with their friends, as young fellows do in football teams and urban gangs; some are ordinary criminals, and many react to a profound sense of moral indignation at the humiliation, disrespect or injustice they have observed in a community with which they identify.

The fact that there is not one profile which describes the person who becomes involved in terrorism does not mean that there are no psychological similarities between people who do get involved and no differences with the 'non-terrorist community'. There are, for example, demonstrable differences between terrorist prisoners and other prisoners. The relationship between colleagues is more supportive; they survive better in solitary confinement; they use educational facilities better; and some groups tend to be quite puritanical and self-sacrificial. Lyons and Harbinson (1986) compared political and non-political murderers in Northern Ireland and found greater stability in those who were convicted of political murders. Marc Sageman (2005) and his colleague Scott Atran piloted a people-based database including background information on many hundreds of global network terrorists and their trajectory within the contexts in which they emerged. This enabled them to look scientifically at different hypotheses about terrorism and has substantiated the view that it is in the context of the group that we are most likely to find pointers in the study of the psychology of terrorism. Atran (2010) suggests that the development of relationships based on 'sacred' values seems important in understanding the radical commitment of these groups to the use of terrorism. This is not meant to imply that the use of terrorism is sacred, or that they are inspired by a particular religious faith or doctrine, but rather that they espouse and share principles which have transcendent value such as 'justice for my people' – matters that are regarded as higher than issues of normal individual morality. Given the perceived inequality of their political position, they come to believe that terrorism is the only effective tactic of warfare available in the asymmetric power context in which the group finds itself.

This work tends to suggest that, with the exception of Israel/Palestine, many violent jihadis live in the diaspora (it is important to note that jihad is *not* necessarily violent). They joined the violent jihad outside their country of origin, and most had no religious education until they became 'born again' in their late teens or early adulthood. Most join through friendship or kinship, and it is a matter of enlistment rather than recruitment in most cases. They create small bands of about eight 'fictive kin' who regard each other as brothers and would as easily die for each other as for any natural parent, sibling or child. This group size is about the same number of family or intimate relationships that people across the world will have on average between the ages of 15 and 30 years. Outside of Palestine, most have a college education, and many are married and professionals. Atran also ascertained that anyone who attempts to join inside Palestine and says that he wants to be a martyr to get virgins in Paradise is rejected by the leaders of Hamas or Palestinian Islamic Jihad as being unworthy of sacrifice (the same is true of Jeemah Islamiyah in Indonesia). There are also other differences from criminal organisations. Terrorist groups usually claim their atrocities. For them the crime is worth committing even if they die in the attempt. The failure of the struggle, rather than their personal capture or death, is the ultimate disaster. Their individual self becomes conflated with their cause, ideal or group – identification with their fellow group members. These are not simply the characteristics of poor, ignorant, lonely, psychologically disturbed or criminal individuals, as is sometimes portrayed by politicians or the press (Sageman 2004).

These findings suggest that to understand causation the psychological fault line must be explored at the level of the group more than the individual. Vamik Volkan described this in his ground-breaking book *Cyprus – War and Adaptation* (1979) and in *Killing in the Name of Identity* (2006) and many other writings; he also shows how the trans-generational transmission of the group identity and the imperative towards reparative violence occurs. The transmission from the parental generation of the sense of being shamed, humiliated and under attack, and the imperative to redress it, is one important element in understanding why suicide bombers and radicals may come from second- and third-generation immigrants who seem otherwise well integrated into their host community.

If indeed the roots of terrorism are to be found in the group, how should we understand the psychology of groups?

Even before Sigmund Freud's pioneering work, Hughlings Jackson, the English neurologist, had described the developmental or evolutionary principle not only in the structure of the brain but also, in his famous Croonian Lectures (Jackson, 1884), in the development of mentation. Organisms as individuals grow and develop from the simple, rigid and reflex, to the more complex, pragmatic and unpredictable, and when they break down, dissolution of function can be observed. The higher, more recently acquired functions are lost, and replaced by the release of the primitive capacities which remain, or by fundamental characteristics of mental life such as the repetition compulsion (Critchley M & Critchley EA, 1998).

Freud and others developed this further in psychoanalysis. They showed how infants and children, as they move through the process of maturation, experience difficulties (e.g., trauma or overstimulation) which mark certain stages in their development as vulnerable points to which they may return in the course of later psychological regression. When individuals in the face of a trauma or threat withdraw from an unacceptable reality, their thinking and behaviour become similar to that seen at various stages in childhood, and they transfer on to people and places in the present, ways of relating which were more appropriate in earlier times. Such thinking may be magical and rigid, and the form of their relationships increasingly by identification – that is to say by imitation rather than attachment.

Something further happens when a patient falls ill with a schizophrenic psychosis. In these disorders, patients display some disturbances of thinking and perception which are not generally seen in childhood but are seen during the dream life of healthy adults. The French evolutionary psychiatrist Henri Ey (1962) called this 'dissolution of the field of consciousness', to differentiate it from dissolution of the development of the personality. Freeman (1981) and Katan (1960) have used analyses of the processes of psychotic thinking similar to psychoanalytic dream analysis to produce reconstructions of the pre-psychotic mental life which have re-established the link and meaning behind a psychotic breakdown. It is important to be clear that while this establishment of a continuity in the mental life of the person between their functioning in normal and psychotic states helps us understand what is going on for our patients in their minds and to connect with them even when they are thinking in a very disturbed fashion, it does not of itself clarify how far the causes of their particular illness are genetic, organic, infective, chemical, connected with vulnerabilities or disturbances in the construction of their personality, or are a result of psychological traumata (disappointments in love, frustrations in life, destabilising successes, etc.). In an analogous way, loss of consciousness (and the appearance of the form of thinking that we call 'dreaming') may be a result of various different physical and emotional factors.

In 1887, when Hughlings Jackson was trying to describe the processes of evolution and dissolution in neurological development and disease in the individual, he used the analogy of the group. He said:

> The higher nervous arrangements evolved out of the lower keep down those lower, just as a government evolved out of a nation controls as well as directs that nation. If this be the process of evolution, then the reverse process of dissolution is not only a 'taking off' of the higher, but is at the very same time a 'letting go' of the lower.
>
> (Jackson, 1887)

It seems to me that that one can take Jackson's analogy with political evolution and dissolution further and actually observe such processes in communities where a terrorist campaign goes through different stages. Elsewhere in this book, we refer in some detail to the experience in Northern Ireland and demonstrate these processes of evolution (group development, including the development of vulnerabilities to breakdown of the group) and dissolution (regression of the group), but for me some of the key learning points are as follows.

Terrorism arises in a particular historico-political context. It usually breaks out after a lengthy gestation, but once released has its own terrible dynamic.

It also has different phases, with an early acute phase being gradually replaced by a period of chronic disturbance. In both stages, however, the community regresses from a myriad of individual differences maintained in a broad mosaic of relationships to a narrower frame of reference. In Northern Ireland, for example, the single difference between Protestant unionist people and Catholic nationalist people assumed pre-eminence, and was reflected in control of land and almost every other aspect of community life. This dynamic whereby the many other ways in which individual people see themselves and differentiate themselves from others are replaced by a single group division is described in detail by Amartya Sen in his book, *Identity and Violence* (2006).

It is not difficult to discern in these references to the process of acute dissolution and regression, emergence of primitive phenomena, chronicity, containment (with security measures rather than medication or in-patient care), and a slow resistance-bedevilled healing process, something analogous to the breakdown and repair of mental health in an individual. The question is, how far one can take this analogy in translating the evolutionary or developmental and psychoanalytical approach beyond the arena of individual intra-psychic conflict and mental illness into the field of intra- and inter-communal conflict – the province of group psychology?

Splitting and understanding

The notion that we should try to achieve some understanding of people and groups involved in politically motivated violence is a challenge to the simple law-and-order approach. The immediate emotional response to a terrorist campaign is often to split the community into bad (the terrorists who are outside the pale) and good (law-abiding citizens who need to be protected from them). This split was clearly observable in Northern Ireland, where it also deepened divisions between Protestants and Catholics. This deepening division was less over the acceptability of terrorism than whether the British government attempts to deal with it were justified and appropriate. There are similarities in the global War on Terror, where the terrorists are not being entirely successfully isolated, but those who proclaimed the war against them have experienced antagonism from erstwhile friends in response to their reaction to the terrorist campaign. The strength and depth of the hatred involved on all sides can overcome any rational appreciation of the damage of communal violence and war, which is self-evidently not in the interests of either individuals or society. Rational argument is a weak lever in the face of profound violence and hate, and in any case splitting into good and bad, and turning the struggle into a moral one of 'good against evil', is the exercise of a psychological defence mechanism against profound anxiety rather than a result of rational analysis.

Some analysts have adopted a different good/bad split, expressing the view that terrorism is a result of post-colonial poverty. ('Terrorism is caused by bad, wealthy imperialists oppressing poor but good natives.') There is clearly a moral impera-tive to address the painful inequalities of education, health and economic well-being in the world, but it is generally not societies at their poorest which fall victim to the tactic of terrorism. Northern Ireland began to experience terrorism as Catholic grievances were being addressed by a more progressive government in the late 1960s. The Middle East became more unstable after oil was discovered and enormous wealth came to the Gulf states. Mr. Osama bin Laden was not a poor man; indeed, he came from an element in the more wealthy Saudi elite. What Bin Laden did demonstrate in his personal life was much of the experience of humiliation and disrespect and their exculpation and repudiation by rage and hos-tile impulses aimed against a designated 'shaming other', which are the emotional driving forces in the group dynamic behind the involvement in terrorism (Robinson, 2001). It is not in the depths of deprivation but at the point of improve-ment that things become most vulnerable to breakdown. This suggests that the link with socioeconomic disadvantage is through the emotional reaction that may come out of the sense that the relative disadvantage is experienced as unjust and disrespectful.

A rationalist explanation by the political left for the emergence of violence as a last resort might read as follows. When people are aware that their relative disad-vantage is the result of poor education or social or cultural differences, they may sometimes accept these as unhappy but justifiable causes of their disadvantage. When their educational opportunities improve and they feel as capable as the next person, they begin to see their disadvantage more in terms of historic cultural, racial or political discrimination and oppression. If they are unable to change this by peaceful political means and non-violent options, the use of physical force, including terrorism, comes on to the agenda.

Those on the political right who espouse what is commonly referred to as 'real-politik' maintain that national leaders and their countries pursue what they per-ceive to be in their own best interests. They propose responses of a simple behavioural kind, giving economic and political favours as encouragement and embarking on punitive operations and war to discourage negative behaviour. The recent US approach to the wider Middle East and Israeli attacks on Palestinians could be seen as being characterised by this approach to the problem.

However, it seems to me that neither of these 'rational self-interest' models entirely work as explanations, nor will the actions that flow from them be success-ful, since we know from our clinical experience that individuals and groups often act against, rather than in, their own best interests, especially when their emotions run high. It is also clear that those on whose behalf terrorist campaigns are appar-ently waged (Catholic nationalists in Northern Ireland, first nation people in Peru, etc.) often suffer profoundly at the hands of their 'protector' terrorist organisa-tions. In addition, most terrorist campaigns are not successful (see p. 166). So if a rational strategic risk analysis were to be undertaken prior to a terrorist campaign, it would almost certainly conclude that those on whose behalf it was to be waged would be highly unlikely to benefit, but would almost certainly suffer a great deal more than their enemies. That such campaigns are undertaken anyway shows that they are not a result of a mere calculus of rational self-interest for the group. Passion is the driver.

The power of feelings, especially humiliation, shame and rage

Involvement in political life enabled me to get to know personally those who represented the different strands of group life in the politics of Ireland, North and South. I was struck by the powerful memories, on all sides of the community, of times when their group, or they as individuals, had been demeaned and their existence threatened. These feelings were profound, especially the sense of humiliation and the shame at having failed to prevent the degrading attacks. These experiences provoked deep anger and fear and created a capacity for responses at least as violent as those that had been experienced.

Subsequently, I have tried to explore whether this dynamic of injustice and humiliation and its relationship to the outbreak of terrorism is confined to Northern Ireland, and have examined a number of other countries that have also experienced violent insurgencies. I will refer very briefly to a couple of examples.

In Peru, there is an historic and, despite recent elections, a current failure by the descendants of the conquistadors to integrate the majority native population into the mainstream of establishment life. They remain generally poor, but also disrespected and excluded from positions of power. This was borne in on me as I participated in a ceremony when the remains of seven of the tens of thousands of those who 'disappeared' during the Sendero Luminosa (Shining Path, Maoist) terrorist insurgency were returned to their families. As I walked with the families through the streets of Ayacucho following the coffins, few people paid any attention. They just went about their business ignoring this multiple funeral. These grieving people and their dead relatives seemed to be of no import; they were split off and disregarded.

In Nepal – the last Hindu kingdom – the upper castes in power excluded the lower castes from positions of respect, and split the community into 'good' and 'bad', with the same toxic humiliation I had seen in Northern Ireland. Even limited moves towards democracy were set aside, and the representatives who then espoused the Maoist strategy only did so after the loss of these modest democratic institutions removed any democratic prospect for them. What is, however, striking about the Maoist response strategy in both Nepal and Peru is that despite their angry violent promotion of the cause of the oppressed, their own abuse of these same people was dreadful. Their lack of humanity in the treatment of those in whose cause they fought powerfully points up that it is not merely a rational response to the socioeconomic plight of the poor.

Although the situations in Northern Ireland, Peru and Nepal are widely divergent when assessed on economic, historical and political grounds, all have experienced violent internal insurgencies characterised by the use of terrorism, and it seems to me that these insurgencies stem from the long-standing sense of humiliation and disrespect felt by a significant section of the population. There is also a deep feeling of shame that is connected to a sense of failure to protect or repair, which is personal but also public, and experienced as a loss of power or agency. While humiliation is characterised by sadism, shame is linked to banishment and the terrible feeling of being wiped out. The narcissistic injuries of shame and humiliation together create the most violent and toxic of responses in the form of terrorism. That aggressive response has also been visited as much on their own section of the community as on the 'enemy'. A rational reaction model is much less helpful in explaining this outcome than one which also takes account of the processes of evolution and dissolution and the power of emotions in the causation of political terrorism.

Analysts of terrorism have often attempted to differentiate between the kind of terrorist insurgencies I have just described and the conflict between Islamists and the West. My own experiences of meeting and talking extensively with the leaders of Hamas and Hezbollah in the Middle East over the past few years have demonstrated to me that, certainly as far as they are concerned, the same key problems are present – severe relative deprivation, a deep sense of injustice especially (but not only) on the question of land, experiences of humiliation and disrespect, and a belief that all non-violent options have been exhausted. In this sense, these movements in Palestine, Lebanon and the surrounding region are local nationalist movements whose purpose is to right perceived wrongs on behalf of their own people. In so far as they turn to co-religionists for help, it is in the service of this primary purpose rather than their being inherently instruments of a wider malign conspiracy. The more they see no peaceful route to resolving the historical as well as the current hurt and grievance of their people and instead experience sanctions and exclusion, the more they will regress into destructive and indeed self-destructive acts. If an alternative route can be opened up, it may be that evolution towards a peaceful outcome can slowly be found, as has been the case in South Africa and Ireland.

A further question arises as to what group psychological processes are at work in the global jihadist networks of al-Qaeda and others. The origins of this movement are complex. At one level, we could observe that a combination of the collapse of the Soviet Union and the stable instability of the Cold War led to regression and the reappearance of the old nationalisms and religious divisions that had been kept in control and subjection for many years. In addition, since humanity has not yet found a way of living without an enemy, the loss of 'the familiar enemy' led to the emergence of Islamism not only *sui generis*, but also, one could argue, as an unconscious result of Western responses to the collapse of the Soviet Union, and the presence of the United States of America as the sole hyper-power (Alderdice, 1991, 2003).

Globalisation consequent on developments in communication, travel and weapons of mass effect produced profound group anxiety and a regression in thinking towards fundamentalism, and culturally to old societal themes and structures. The reaction is, however, deeply ambivalent because mixed with antipathy towards domination is a wish to possess all the benefits of education, healthcare and economic prosperity represented by Europe, but more especially its offspring, the United States of America. There is also the haunting problem of why Islamic society, which was once fertile in ideas and innovation, suffered such reversals and humiliation. Part of the answer given by Islamist fundamentalists is not just Western imperialism, but what is seen as Muslim betrayal, in the form of Arab royal families and the regime in Egypt enjoying oil wealth and the alliance with the West rather than sharing it with their own people. The reciprocal hypocrisy, as they see it, of Western powers proclaiming an attachment to democracy and human rights while allying themselves with undemocratic regimes and disregarding the results of free and fair elections adds to the shame, humiliation, sense of injustice and rage, and opens up the dangerous possibility of a regression beyond the split between Islam and the West into the communal split and sectarian bitterness of Shiite against Sunni.

These observations about the origins of terrorist violence are reminiscent of the work of Gilligan (1996) with mentally disturbed individuals who had committed serious violent crimes in the United States. He made observations about what he described as 'shaming' in prisoners who had committed very violent crimes against other persons, similar to what I am describing in the origins of the terrorism in various parts of the world. Despite the awfulness of their crimes, his prisoner patients also believed themselves to be justified; righting some terrible wrong, or some deep disrespect done to them. This is similar to the thoughts and feelings of those who engage in terrorism. While the rest of the world may see them as evil, those who engage in terrorist attacks believe that theirs is a moral and courageous activity motivated not by personal material gain but by principle. Those against whom they pit themselves are seen as the immoral ones, and they cite not only the political oppression noted earlier, but also the falling away of a sense of meaning and moral purpose and commitment in the West. This latter strand of their critique is actually a view shared by Christian fundamentalists in the West.

This shared view of groups that would otherwise regard each other with deep suspicion brings another issue into view. The analysis given above could easily be misused to serve a stance that simply condemned Israel and the United States of America; however, this is to fail to take the history of these two communities into account. The formation of the state of Israel was an attempt to find a safe haven for a religious group and nation which had been persecuted by Christendom for much of the last two millennia. The United States of America too was, for many of its citizens, a place to escape from religious and political persecution and economic hardship and misery in Europe. That both groups gave scant regard to the welfare of the indigenous people they found there, treating them as badly as they themselves had been treated in Europe, was a group manifestation of 'identification with the aggressor'. The gross appearance of such a psychological defence in the politics of today suggests that any process to address the problems of 'anti-Western' Islamist terrorism must also enable Israel and the United States to explore the origins of these difficulties in their history.

Primitive thinking, emotional responses and the process of making peace

Professor Gilligan's patients were individuals suffering from psychoses. As I have outlined earlier, this is not the case with individual terrorists, but is it possible to interpret the thinking of their group as analogous to a psychotic process? Certainly, terrorist groups can at times present a primitive mode of thinking which is difficult to engage in rational debate or argument. There is a denial in word and action of the individual humanity of those who are about to suffer at their hands. The perception of the people who will die in the Twin Towers or a bomb in Belfast or Tel Aviv is that they are Americans, Protestants, or Catholics or Jews, and that this is all that is to be said. Just as in psychotic thinking, the part stands for the whole, and the humanity and difference of the other is lost. There is little appreciation that those they kill may not even be their enemies. They may not as individuals share the position of their government or state. They may even have campaigned for the cause espoused by the terrorist who will now kill them as symbols of the hated Other. These possibilities are shut out from thinking. The people who will die are dismissed as the 'unfortunate collateral damage of war'. In using such a phrase, we become aware that the need to set aside the individual humanity of the victim of our violence is also a necessary defence for all soldiers, including those who respond militarily to terrorist attacks with orders to 'destroy the terrorists'. The attachment to a hard-won rational system of law and liberal democracy is always in danger of being loosened by the powerful emotions unleashed in the community by the terrifying nature of terrorism and war. Terror is a result of the regression into violence, but terror is not a mere side effect of these attacks. It is the terrorist's purpose not just to blow away people and buildings but also the institutional and mental structures of freedom and order that a group worked for centuries to put in place. As we shall see in Part II, an angry terrorism often provokes an emotional response rather than a calculated one.

In Northern Ireland, the failure of the terrorist campaign led eventually to the profoundly regressive behaviour represented in the 'dirty protest' and the hunger strikes of 1981, which created martyrs because of the character of the response of the British Prime Minister, Margaret Thatcher (see pp. 116–117). This helped make their deaths into a symbolically powerful 'blood sacrifice' and contributed in very significant measure to the political rise of Sinn Fein, which now represents the majority of the Catholic nationalist community in Northern Ireland. This increase in the strength of the republican movement's political wing began even while its military wing (PIRA) was still involved in violent criminal activity, though not, after 9/11, in overt terrorist tactics. In the Middle East, the reactions to the suicide bombings have also contributed to the creation of a generation of martyrs with their conscious, voluntary 'blood sacrifice'. By treating themselves in a less than human fashion, they become glorified. While their enemies respond with a mistaken analysis that punishment will stop the bad behaviour, Islamists have grasped the psychological transcendence and paradox on the other side of dehumanisation.

In South Africa and Northern Ireland, it was finally discovered that only a long process of containing difficult emotions, building relationships and untangling the historic repetitions of hurt and humiliation gave any hope for the future. It was remarkably similar to the process of individual and group psychotherapy. In pursuing and being involved in this process, I was struck by the work of the French Canadian Rene Girard (1977), who has written extensively and with considerable insight about the connections between group violence, sacrifice, law, religion, culture and the scapegoat mechanism. He acknowledges the insights of Freud, who realised that while the evidence of the clinic had led him to valuable understandings about the vicissitudes of the libidinal drive in the individual, the inescapable tragedies of the First World War required him to re-evaluate his understanding of aggression and the importance of the group. Girard, however, draws attention to Freud's reference, in *Group Psychology and the Analysis of the Ego* (1921), to the inescapable conflict arising from identification in the relationship between the boy and his father. The inevitable emergence of hostility when the boy imitates the desire of his father in relation to his mother leads to the Oedipus complex. Freud notes in the paper that 'identification, in fact, is ambivalent from the very first' (Section VII, Identification, p. 134, para 2). Girard's complaint is that Freud does not then follow this insight through to what he sees as its logical conclusion, which is the relational and imitative nature of aggression and its outcome in violence, though other analysts including Klein, Bion and Rosenfeld have gone on to address this. Girard himself further explores the ways in which the mechanism which he refers to as 'mimesis' leads inevitably to violence unless the social boundaries of religion, law and culture are respected. Mimesis is the precursor to identification and individuation, that is to say the development of the individual self, albeit always in relationship with others. It is a primary activity. Perhaps the 'holy' or 'sacred' characteristic of martyrdom in the regression of suicide bombing and hunger strikes in particular, and terrorism in general, is linked to going back to first principles and primary relationships – redrawing the map in the most 'pure' manner possible.

The implication of Girard's approach is that it is not religion that is the cause of violence, not even fundamentalist religion – though it is along the regressive road – but rather it is the breakdown of the 'cultural' boundaries established through religion and law that results in the release of violence. This argument implies that after the breakdown of the horrible but stabilising boundary of the Cold War, the emergence of a new and peaceful world order depended on putting new boundaries of various kinds in place. Without that, the positive opportunities of globalisation with its freedom to trade, travel and communicate could only be perceived as a threat. The current regression to fundamentalist ways of thinking in the West as well as the East is then a flight from and defence against this modernity in the absence of other more healthy defences. The Islamists make this clear when they proclaim that the solution is for the great evil which is America to leave their part of the world, that is to say for a new East/West boundary to be established. This is a profound and dangerous regression, but without alternative boundaries such as those set by the United Nations and international law, reciprocal violence seems almost inevitable.

The appearance of terrorism can therefore be reinterpreted not as a moral issue (on either side) but as a symptom of psychotic-like regression to acting out a fantasy of a primary, idealised 'object' (the wish-belief of a past perfection) with which the terrorist mimetically identifies – a kind of group equivalent of psychosis. We are well aware as psychiatrists of the need from time to time for appropriate and sensitive containment (pharmacological, physical and social) if a patient with psychosis and their family are to be able to benefit from psychological therapies and find healing. By analogy, we could make the proposition that the important role of containment and boundary setting in the national and international sphere should not be portrayed as a moral intervention, but rather the creation of a context in which the disturbed thoughts, feelings and behaviour of all the groups involved, as well as the causes of the disturbance, can be addressed.

4

THE ROOTS OF CONFLICT IN NORTHERN IRELAND

Nora Gribbin and Rodney Turtle

But as the deluge [of the First World War] subsides and the waters fall short we see the dreary steeples of Fermanagh and Tyrone emerging once again. The integrity of their quarrel is one of the few institutions that have been unaltered in the cataclysm which has swept the world.

Sir Winston Spencer Churchill addressing the House of Commons on 16 February, 1922

Introduction

The Troubles is the name given by the people of Northern Ireland to the times when the long-standing conflict between the two polarized communities erupted into a violent conflict that was to last some 30 years. Many commentators trace the start to the late 1960s when a series of marches demanding equal rights for the Catholic minority community were met with at least containment and often violence by government forces. Conflict spilled over into the wider community, resulting in some 3,500 deaths and 35,000 injuries in the 30 years. New security measures and a large increase in the presence of security forces impacted the people. Some accepted personal freedoms were curtailed. Anxiety levels increased, and a lack of business confidence and investment contributed heavily to a period of relative economic stagnation.

Let us first take a look at the history of the Northern Ireland before considering the onset of the Troubles. In chapter 7, we focus on a single day, Bloody Sunday, which aggravated a cycle of violence. In chapter 14, we ask if the peace process can truly offer continuing hope.

A brief history of the Northern Irish conflict

Since the earliest settlement of Ireland, the northeastern Irish people maintained a sense of separateness, always feeling closer to those across the channel in Scotland, than they did to people in the rest of the island. In an age when roads were few and often impassable, the stretch of water between Antrim, in the north of Ireland, and Galloway, in southern Scotland, became less of a boundary and more a channel of communication enabling people to move back and forth with relative ease.

Superimposed on this relationship between some of the people in Ireland and Scotland was England's historic struggle for control of the whole archipelago of islands. Much of the history of the islands is of violent struggle for control of territory. The same political debate is still very much alive today though fortunately promoted largely if not exclusively through democratic politics rather than physical force.

Religious adherence had no small part in these struggles. Relations between the Roman Catholic Church with the British state, from the time of Henry VIII and the English Reformation in the early 16th century, were very difficult. Political and religious affiliations gradually came together in Ireland at that time too. Scotland's own Presbyterian form of church was based on Swiss Calvinism, and quite distinct from the episcopacy of the Anglican Church.

British attempts to subdue Ireland increasingly involved the settlement or 'planting' of Scots and English colonists who, it was hoped, would be loyal to the British Crown and defend their new homeland, as well as promote the Protestant strand of the Christian religion in Ireland.

Economic necessities mainly drove the Irish diaspora. During the mid-1800s, the Irish potato blight brought starvation. A quarter of the population died, while many survivors emigrated to the eastern United States. Those emigrants, the majority of whom were of Catholic origin, retained great attachment to their motherland and were a kindred spirit to the Irish people still at home.

In 1916, in Dublin, an unsuccessful rebellion by republicans became known as the Easter Rising. Support for the defeated rebels only strengthened when British forces executed the leaders. Padraig Pearce immediately became an enduring Irish martyr to the cause of Irish freedom. In 1919 the Anglo-Irish war (or Irish War of Independence) broke out. This ended with the 1921 Anglo-Irish Treaty which set up the Irish Free State but ' ... allowed the Parliament of Northern Ireland to exclude Northern Ireland from the powers of the Parliament and Government of the Irish Free State' (Saville, Hoyt & Toohey, 2010, vol. 1, para 7.8). This resulted in the partition of Ireland into six predominantly Protestant northern counties and 26 predominantly Catholic southern counties. The northern province remained part of the United Kingdom and subject to the British parliament in Westminster. This division sparked the Irish civil war, largely fought in the South, while the unionist North established the Northern Ireland Constitution as a self-governing dominion. Partition was the chief herald of the future conflict in the north between the Protestants and Catholics.

In 1936, the Irish Free State Parliament introduced the External Authority Act, and the Bunreacht na hÉireann (Irish Constitution) was enacted in July 1937, renaming the state Éire or Ireland. Articles 2 and 3 laid territorial claim to all 32 counties of the island of Ireland. Westminster responded with the Ireland Act 1949 clarifying dominion over Northern Ireland: 'In no event will Northern Ireland or any part thereof cease to be a part of His Majesty's dominions and of the United Kingdom without the consent of the Parliament of Northern Ireland.' Little was done by way of cross-border cooperation of any kind, and the two states developed separately.

The Southern Irish state emphasised and developed its independence by leaving the British Commonwealth, becoming a republic, remaining neutral during the Second World War, and refusing to join the NATO military alliance.

After 50 years of partition, the percentage of Protestants in the Irish Republic had fallen from just over 10% to around 3%. Divisions between the Protestant North of the island and the Catholics in the rest of the country seemed unbridgeable, and the substantial Catholic minority in the North (as it came to be called) began to feel isolated and alienated.

The Troubles (1968–1998)

At the start of the era of mass communication, civil rights marchers of the late 1960s took to the streets inspired by the international recognition of human rights and equality movements in countries such as South Africa and the southern states of the United States. Key issues were the sense of alienation from the state and the problems of political and religious discrimination against Irish nationalists, especially Catholics, in terms of unfair housing policies, employment and voting rights. Hard-line Protestant elements greeted the civil rights marches with violence, which sparked serious urban unrest in certain pockets of Belfast and Derry. While the trouble was still contained within Northern Ireland, the context was the territorial dispute between the North and South and the unresolved relationship between Great Britain and Ireland.

This breakdown quickly became bloody. In the subsequent violence, 3,500 people were killed, and tens of thousands injured in a population of just 1.5 million (in the United Kingdom, the same proportion would represent hundreds of thousands). The government's first reaction was to deal with the problem purely as a matter of internal security. However, the Northern Ireland Government and the police (the Royal Ulster Constabulary) failed to stem the violence. The Civil Authorities (Special Powers) Act of 1922 and the Emergency Powers Act of 1926 – legislation which had been introduced as an emergency measure immediately after the Irish civil war – gave the government extensive powers. It remained in force and was periodically used over the following 50 years. In 1971, its use was manifest in detention without trial, internment being a last-ditch attempt at internal management. As many observers had predicted, the security situation deteriorated disastrously. There were perpetrators on both sides, but it was mainly Catholics who were arrested and detained. There were 2,400 arrests in the first six months; most of those arrested were not implicated in illegal groups and were soon released. There were abuses and affronts: interrogation techniques used at the time were later to be condemned by the European Court of Human Rights as 'inhuman and degrading' treatment.

It came to be almost universally regarded as a misjudgement of historic proportions which inflicted tremendous damage both politically and in terms of fatalities.

(McKittrick & McVea, 2001, p. 69)

Internment had a counterproductive effect: it acted as a recruiting sergeant for the Irish Republican Army (IRA), whose Provisional Wing (PIRA) became the main republican terrorist group. The IRA of an older generation known as the OIRA – the official IRA – had been largely inactive. Now PIRA emerged, partly to help protect Catholic areas against Protestant mobs.

The Troubles continued for over three decades in cycles of violence involving Catholics, Protestants and the various security forces, before some kind of realisation prevailed to allow the Good Friday Agreement to be signed (1998) and to offer hope of peace and reconciliation.

In the context of this historical overview, we now consider some of the relevant events in Derry City leading up to Bloody Sunday.

Voting rights in Northern Ireland were linked to house ownership, which favoured the Protestant community and disenfranchised the many Catholics living in rented accommodation. This was particularly relevant in Derry, the second city in the Northwest of Northern Ireland, which had a 60% Catholic population but quite remarkably a unionist council. Gerrymandering was as rife as discrimination in employment and housing. Derry is divided by the River Foyle into the west bank called the Cityside and the east bank known as the Waterside. Catholics dominated the west Cityside, whereas Protestants held sway on the Waterside. Activists from both sides of the community sought equal rights for the disadvantaged and unemployed, who often lived in poor housing conditions. Both communities often had the same problems.

Saturday, 5 October, 1968, is the Troubles' official start date (McKittrick & McVea, 2001). It followed the RUC's heavy-handed response to a civil rights march in Derry organised by activists with some input from the Northern Ireland Civil Rights Association (NICRA). Unionists strongly opposed this march, and there was talk of a counter march by the Apprentice Boys of Derry (a pattern of counter demonstration was a recognised tactic). A last-minute ban by the Stormont government's Minister of Home Affairs had been disregarded.

Worldwide communication was now instant, and as the response to the march was captured on film and the television footage and shown around the world, it provoked an overwhelmingly hostile reaction outside Northern Ireland. The United Kingdom Government increased pressure on the Northern Ireland Government to step up the pace of reform, and the long-standing convention that Northern Irish affairs were not discussed at Westminster was finally abandoned. Within Northern Ireland, the Catholic population was outraged to hear that the Stormont Cabinet tabled a motion congratulating the Royal Ulster Constabulary (RUC) on their policing.

In January 1969, another march was notoriously ambushed at Burntollet bridge near Derry City by Loyalists and off-duty volunteer police (B Specials).

....The police had become regarded by many in the nationalist community not as impartial keepers of the peace and upholders of the law, but
rather as agents of the unionist Northern Ireland Government, employed
in their view to keep the nationalist community subjugated, often by the
use of unjustifiable and brutal force.

(Saville, Hoyt & Toohey, 2010 – section 2.2)

Seven months later, a riot broke out when the annual Apprentice Boys Parade in
Derry skirted the Bogside and ended in a stand-off between the rioters and over
1000 police in armoured cars who deployed water cannon and tear gas to subdue
the crowd. The Battle of the Bogside raged for three to four days and convincingly
demonstrated the ineffectiveness of the RUC. British PM James Callaghan sent in
the army as a short-term strategy to restore law and order in Derry City.

At first, the army was welcomed by the Catholic population in both Derry and
Belfast as a protective force against the discriminatory policing. Two years later,
this trust had been shattered. As the violence escalated, army numbers in Northern
Ireland were increased to 7000.

As Colin Parkes notes on p. 84, violence leading to deaths has the greatest
impact on the community. The Saville inquiry concluded that 'the increased level
of violence, and particularly fatal violence, in Northern Ireland in the period to the
end of July 1971 is shown starkly by the figures ... In 1969, 18 people were killed
in incidents related to the Troubles; in 1970 there were 28 deaths. In the first seven
months of 1971, 31 people were killed' (Saville, Hoyt & Toohey, 2010, vol. 1,
para 7.114). In Derry, the British army shot and killed two unarmed rioters in the
Bogside. At the time, Brigadier Alan Cowan noted: 'Oversimplifying, we handed
the IRA on a plate on 7 and 8 July what had been denied them for 18 months, i.e.,
we were sucked in, used our weapons for the first time in Derry and that turned the
population against us and towards the IRA ... We have broken rule one in the
internal security book; instead of having a friendly population, or at least one that
practices benevolent neutrality, we now face an entirely hostile community.'

In August 1971, the reintroduction of internment escalated the violence and led
to a further upsurge in support for both wings of the IRA in Derry. 'In the four
days after the introduction of internment, the continuing unrest led to 25 deaths
and many injuries' (Saville, Hoyt & Toohey, 2010, vol. 1, para 8.53). Within days,
'Free Derry' was established; in the Bogside, Brandywell and Creggan, both
wings of the IRA, the Provisionals and the Officials, operated openly with widespread popular support, patrolling the area in armed patrols and establishing
offices throughout the area. Free Derry also served as a secure base for operations
throughout the rest of the city, and its existence proved a consistent embarrassment both to the unionist government at Stormont and the British Army.

A further ban on parades and marches imposed on 18 January, 1972, was flouted
four days later at Magilligan Strand County Derry when a demonstration against
internment took place. This march was met with force from The Parachute
Regiment (Paras) of the British Army.

Nigel Wade described to the Saville Inquiry: 'I recall seeing paratroopers firing baton rounds into the chest of marchers at very short distance and that the regiment's NCOs had to use riot sticks to control their own soldiers' (Saville, Hoyt & Toohey, § 9–207).

The nature of the differences between the two communities

We now consider some of the influences on the mindset of those living on each side of the divided society in Northern Ireland in the 1970s when 'Bloody Sunday' occurred.

On many issues there is a striking similarity of views between the two communities where they report similar reactions to questions posed by researchers on topics such as reasons for liking and disliking Northern Ireland, their thoughts on emigration, the role of the trade unions and views on class in Northern Ireland. Attitudes to the English and the southern Irish were also surprisingly similar.

This large amount of common ground goes some way to explaining how civil society has remained so cohesive and coexisted alongside political discord and violence. We see a population that, from an objective viewpoint, seems to have more to bind them together than to cleave them apart though, evidently, there are two distinct communities with important and deep divisions which influence how they feel and think about themselves, their own community and the 'other' community. These are powerful fault lines which contribute to the sense of 'us' and 'them' which are necessary for popular acquiescence and support of terrorist motives and actions. This division is best seen as reflecting two patterns of attachment to complex identities which are partly defined by their differences. Viewed in this light, any attempt at reconciliation is felt as a kind of abuse of the object of attachment.

Idealistically, (stereotypic) Irishness embodies ethnically Gaelic ancestry, a traditional language and music within a Gaelic culture, adhering to Catholicism (since the conversion from Paganism by St Patrick in 600 AD) though with loss of the native Gaelic tongue through the enforced use of the English language by the elite in the 14th century Pale, in Dublin. For centuries it has been difficult to separate religion from nationhood as the church and state were entwined, and religion played such a central role in the Irish community. This identity is compounded by the historical grievance of subjugation and disadvantage by an oppressive and discriminating colonial enemy and Protestant power. While many Protestants in Northern Ireland have a different sense of Irishness, without certainly the Catholic dimension and without the Gaelic heritage, there may be less solidarity or security within this group owing to differing Protestant religious denominations and historical origins. Many refer to themselves as British rather than Irish, and many seek an affiliation to Britain for a sense of belonging as a group. In this sense, they are just as nationalistic as the Irish 'nationalists', the essential difference being the entity to which they were attached.

Primary dimensions of dichotomy

Thus, we have a nationalist group which believed that the island of Ireland was their true homeland, one nation with a shared culture and heritage which should never have been divided and which should be reunited. On the other side, the unionist group saw their roots and security in the strength and legitimacy of the union with Great Britain; they associate themselves with British culture and values. This dichotomy was challenged in the 1960s by developments in both the unionist and nationalist camps when the civil rights movement sought an end to discriminatory practices in voting and housing allocation and demanded 'British rights for British citizens' as a primary policy objective (Whyte, 1991, p. 195): this seemed to have little in common with old-fashioned nationalism. Two strands formed in the unionist camp into those whose main attachment was to Great Britain (the British nationalists) and those whose main attachment was to their Protestant religion, which they saw as being best defended by the link to Great Britain. The former were represented by the Official Unionist Party, and the latter supported Ian Paisley's Democratic Unionist Party.

As we saw in chapter 1, both attachments to God and attachments to homes and territories expand to include many associated persons, places and assumptions. Indeed, as in some Muslim countries, church and state can merge. In Northern Ireland too, church and culture are intertwined so that social activities such as sports clubs, women's guilds and youth clubs develop along religious lines as do voluntary organisations, dramatic societies, old people's homes and craft clubs.

There is extensive reference in the literature and indeed widespread agreement within Northern Ireland that it is possible to place individuals as belonging to the Protestant or Catholic community by how they look, talk and deport themselves. Whyte concludes that 'a complex interplay of clues – name, face, dress, demeanour, residence, education, language, and iconography – provided the evidence' permitting this attribution with great accuracy (Whyte, 1990, p. 21).

Paradoxically, both sides regard themselves as minorities. Protestants, though a majority in Northern Ireland, know they are a minority in the island of Ireland, whereas Catholics are well aware of their minority status in Northern Ireland yet know that they are part of the majority population of the island as a whole. Both sides may then regard themselves as threatened minorities with behaviours and attitudes which reflect this mindset (see pp. 17 and 73 for further consideration of the psychology of victims).

The Protestant community, most notably the Orange Order, organises an extensive series of marches and parades annually to commemorate and celebrate their various historical victories, a tradition they wish to perpetuate. During the annual 'marching season', many thousands of band parades take place across Northern Ireland. They are often routed close to, or even through, Catholic areas. Protestants who take part in these marches view these as a legitimate celebration of their history and legacy, whereas Catholics regard them as insensitive and often provocative triumphal displays of superiority and dominance. These celebrations could be construed as a psychological defence in the collective psyche of those participating, reflecting the insecurity of their attachment to the union and, as a minority in Ireland, to the inferred threat from the Irish Republic (see p. 50). Any change in the routine of the marching route is resisted, and there is no compromise – 'not an inch' – a resonance with the former attitude of leaders such as Paisley to a united Ireland. Prejudice, attitudes and assumptions are evident in the observation that 'northern Protestant businessmen feared that a Dublin Parliament would be dominated by farmers neither competent to administer industrial Ulster nor concerned about its welfare' (Bardon, 1992, p. 405). Painted pavements and associated bunting in the Union colours clearly demarcate Protestant areas just as surely as the gable ends of houses in 'Free Derry' are covered with murals depicting a Catholic view of the armed struggle.

Thus, we have a dichotomy that cannot describe the full range, variety and nuance of the views held by all individuals within the communities but is nonetheless deeply descriptive and illustrative of a complex situation in a divided community. These two communities have belief systems underpinned by a set of secondary dimensions stemming from their own heritage and the role they see for their communities in Northern Irish society.

Secondary dimensions of dichotomy

Although the labels 'Protestant' and 'Catholic' have come to stand for the two sides in Northern Ireland, there are a range of other dimensions which add colour and meaning to the differences between the two communities and how they view themselves. They have given rise to myths of superiority and inferiority as described on pages 81–84.

One of the more obvious is a myth of ethnicity which stems from the perceived geographical and cultural origins of the two communities. Many in Northern Ireland think that the Protestant community comprises the successors of the Protestant landowners and agricultural workers from the waves of settlement in Ireland and especially Northern Ireland from the 16th century. This 'Plantation of Ulster' brought Protestants from England and Scotland who had a different religion, culture and traditions from the indigenous Irish Catholic population whose land they occupied and whose livelihoods they diminished. Invariably, the settlers regarded themselves as cultured, civilized and clearly superior to the native Irish, whom they regarded as little more than backward barbarians. They held themselves aloof from the Irish population for their own security and by their own preferences, so there was initially limited contact between the planted and native stock. While this myth is compelling, it is far from complete. For a start, it downplays differences within the settlers. More of them came from Scotland, but the majority of the landowners were of English origin and had all the differences entailed by history, outlook and culture. There was also a complex stratification among the settlers: the elite landowners adhered to the Anglican faith, and the tenants hailed from Scotland and belonged to more fundamental faiths such as

Presbyterianism or Methodism (Bardon, 1992). Over the coming centuries, the settlers certainly assimilated much of the culture of their new surroundings but remained profoundly aware of their origins.

This mythology forgets that there were major waves of settlement of Ireland from Wales, Normandy and England after the Norman invasion of Ireland in 1169–71. These so-called 'Old English' were gradually assimilated into Irish society and acquired its indigenous culture over the centuries. By the time of the Plantation, in the mind of the settlers, they were much more closely identified with the native population than with their origins and were deeply distrusted owing to their Catholic religion and regarded as degenerate owing to their long association with Irish culture. Native Irish elites began to speak English from the 14th century, when the ruling English introduced laws to require English to be spoken. Old English and the Irish elite communities viewed each other with mistrust, but both looked down on the mainly low-class Gaelic speakers.

Recent scholarship reveals that native and planted peoples did not hold themselves as far apart as previously thought: significant intermarriage and changes of religion occurred. As Jonathan Bardon (1992) notes, 'by the late nineteenth century descendants of natives and planters had become so intermingled that it would be quite wrong to conclude ... that the majority of Catholics are of Gaelic origin and that most Protestants are of British colonial stock.' Yet, this persistent division proved a remarkably resilient belief (Ruane and Todd, 1996) that would become further elaborated as Northern Ireland developed.

Several other themes define and polarize the two communities. These may have less significance than the religious and political differences between the two communities but have a profound influence on their collective psyches and how each side perceives the other.

Economic Differences. A consensus has yet to emerge on the reasons for the gap between the relatively more affluent Protestant community and the less affluent Catholic community; there is broad agreement that the gap was real (though now narrowed) and a painful reminder of discrimination against Catholics. According to Whyte, the gap 'is sufficient to embitter relations between the two communities'. (Whyte, 1990, p. 64). The perception of economic disadvantage persists despite changes in the patterns of employment opportunities in the latter decades of the 20th century.

Housing. In Northern Ireland, the issue of unequal access of the two communities to public housing was a well-known and divisive issue. Separation of the two communities is most distinctly seen in working-class areas of Belfast, Derry and some of the larger towns. Research shows that 'in round figures, about 35% to 40% of the population lives in segregated neighbourhoods' (Gallagher & O'Connell, 1983, p. 34). Where segregation exists, it can be a powerful contributor to misunderstanding between the two communities through ignorance of each other.

Another potent source of complaint came from Catholics seeking access to public housing controlled by local authorities. Bardon (1992) notes that in western counties, battling for political control of councils' 'provision of local authority housing was only made where it would not affect the electoral balance'. Discrimination was rife. Referring to Catholics in local council houses, 'One and that's too bloody many,' commented the mayor of Portadown (Gallagher and O'Connell, 1983, p. 19). The behaviour of local councils was largely condoned by the Northern Ireland government, which would not overrule them. This powerful source of anger and injustice significantly contributed to the birth of the Civil Rights movement.

Throughout Northern Ireland, there is a deeply ingrained rule and practice of not selling property or land to 'the other side', often enforced by intimidation, for fear of losing ground, so to speak. In business, this is manifested by only trading with your 'own side'. For example, in Derry, many Waterside residents would prefer to drive 30 miles to the market town of Coleraine to shop than venture across the river to the Cityside. These sorts of behaviours and attitudes maintain the divide.

Education. 'A striking feature of Northern Irish society has been the existence of two parallel sets of schools' (Whyte, 1990, p. 42) with the 'controlled' or state schools being multi-denominational but in practice Protestant and the 'maintained' schools supported by public money too, open to all, but set up and controlled by the Catholic church. Those attended by Protestants stress Britishness and British culture, whereas Catholics attend schools which emphasise the Catholic observances and traditions. State schools, attended mainly by Protestants, play rugby, cricket and soccer, which the Catholic community regards as British sports. Catholics are introduced to Gaelic football in their parishes and through their schools and are closely associated with county teams that partake in annual all-Ireland leagues. The only truly integrated educational establishments were the universities.

Conclusions

We have outlined the history of Northern Ireland and how it became populated by two distinct groups – the majority regarding themselves of settler origin, adhering to the Protestant religion, and the minority seeing their origins in the native Gaelic population of Ireland and following the Catholic religion.

In our analysis of this situation, we have seen how each group developed distinct sets of attachments and assumptions which each believed to be essential sources of security. Protestants saw their security as rooted in their British nationality and power, earned by conquest and supported by the British queen and government. That myth had been challenged, within recent memory, by the secession of the major (Catholic) part of Ireland. As a result, the Protestant attachment pattern in Northern Island had become insecure and fearful, with the predictable result that they clung harder than ever to the old mythology, idealising it and denigrating those whom they perceived as threatening the myth. Catholics, on the other hand, saw their security as rooted in their attachment to God and to their

God-given right to an Irish identity. Those in Northern Ireland had witnessed secession of their brothers and sisters in the South and now saw themselves as second-class citizens in Northern Ireland. They too felt insecure, clung to their attachments and distrusted the dominant party.

We have examined how this conflict was aggravated by segregated employment, housing, religion, education, sports and leisure and by triumphal demonstrations and injustices. As the Troubles continued, a pattern of civil disorder leading to counter-violence escalated from the actions of a few extremists to involve much of the population in some of the poorer urban areas, including 'Free Derry', where a near insurrection had taken place.

5

THE ROOTS OF CONFLICT
IN RWANDA

Peter Hall and Colin Murray Parkes

The 1994 Rwandan genocide is one of the defining events of the twentieth century. It was a genocide characterised by mass participation by the majority civilian Hutu population, the bloody slaughter of neighbours and former friends, and the cruelty of the methods of execution. Although the underlying causes were multifactorial, the event that triggered the genocide was the assassination of President Juvenal Habyarimana.

In this chapter, we trace the events leading up to the assassination. In chapter 8, we describe the consequent escalation of deadly violence that led to the killing of about 800,000 people. In chapter 15, we consider the subsequent peace process. Apart from the references quoted, our information for all three chapters comes from our visits to Rwanda in 1994 (Peter Hall – PH), 1995 (Colin Murray Parkes – CMP) and 2012 (CMP). Ten interviews were recorded in 2012 and will be identified by the first name of the interviewee in italics.

Historical context and the development of negative codes, prejudices and assumptions

Rwanda is a hilly country, the size of Wales, in central Africa. Surrounded by Uganda, Tanzania, Burundi and the DRC (Democratic Republic of the Congo. Its destiny has been heavily influenced by its neighbours, and by its colonial history. With a population density similar to that of the United Kingdom but no industrial base to support it, it is one of the poorest countries in the world. It has few mineral resources and relies on subsistence agriculture and two harvests a year to survive.

Before the genocide, 84% of the population were ethnic Hutus, 15% ethnic Tutsis, and 1% Twa (pygmies). During the 19th century and the first half of the 20th century, it was dominated by Tutsis, who typically owned cattle, and considered themselves, and were seen by their Belgian colonial masters, as a superior caste. Kamukama (1993, pp. 12, 13) suggests that their occupation as herdsmen accustomed them to protecting their herds from animal and human enemies, and collectively raiding and counter-raiding other groups had enabled the Tutsis to develop military skills and, eventually, mobile armies. In contrast, the majority Hutus were agriculturalists, farmers whose settled family communities had seldom depended on their skill as warriors. Rwanda has historical links with groups who speak the same language, Kinyarwandan, living in neighbouring countries. As a former Belgian colony, it remained within the Franco-Belgian sphere of influence and, latterly, developed a defence pact with France. Among colonial influences were a system of Catholic schooling with a strong influence on obedience and firm opposition to the use of birth control. Their communities were tightly organised on a hierarchical model that enabled strict government control to be maintained.

In 1959, as the Belgian colonialists were planning to leave, a Hutu uprising toppled the privileged Tutsi aristocracy and the populist Hutu administration depicted all Tutsis as scheming, treacherous, speculators in their overpopulated country. Just as Hitler had blamed the economic plight of Germany after World War I on the Jews, so the Hutu governing elite made the Tutsis the scapegoat for the economic plight of Rwanda. Thereafter, grassroots antipathy between the ethnic groups gave rise to growing prejudice.

Eugenie, M: 'Among the students there was discrimination … some nuns were really, really bad.'

Albert: 'I remember in the mid-1960s I was at school and I remember my teacher, whom I loved, and there was fighting. I remember this teacher pinching my nose and saying "You are finished now" and I had admired him, he was my hero, and he said "you are dead" (sighs).

A series of massacres took place.

Albert: 'When I went home … the whole village was empty and they were all hiding, and my father took me by the hand into the bush. I thought it was kind of a picnic, you could see the moon in the night, but you could feel the fear around you. People from the other part of the country were attacking. … My worst memory is seeing my father trembling for his family.'

Three hundred thousand Tutsis fled the country.

During the 1960s, incursions into Rwanda by exiled Tutsis provoked reprisal massacres, led or instigated by officials, in which nearly 20,000 Tutsis still resident in Rwanda were killed (Human Rights Watch, 2006). Some exiled Tutsis joined local armies and began to plan for their return. Among them was the future leader, Paul Kagame, born an aristocratic Tutsi, whose family escaped to Uganda when he was two. 'His earliest memories are of houses burning on a hill, shouting and commotion, his desperate mother, the family scrambling into a car as a Hutu death squad came running down the hill towards them' (Grant, 2010).

As we saw on pages 23–5 forced expulsions from homes and homelands give rise to intense grief and homesickness that can become prolonged and remain intense if the new environment fails to provide the security that is the essence of a home. Conditions in the refugee camps were bad, and the lot of refugees in Uganda was worst of all. In contrast to Tanzania and Zaire, Uganda denied citizenship even to the children of refugees (Mamdani 2001). Repeated appeals to President Habyarimana to allow exiled Tutsi to return to their own country came to nothing, despite the involvement of UNHCR in the negotiations. 'Having been a refugee informs much of my thinking. It's very close to being dehumanised,' says Kagame (Luscombe, 2011). In 1982, he, along with many fellow Tutsis, joined the rebel National Resistance Army (NRA) of Yoweri Museveni that, by 1986, had won control of Uganda. He gained extensive military experience and had been appointed as Museveni's Chief Intelligence Officer. Three years later, Amnesty International reported violations of human rights by elements of Museveni's army against the Acholi tribe. They included the torture and killing of prisoners without trial. While Kagame's name was not mentioned, he fled Rwanda when Tutsis were being massacred and so might have learnt then how to 'tolerate' revenge.

> There was ... a hardening that is still there in the way I approach many things. You can't shock me, because what can be worse than what I have seen and lived through?
>
> (Interview with Paul Kagame; Grant, 2010)

The growing influence of Rwandans in Museveni's army had concerned many Ugandans. To allay their suspicions by removing a leader from the scene, Kagame was sent abroad. He was posted in 1990 to Cuba, then to Fort Leavenworth in the United States to undergo training in guerrilla and other warfare. The distrust had been justified – Kagame and his colleague, Fred Rwigyema, had established the Rwandese Patriotic Front (RPF) – a secret army within the Ugandan national army, with Kagame as second in command. In October 1990, the RPF invaded northern Rwanda, where they were met by a combined force of Rwandan government and French troops. The RPF's charismatic leader, Rwigema, was killed on the second day, and Kagame's dash home proved too late to prevent a collapse in morale and the rout of the invasion force.

Twenty years previously, Major-General Habyarimana had seized power in Rwanda in a coup d'etat, and set up a one-party state with tight central control headed by the Mouvement Revolutionnaire National pour le Development (MRND). The party was dominated by a close circle of Hutu extremists, at the centre of which was his politically active wife, Agathe. It was this court within a court, known as the 'akazu' (little house), which comprised relatives in key political positions and a network of associates and informers, that two decades later would mastermind the genocide (Gourevitch, 1998).

Initially, Habyarimana had promoted genuine national development, but after nearly twenty years in power his popularity was waning. The governing elite could extract only limited surplus value directly from the peasant masses. In addition to taxes, they had two other potential sources of enrichment: skimming export revenues and foreign aid. During the late 1980s and early 1990s, the three sources of export earnings (coffee, tea and tin) declined. Coffee export receipts fell from $144 million in 1985 to $30 million in 1993, government budgets were cut, and the only remaining source of enrichment was foreign aid. Those who could benefit from it had to be in positions of political power. Consequently, elite Hutus engaged in a fierce competition for control of the rapidly shrinking economy.

The timing of the RPF invasion was unfortunate for Habyarimana because donor countries' demands for austerity measures and the collapse in coffee prices had weakened support for the government. He found himself torn between pressures from the donors countries to move towards a more democratic form of government and pressure from his main source of domestic political support, the akazu, to maintain the status quo. Much of what power the President retained was concentrated within the 'akazu' (OAU Report 2006).

Under Kagame's effective command, the defeated RPF regrouped among the mountains of northern Rwanda and grew steadily stronger. Meanwhile, President Habyarimana and close colleagues began to spread exaggerated reports of the threat the RPF represented, claiming that '... an RPF victory would mean death or enslavement for every Hutu' as a means to attract dissident Hutus back into the MRND (Kinzer 2008, p. 92). Over the next three and a half years, they used government-owned media to redefine the population as 'Rwandans', meaning those who backed the president, and the 'ibyitso', or 'accomplices of the enemy', meaning the Tutsi minority and those moderate Hutu who were opposed to the president.

In the campaign to create fear and hatred of the Tutsi, Habyarimana's regime played upon memories of past domination by the Tutsi minority and on the legacy of the revolution that overthrew their rule and drove many into exile.

The Belgians had long ago required everyone to carry an identity card denoting the owner's ethnic group. Residents of the countryside, where most Rwandans lived, generally knew who were Tutsi even without such documentation, and some Tutsi were recognisable from their physical appearance. But breaking the bonds between Hutu and Tutsi was not easy. For centuries they had shared a language, a common history, and the same Christian religion and cultural practices. They lived next to one another, attended the same schools and churches, worked in the same offices, and drank in the same bars. Many Rwandans were of mixed parentage, the offspring of Hutu–Tutsi marriages.

From the start, Habyarimana's regime were prepared to use physical as well as verbal attacks to achieve their ends. They organised massacres of hundreds of Tutsi in mid-October 1990 and in five other episodes, before the start of the 1994 genocide. A District Leader of the Interahamwe said to Jean Hatzfeld:

> We told ourselves that we didn't want to be demeaned any more, made to wash the Tutsi minister's air-conditioned cars, for example, the way we used to carry the kings in hammocks. I was raised in the fear of the return of Tutsi privileges, of obeisance and unpaid forced labour, and then that fear began its bloodthirsty march. I came to manhood at the worst moment in Rwandan history, educated in absolute obedience, in ethnic ferocity.
>
> (Hatzfeld, 2007, p. 95)

In some incidents, Habyarimana's supporters also killed Hutu opponents – their principal political challengers – as well as Tutsi, their declared ideological target.

> Ngoga: 'Many of my family were killed in 1991, but nobody could be brought to justice. It is not only my family, many were killed at that time. After my father was hit – in 1992 an organisation for human rights raised the issue … they threw them in the hole that was nearby, very deep, no one knew how deep. Up to now nobody can know who is there. They erased their name in the register so that if organisations came later they showed they did not exist.'

In 1991, Habyarimana was obliged to end his party's monopoly of power, and new rival parties developed, and contended for popular support. Several of them created youth wings ready to fight to defend partisan interests. Rather than negotiate in earnest with the RPF, Habyarimana chose to increase the size of his armed forces (from 5,000 in 1990 to 30,000 in 1992), thereby diverting scarce resources from needed food imports, health care and education. By early 1992, Habyarimana had also begun providing military training to the youth of his party, who were thus transformed into the militia known as the Interahamwe ('Those Who Stand Together' or 'Those Who Attack Together'). Massacres of Tutsi and other crimes by the Interahamwe went unpunished, as did some attacks by other groups, thus encouraging a sense that violence for political ends was 'normal'.

As a result, through attacks, virulent propaganda, and persistent political manoeuvring, Habyarimana and his group managed to polarise divisions between Hutu and Tutsi by the end of 1992. However, his fear of an attack from without was not unjustified, and in 1993 a dramatic military advance by the RPF threatened the capital city, Kigali, where it was halted by an alliance of Rwandese, French and Zairean (now DRC) troops. Thereafter, as a result of international pressure, a body of over 600 RPF troops was permitted to remain in Kigali and on 4 August, 1993, Habyarimana signed the Arusha Peace Accords. These comprised a series of protocols on the rule of law, power sharing (which advantaged the invaders), the repatriation of refugees, the resettlement of displaced persons, the integration of the armed forces, and an interim government intended to represent a step towards democratic elections. Crucially, the Accords stipulated that officials, including the president, could be prosecuted for past abuses – thus confronting Habyarimana and his supporters with potential criminal convictions and inevitable loss of power. Furthermore, tens of thousands of the estimated 35,000 soldiers of the Rwandan army, including a majority of officers of Habyarimana's generation, were threatened with demobilisation and loss of income.

These events heightened concerns among a wider circle of Hutus, including some formerly indifferent towards Habyarimana. Increasingly anxious about RPF ambitions, this expanding group was attracted by the new, extremist private Radio Télévision Libre des Mille Collines (RTLM) and by a movement called

Hutu Power, which cut across party lines and embodied the ethnic solidarity Habyarimana had championed for three years.

In late October, Tutsi soldiers in neighbouring Burundi murdered the then Hutu president, who had been freely and fairly elected only months before. In massacres touched off by the assassination, tens of thousands of both Hutu and Tutsi Burundians died. The crime, vigorously exploited by RTLM, reinforced the fears of many Rwandan Hutu that Tutsi would not share power, and swelled the numbers supporting Hutu Power.

Soldiers and political leaders distributed firearms to militia and other supporters of Habyarimana in 1993 and early 1994, but Bagosora and others decided that firearms were too expensive to distribute to all participants in the 'civilian self-defence' programme. They advocated arming most of the young men with more rudimentary weapons such as machetes. Businessmen close to Habyarimana imported enough machetes to arm every third adult Hutu male.

Aware of these activities, the RPF prepared for further conflict. They too recruited more supporters and troops and, in violation of the peace accords, increased the number of their soldiers and firearms in Kigali. They understood the risk that renewed combat would pose to Tutsi, particularly those who had come out publicly in support of the RPF in the preceding months, and warned foreign observers to this effect (Human Rights Watch, 1999, p. 9).

Meanwhile, in October 1993, the UN had deployed a small and poorly equipped peacekeeping force of 2,615 troops (8,000 had been seen as optimal) to oversee the peace process. Kofi Annan, then Under-Secretary General for Peacekeeping at the UN, explains that even this number had been opposed by the United States following the killing of 18 US soldiers in a disastrous failed attempt to capture a warlord in Somalia. This had led to the withdrawal of US troops and the collapse of the UN mission to Somalia. 'The world abandoned Somalia, allowing it to create for the world whole new forms of civil chaos and human suffering' (Annan, 2012, p. 45).

In January 1994, Lieutenant General Dallaire, in command of the UN forces, informed the secretary general that '… a top-level trainer of the Interahamwe who disagreed with the policy of exterminating Tutsis had warned him of a plan to provoke a civil war, assassinate the members of the interim government and kill any Belgian [UN] troops who resisted. The trainer offered to disclose the location of a large cache of arms. Dallaire requested permission to raid the arms cache, but this was refused on the grounds that it might trigger '… the collapse of the entire peace process.' Annan discloses that a senior Rwandan official later admitted that they knew that '… the death of just a few foreign peacekeepers would be enough to end the appetite for intervention and allow them to get on with their murderous plans' (Annan, 2012, pp. 54, 57).

By late March 1994, Hutu Power leaders were planning to slaughter massive numbers of Tutsi and Hutu opposed to Habyarimana, both to rid themselves of these 'accomplices' and to shatter the peace agreement. They had soldiers and militia ready to attack the targeted victims in the capital and in such outlying areas as Cyangugu in the southwest, Gisenyi in the northwest, and Murambi in the northeast. But elsewhere they had not completed the arrangements. In the centre of the country, they had successfully disseminated the doctrine of Hutu Power, but they were unsure how many ordinary people would transform that ideology into action. In other areas, particularly in the south, they had not won large numbers of supporters to the idea, far less organised methods of enforcement (Human Rights Watch, 1999, pp. 9–10).

Despite the signing of the Arusha Accords in August 1993, it had not been implemented owing to the deadlock and the climate of insecurity fostered by the MRND and its allies, particularly the Coalition pour la Defence de la Republique (CDR) and the hard wing of the Rwandan Army. On 15 March, 1994, five non-governmental human rights defence organisations:

> … deplored the fresh upsurge of violence in Rwanda, the distribution of weapons, the delay in the implementation of the Arusha Accords, and the attempts of the MRND to obtain a promise of amnesty for those who were involved in previously perpetrated breaches of human rights.
>
> (Amnesty International, Human Rights Watch,
> Inter-African Union of Human Rights, International Center
> for Human Rights and Democratic Development, and International
> Federation of Human Rights Leagues, 1994)

At the beginning of April 1994, after much equivocation, Habyarimana had accepted the democratisation of the regime and the implementation of the Arusha Accords, which had to be finalised by an oath taken by the members of the broad-based transitional government and the transitional parliament. A regional summit held in Dar es Salaam on 6 April, 1994, was intended to facilitate the implementation of the institutions arising from the Accords (Communiqué issued at the end of regional summit meeting held in Dar es Salaam on 6 April,1994). Habyarimana, who had received several warnings from countries that had backed the Accords, as well as from the UN, was ready to put them into practice.

To sum up, by April 1994, three substantial groups faced each other in an unstable alliance; an army of Tutsi émigrés, who shared a myth of tribal superiority as members of a warrior caste that had been viciously persecuted, driven from their country, and taken part in a successful rebellion in Uganda without receiving due reward; a ruling Hutu elite, with wide support in the northern provinces, who bore a historical grudge against their former rulers whom they now denigrated as impure 'cockroaches'; and a mixed group of Hutu and Tutsis, mainly centred on the southern provinces, who tolerated each other and supported the UN-brokered peace accord as the only logical solution to their endemic problems. Each of the first two groups fit Alderdice's preconditions (pp. 43–4) and Moghaddam's model of the *staircase to terrorism* (p. 17). Both had suffered narcissistic injuries of shame and humiliation, severe relative deprivation, felt a deep sense of injustice and disrespect and shared a belief that all non-violent options have been exhausted (the RPF by forced expulsion from Rwanda, the Hutu extremists by the signing of the accord); both had been recruited into 'parallel' organisations that sanctioned and even saw moral value in illegal acts (in the RPF by rebel activities and in the Hutu extremists by massacres); in addition, both had been indoctrinated into a secret group with strong charismatic leaders who rewarded conformity and insisted on absolute obedience and unity (the RPF and the interahamwe); and both had learnt to distance themselves psychologically from the 'enemy', thereby counter-acting normal inhibition of taboos on killing or extreme violence (p. 96).

Part II

RESPONSES TO A TERRORIST ATTACK

6

RESPONSES TO TERRORISM THAT FEED CYCLES OF VIOLENCE

A model

Colin Murray Parkes

In part I, we focused on the psychological factors that lie at the root of terrorism. While this understanding may enable us to reduce the risk, it may never be possible to prevent all acts of deadly violence from taking place, and we must be prepared for those that do. We turn now to the main theme of this book, which is to consider the responses that follow terrorist attacks. Here, in part II, we consider responses that may feed into or aggravate cycles of violence, and in part III we consider responses that may break these cycles.

It is as naive to assume that the problems of terrorism can be stamped out by punishing the terrorists as it is to believe that the bad behaviour of children can be stamped out by punishment alone. Clearly, it is important to apprehend suspects, give them a fair trial and punish those who are guilty of criminal offences; but these procedures alone are unlikely to solve the problem. Some terrorists cannot be found, others are seen in their homelands as heroes whose trial and punishment aggravate hatred of their captors, and suicidal terrorists are already beyond the reach of our justice; indeed, they may even be seen as martyrs.

Many parents find it easier to blame the children than to listen to their complaints and to admit the possibility that parents may themselves be culpable to some degree. By the same token, it is always difficult for victims of attack, and their leaders, to recognise their own contribution to the conflicts.

Those who plan successful terrorist attacks are seldom foolish. They know what they are doing and have considered the consequences. They may be deliberately provoking a response from the attacked side that will strengthen their support at home and, in their eyes, provide moral justification for their behaviour. Acts of terrorism may then escalate into sub-wars or wars that disturb the balance of power. Others may intend to undermine support for their political or military opponents by terrorising or punishing their electorate back home. This is most likely when they see their enemy as foreigners occupying their land and the foreigner's political leaders as vulnerable to public opinion. If we are to prevent such disasters, it is necessary to understand just how acts of terrorism can easily trigger responses that cause or aggravate cycles of violence.

One group that has studied how people react to violent deaths is the International Work Group on Death, Dying and Bereavement (IWG). This organisation was founded in 1974 and comprises teachers, researchers and clinicians, with special knowledge of the problems to which deaths can give rise. Over the years, their members have included many of the pioneers of hospice and palliative care whose work has greatly improved the care of people approaching death and of their families before and after bereavement (iwgddb.org).

Members of the IWG meet in a different part of the world every 18 months or so for five days. They divide into work groups of varying sizes, each focused on a particular topic chosen by the larger group as a suitable focus for consideration. Among them have been work groups on 'Disasters', 'Violence and Violent Death', and 'Breaking the Cycle of Violence', each of which has published documents, further details of which are given in the list of references (IWG 1997–1998, 2005, 2011 & 2013). A workgroup on 'Armed Conflict' was set up in 2005 in Hong Kong, China, and continued in other countries until 2010. The group published two papers, one of which posed the question: 'Can specialists in death, dying and bereavement contribute to the prevention and/or mitigation of armed conflicts and cycles of violence?' (IWG 2011). This was directed at the specialists and concluded: 'Professionals with training and experience in the care of traumatized, dying, and/or bereaved individuals possess knowledge and insights that are relevant to educating and supporting people before and after armed conflicts. Through their clinical work, military service, assistance in disasters, consulting, and research, these professionals have a depth and breadth of understanding and experience that positions them to intervene in constructive ways that may well reduce the risk of further armed conflict.'

In the Armed Conflict group's second paper (IWG 2013), a model for analysing responses to armed attack was developed. It is this that forms the basis for the analysis of responses to terrorism that is used here. It has been modified to recognise one of the limitations of the IWG's model: it did not include an account of the background and context in which the attack had arisen. This takes place before the terrorist attack and belongs in an introductory section that explains the development of negative codes, prejudices and assumptions held by both sides in the conflict.

The context of terrorism

As we saw in the previous chapters, terrorist attacks occur for reasons that can be analysed and the responses to them are influenced by psychological predispositions that are themselves contextual and open to analysis. Some of these are logical responses to the situation, whereas others more driven by emotion. It is the latter that are the main concern of this volume. They may give rise to the following.

Negative codes, prejudices and assumptions

All of us are prejudiced, however hard we try not to be. Our nervous system works by being selective, by simplifying the enormous complexity of the world into bite-sized chunks or packages, patterns that we can recognise and use (see pp. 30–33. It is, in effect, a coding and decoding machine.

It includes the higher functions by which we group these packages together and create ideas or constructs (links between packages that, together, give rise to meaning), codes (short forms that symbolise a larger package of associated ideas), and assumptions (yet larger constructs) that, together, give rise to an internal model of the world that we assume to be true, the 'assumptive world'. Together, these overlapping ideas, codes and assumptions enable us to accord different degrees of salience to particular sensory input, valuing some above others and warning us of potential dangers. Thus, I may identify a package of sensations as a strange person (idea), classify that person as an 'enemy' (code) and assume that I am in danger (assumption). In the environment in which we evolved, dangers abounded, and even today there are many parts of the world where few people survive to old age.

To a greater extent than other creatures, we spend much of our time communicating with our fellows in order to expand our repertoire of codes. Much of our education presents us with information in ways that make sense of the world that we then meet and the greater world that we might meet. Inevitably, this involves simplifying complex data about potential dangers and sources of reward.

Stereotypes are compact ways of classifying groups of people. They ignore individuality and often belittle entire populations. Even positive stereotypes are dangerous as they give rise to ideal expectations and ignore imperfections: there is no virtue in loyalty to a corrupt cause (e.g., 'my country, right or wrong'). Prejudices are often reified as slogans, easily remembered codes that are used to promote a simplistic view (e.g., 'the only good Indian is a dead Indian'). Lack of interest in other individuals, cultures and nations leads to ignorance that is easily turned to hostility by exposure to biased opinion.

By the time we reach adolescence, we have learned enough about the world to venture away from home and parents. At this time, friendship links usually become more salient than familial attachments, and conflicts of loyalty often arise. For a while we move back and forth between our old and new worlds as we test our strength and discover new places in the world.

Of particular importance to the perpetuation of armed conflict is the education of children and young military personnel. For most people, education in the use of violence and armed conflict begins in childhood and continues throughout life. Children and other young animals find aggressive play very enjoyable; indeed, in the environment of evolution, it increased their fighting and survival skills. In some circumstances, this assumption may still be justified (See Hatzfeld's and Parkes's interviews with Tutsis who survived the genocide, p. 130. When teaching history, teachers often overprotect children by glossing over the horrific consequences of armed conflict. As a result, children learn to see the glory, but not the cost, of war and death.

Some parents are indifferent, neglectful or abusive of their children; these attitudes have been shown to sow the seeds of violence (Hunter, Kilstrom, Kraybill & Loda 1978; Widom 1989). Parents and teachers may stereotype children with misattributions of wickedness. Some parents ignore their children except when they are bad; as a consequence, the children learn to be bad in order to get attention, and they may commit violent acts throughout their lives. Service in the armed forces is an attractive option for these young adults, who are then likely to abuse the power that is placed in their hands.

This is a time when new attachments are often insecure, and youngsters feel, and often are, in danger. For some, conflicts between sexual, territorial and other goals give rise to high levels of anxiety which interfere with their ability to learn and to work just at a time when these skills are most needed. They may also be exposed to pressure from their parents and teachers. At such times, they become more open to 'dropping out' or to recruitment into new social units including gangs, religious sects, military and other 'causes', including terrorism.

Although we may all live in the same world, each person's experience of that world, being unique to them, gives rise to a different internal model, and because we are mobile, moving from one place to another as we search for new friends, places and roles, we must switch from one world to another. Most young adults learn to adapt their assumptive world to fit the world that they meet. It is as if we build a repertoire of identities on top of the core identity of our childhood while remaining children at heart. Out of these elements, we each build our own mythology.

Even the history that we learn at school reflects the bias of our teachers, and we select the news we want to hear and remember the happenings in our lives that show us in a good light. The fact that these are myths does not mean that they are necessarily harmful. In fact, our world would be poorer without them. On the other hand, they play a significant part in causing and perpetuating cycles of deadly violence and are transmitted both in day-to-day interactions and in more formal education.

Myths of virtue

These tend to establish the moral superiority of one group and to justify their superior power, rights and exclusivity. We saw in chapter 1 how people tend to idealise those to whom they are attached. This explains the *myths of nationalism* described on p. 22. Most nations believe that they are better than other nations in most ways. This myth enables people to assume that the death of an opponent is less important than the death of a person on one's own side. Given the prevalence of myths of virtue, it is not surprising that they are often associated with myths of *divine preference and protection*. God is on the side of the good, we are good, and therefore God is on our side.

True bravery and endurance deserve respect but not worship or idealisation into myths of *heroism*. Since many of our heroes are warriors, they receive greater publicity and adulation, and are more likely to be adopted as role models than those who 'saw the thick planks of peace' (Weber 1946).

Likewise, deaths of terrorists and soldiers often give rise to myths of *martyr-dom* on their own side:

> ... A martyr's privileges are guaranteed by Allah; forgiveness with the first gush of his blood, he will be shown his seat in paradise, he will be decorated with the jewels of belief (Imaan), married off to the beautiful ones, protected from the test in the grave, assured security in the day of judgement, crowned with the crown of dignity, a ruby of which is better than this whole world (Duniah) and its entire content, wedded to 72 of the pure houris (beautiful ones of paradise) and his intercession on the behalf of 70 of his relatives will be accepted.
>
> (quoted by Osama bin Laden in his fatwa of August 1996)

These promises may be so seductive that they give rise to suicidal terrorism (see p. 16). The deaths of martyrs come at high cost to their families, who are then condemned to become a living memorial to them. In Turkey, a long-standing separatist movement led by the Kurdish Worker's Party (PKK) gave rise to an estimated 37,000 deaths during the 1980s and 1990s with extra-judicial killings by terrorists on both sides. A research study compared three groups: mothers of sons killed in the Turkish army, Kurdish mothers of sons who had 'been disappeared' or died fighting for the PKK and mothers who lost a young child from leukaemia. At the five-year follow-up, findings showed that the mothers of 'martyrs' on both sides of the conflict were still showing high levels of persistent depression compared with mothers of children who died of leukaemia (Yuksel & Olgun-Özpolot 2004).

Groups or nations that feel victimised and may in the past have been victimised perpetuate a *myth of victimisation* that is assumed to justify complaint and retaliation against the supposed victimisers or their descendants. In Northern Ireland, as we saw on p. 59 both Protestants and Catholics see themselves as minority groups and victims. Protestants, fearing union with the Catholic south, hold provocative and triumphalist marches, whereas the Catholics, who are a minority in the north, complain that they are the victims, and many have supported terrorism. Likewise, the forebears of Hutus were victimised by their Tutsi masters during the 19th century, which engendered the hatred that was later seen as justifying repeated massacres by Hutus of Tutsis in Rwanda (African Rights 1994).

While such myths help us to preserve our self-respect, and may indeed justify our pride, they run the risk of leading to illusions of grandeur, arrogance, aggression and, perhaps most dangerous of all, a tendency to overestimate our strength, bravery and resources, and to underestimate the strength, bravery and resources of others:

> Resorting to fundamentalism, with its cognitive simplification of right and wrong, true and false, black and white, and its emotions that find release in this simplification, creates a particular state of mind ...

insulated against reality, and one acquires a new identity and a secure sense of righteousness and moral superiority.

(Stein 2010)

Myths of vice

These are even more dangerous. They represent the downside of the myths of virtue, which need to be maintained by contrast with the vices of others. If we are strong, others are weaker, and if we are good, others must be bad.

Myths of enmity are common, especially after an attack. They often reflect ignorance of the motives of our assumed opponents. Once others are identified as 'enemies', it becomes dangerous to associate or communicate with them. Indeed, those who continue to communicate with them are themselves suspect. Consequently, the hostility tends to persist. It is easier to attribute hostile motives to strangers than to friends, and, when conflicts break out, it is easier to kill them.

And if God is on our side, it is logical to conclude that our opponents are supported by the devil; in its most extreme form, they may actually become or be led by the devil. Anyone who is identified as *diabolical* deserves any harm that we do to him (or her), and we can expect to be rewarded in heaven for such acts. In his fatwa of 23 February, 1982, Osama bin Laden referred to 'Satan's US troops and the devil's supporters allying with them' and after 9/11, Bush denounced nations that he saw as enemies of America as an 'axis of evil'. Other people's sins are always worse than our own, and the attribution of an entire race of people as evil provides an excuse for brutality and killing that leaves our conscience clear.

More complex are the *myths of impurity* of which our enemies are often accused. The virtue of cleanliness is another human characteristic that we share with other species. It strengthens and reflects social bonds in birds, mammals and some insects as well as protecting them from pathogens. Human beings teach their children to clean themselves from an early age, and cleanliness is rewarded with approval. Indeed, 'cleanliness is next to godliness', and rituals of purification soon provide us with a means to wash away sins as well as dirt. But those who fail to perform such rituals are impure and run the risk of becoming alienated from God. Non-believers are impure. Sexual behaviour, because it involves organs that are also used for excretion, is closely allied with impurity and hedged with prohibitions and rituals of purification. Relationships with the impure are dangerous, particularly if they lead to love. Such relationships threaten not only the immortal soul of the apostate, but that of the entire sect, which may be contaminated by association. Genocidal killings and 'ethnic cleansing' are assumed to be necessary to cleanse the world of impurity. Hitler's 'Law for the Prevention of Offspring with Hereditary Diseases' led to compulsory sterilisations and, by logical progression, to the 'euthanasia' (i.e., genocide) of citizens who were perceived as a threat to the purity of the German nation (Goldhagen 2009, p. 71).

Allied to this is the *myth of apocalypse*, which implies that it may be necessary to destroy the world in order to save it from corruption. The idea that 'it's better to die than to live and compromise', or that it is a sacred duty to destroy the enemy even if this means destroying the world, is particularly dangerous in the minds of those who control weapons of mass destruction.

> Acquiring weapons for the defence of Muslims is a religious duty. If I have indeed acquired these weapons [of mass destruction], then I thank God for enabling me to do so. And if I seek to acquire these weapons, I am carrying out a duty. It would be a sin for Muslims not to try to possess the weapons that would prevent the infidels from inflicting harm on Muslims.
> (Osama bin Laden interviewed for *Time* magazine 12/98)

Bush had (has?) a similar belief that 'God is on the side of America' and that this might have entitled him to make use of nuclear weapons against the evil enemy (Lifton, 2003).

The cycle of violence

In the light of these preconceptions, it is now time to look at the model of the cycle of violence that can be triggered by a terrorist attack.

The model is shown in Figure 6.1. At each point in the cycle, powerful emotions and pre-programmed responses play a part in determining what happens next. The psychological factors coming to bear at each of these points in the cycle will be examined, and we shall see that they easily steer events in the direction of aggravating or perpetuating the cycle. We shall also see, here and in part III, that they are choice points at which the cycle may be broken.

(1) The cycle starts with an *act of terrorism,* a violent attack that has led to one or more deaths. Some attacks are more likely to generate a cycle than others. (2) In most instances, the attack will be witnessed and *perceived,* by the public and the leadership, through the eyes and ears of the media of communication. Some

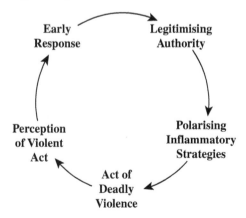

Figure 6.1 The cycle of violence.

perceptions are more biased and distorted than others. These perceptions will influence (3) the impact and *response* in the affected population. Some responses are more emotional than others. Whatever the immediate response, the event is unlikely to trigger a cycle of violence unless (4) it is permitted or fostered by a *leader or leaders*, and (5) *polarisation* follows and people are pressed to take sides and move to increasingly extreme positions favouring (6) forms of *retaliation* that may perpetuate the cycle.

While this model makes logical sense, a word of caution is needed. The sequence is not as clear-cut as it may, at first, seem; some cycles of violence are triggered by an accumulation of threats or multiple events occurring over many years that bring about a gradual build-up of tension. In addition, people move back and forth through the cycle, public reactions influence leaders, leaders influence public reactions, and all may contribute to polarisation or depolarisation. The devil is in the detail.

In analysing this cycle in more detail, we need to recognise that most terrorist attacks are aimed at two main audiences, the attacked population and at least one other population that is seen by the terrorists as likely to be sympathetic to their cause. At each point in the cycle, it is useful to consider both of these points of view. To make this clearer, the attacked 'side' will be considered first followed by the potential allies of the terrorists.

The attacked population

When our survival and that of those we love is threatened, we may not wish or be able to explore, withhold judgement, play games, or try to understand the point of view of strangers.

1. The terrorist attack

The intensity of the response is greatly influenced by both the number of dead, and, as we saw in chapter 1, the strength of our attachment to them. These include both nurturant attachments (to women and children) and attachments to those on whom our security depends; secular and religious leaders, places, gods and symbols that are assumed to keep us safe in the world. Consequently, we react much more strongly to attacks on these than we do to attacks that do not threaten our security.

Attacks that target political leaders, monarchs or celebrities and those that take place on sacred occasions or destroy important places within the homeland will result in more powerful reactions than attacks on small numbers of unknown persons and attacks that take place abroad.

In India, attacks on mosques and other holy places keep alive the conflicts between Muslims and Hindus; in the United States, the 9/11 terrorists chose the Pentagon, the World Trade Centre and (unsuccessfully) the White House for their targets, each of them symbols of American power.

In Sarajevo, in June 1914, Gavrilo Princip, a member of the secret terrorist organisation The Black Hand, assassinated the Archduke Ferdinand, heir to the throne of Austria/Hungary. This was an unstable, dynastic state led by Emperor Franz Josef, aged 84. He was shaken by the assassination and fearful for the future of the monarchy. The government were convinced that Serbia had orchestrated the attack and sent an ultimatum to Serbia; Franz Josef then declared war. At this time, Europe was in a state of flux. Russia mobilised, triggering a declaration of war from Germany, whereupon Britain and France declared war on Germany. Thus began World War 1.

The number of attackers and their motives are also important. Solitary terrorists are much less of a threat than organised gangs with hostile plans and a substantial following. Anders Breivik, in 2011, evoked horror by his massacre of 77 people, mostly adolescents, in Norway, but the danger of his triggering a cycle of violence was much less than the examples given above, in all of which the terrorists were backed by others.

2. The perception of the attack

Terror is a rare response to terrorism, but this does not mean that the attacked population are not disturbed by terrorist attacks. We human beings like to think of ourselves as calm, rational beings who see the world the way it is, draw logical conclusions and behave appropriately – and much of the time we do. Deadly attacks, however, are often misperceived, and these misperceptions can have disastrous consequences. People who have been attacked typically overestimate the danger. As Horowitz puts it (2000, p. 179): 'Anxiety limits and modifies perception, producing extreme reactions to modest threats.' Here, we consider the sparks that can set off the 'fire' of traumatic responses and trigger, inflame or perpetuate a cycle of violence by influencing the way in which an attack is perceived.

We saw, in chapter 2, how threats to life and other traumatic events trigger alarm reactions in the nervous system that often overrule logical responses. For most people, it is the news media that expose us to the news of a terrorist attack. They often do this in ways that can easily cause us to misperceive its salience. As Dettmer (2004) puts it, the mass media supply terrorists with 'the oxygen of publicity'. One of the limitations of modern methods of communication is the ease with which dramatic and horrific events can be brought into the living rooms of the general public without being put into perspective. A single death witnessed on television can have a greater impact than a thousand unseen rapes and murders. Terrorist attacks cause very few deaths by comparison with motorcars, influenza and global warming, yet they give rise to disproportionate fear.

The two aircraft that impacted the Twin Towers on 9/11 crashed into every home with a television set. We were all alerted to danger, horrified and, to some degree, traumatised, and we are still suffering from the consequences of that event. At the time of writing, few further attacks have taken place in the United States, and it appears that the tightening of security that has taken place has reduced the risk. Yet a sense of risk is still pervasive.

It is inevitable that news media will show images of death and destruction, carefully chosen to stir us, but within the limits of tolerance of a public who are growing daily more accepting of such imagery. More questionable is the slant given to such news, which tends to feed anxiety and fear in the attacked, or aggression and triumph in the attackers, rather than to help people to get the news in proportion. Headlines have the function of attracting attention and stimulating emotions.

For example, the following headlines that appeared on the front pages of American newspapers on 12 September, 2001, are typical; they both reflected and stimulated the public perception of 9/11: 'TERRORIZED' (*Times Record News*), 'PURE EVIL' (*Herald Sun*), 'UNDER SIEGE' (*Daily Record*) and 'WE'RE AT WAR' (*NY Daily News*).

While most responsible journalists are scrupulous about the veracity of the information they report, that information is often selected to reflect a particular point of view, and the comment that accompanies it has a similar purpose. Even solitary terrorists may be depicted as representing groups that are assumed to share their views. As we saw on p. 32 et seq., the public are themselves primed for alarm by attack and pay more attention to alarmist reports than by objective, statistical assessment of risks. Negative information is seen as more informative (salient) than positive information (Breckenridge and Zimbardo 2007); as a result, anxiety sells papers, and some editors become skilled at stirring it up.

The internet is now another source of information that lacks the codes of ethics followed by most journalists. Here, bigots and extremists of all kinds can find support for their views.

> ... The building of a mosque, especially at Ground Zero, is viewed by Muslims as a decisive victory over the infidels in Islam's march to establish its ultimate goal: the submission of all others to Islam and to Sharia Law.
> (Wafa Sultan in *Hudson New York* 19 May, 2010)

Attackers and attacked will see the event in very different ways. Attackers, who seldom perceive the impact of bombs detonated from a distance, may see it as a triumph over an evil enemy. Neither side is likely to understand the other's point of view, nor do they wish to. More important is the perception of the attack by potential allies of the attackers. Attacks that kill innocent persons may evoke disgust among those formerly sympathetic to the terrorist cause.

In 1993, Ayman Zawahiri was a member of a group that carried out an attack on a motorcade containing the Egyptian prime minister. The minister was slightly injured, but a little girl was killed by debris, and this outraged the Egyptian population, who took to the streets in revulsion. This single event seriously damaged Zawahiri's group (Wright 2006).

Here too, the local media have a major influence on the public response, and it is no coincidence that people select the information channel with which they most closely identify and which is likely to interpret the attack in ways that they find acceptable.

3. The response to the attack

To minimise danger, individuals who have been attacked must *remain alert* to possible dangers, and this may increase fear. We are much more aware of the threat from others than we are at recognising the threat that we represent to them: 'Paranoia is the logical endpoint of obsession with security' (Buzan 1991). Terrorist attacks may threaten the lives of a few individuals, but they rarely constitute a serious risk to most members of the attacked population. In her thorough review of studies of 457 terrorist groups, Audrey Cronin draws the conclusion:

> ... A wide range of statistics demonstrate that terrorist groups, typically neither enjoy longevity nor achieve their desired outcomes, [however, she adds] ... *except* when a state overreacts or a group becomes strong enough to transition into another form of violence ... The crucial mistake after 9/11, as after countless other terror attacks throughout history, was an overreaction and treating a terrorist campaign as though it were part of a traditional military campaign in which the application of brute force would compel the enemy into submission.
>
> (Cronin 2009)

Overreaction

The nervous pathways that link many a dangerous stimulus with an immediate response are extremely rapid and take place largely outside of conscious control. It is a consequence of these developments that, when we feel threatened or trapped, we often revert to simple, more primitive, responses. Given these influences, it is likely that the attacked will overreact to the supposed danger. Bewilderment and hyper-alertness are natural reactions to all threats and rapidly give place to fear, anxiety and anger, sometimes amounting to rage, as the news sinks in. Difficulty in sleeping, nightmares, and the bodily symptoms that accompany anxiety and tension are common.

Terror may be unusual, but fears are often disproportionate to their cause.

> Following 9/11, widespread fear of further bombs in public buildings in the USA brought about a drop in use of large shopping malls. Yet, if terrorists were to destroy one US shopping mall every week the odds of dying in a shopping mall would still be only 1.5 million to one.
> By comparison:
> The odds of dying in a road traffic accident in the next year are 7,000 to one.
> The odds of dying of cancer are 600 to one.
> The odds of dying of heart disease are 400 to one.
>
> (Rothschild 2001)

The magnitude of these psychological reactions varies greatly. Among those who are used to danger or who have been well trained to cope with it, reactions may amount to no more than an increase in alertness, rapid processing of information about the danger and an increase in efficiency. Police, medical and military responders may be well able to cope. To the extent that the attack fits their expectations, they will know what to do and how to do it. They will be alert but not unduly fearful.

But people without prior experience or training, when exposed to an attack, are more likely to become disorganised in their thinking; they tend to feel helpless and fearful, cling to others and talk endlessly; occasionally they may panic (a reaction that is most likely to arise if people feel trapped and unable to escape), or they may hit out wildly and inappropriately at anyone remotely associated with their supposed attackers. Group influences may cause these reactions to escalate, crowds gather, and there is a danger that violence will break out.

Anger and aggression

Anger is a natural reaction to threat and, in the environment of evolution, it often enabled those attacked to survive. But aggression was not the only way of surviving; some survived because of their ability to perceive danger and to make their escape (see p. 130. Human beings have the capacity for fight or flight when faced with acute danger, and they have brain pathways, involving deep nuclei that evolved early in evolution, that come into operation in such situations. These are less under the influence of the will than the cerebral cortex and are responsible for 'gut' reactions that may be inappropriate. The soldier who drops on his belly in a firing position when he hears a shot may do the same when a car backfires, or he may mistake a tripod for a gun and shoot a cameraman; these are responses that may be automatic. Although they are learned responses, they have become ingrained by repetition and may be triggered by fear. Without the cortical control that would come from greater experience and maturity, mistakes are likely.

Whenever deadly weapons are placed in the hands of large numbers of inexperienced youngsters, or experienced soldiers placed under extraordinary stress, there will be a few mistakes of this kind. Repeated exposure to attacks, such as those occurring in some combat situations, along with preexisting vulnerability, explains many of the problems of traumatic stress that arise in current military service (see chapter 7). Sadly, they often serve to aggravate deadly conflict.

Individuals vary in the extent to which they can control impulses to action. Among people who are innately aggressive or have learned to meet threats by fighting, an aggressive response is likely, while others will attempt to distance themselves from the attack.

Psychiatric problems

Grief will be triggered by any losses that result from an armed attack, but in emergency situations, it is often necessary to inhibit or postpone grief, and this may increase the risk of irrational outbursts later. It may even lead to physical and mental health problems in the long run (Parkes CM & Prigerson 2010, pp. 127–129).

Repression of grief is not the only cause of *psychiatric problems*; these may arise in people already vulnerable, or as a response to extreme stress. They include anxiety and panic disorders, *post-traumatic stress disorders* (PTSD) – in which people are haunted by recurrent memories or horrific images and go to great lengths to avoid any place or situation that will evoke them – and *dissociative syndromes* (such as amnesias and wandering fugues); together, these are termed *traumatic stress reactions*. People with prior vulnerability to *depression* may plummet into major depressive disorders with a risk of suicide, consumption of alcohol or other *drugs* may increase and lead to acute intoxication or chronic addiction, and a wide range of other psychological problems and vulnerabilities may be aggravated. These difficulties are most likely to arise in those most directly affected by the attack.

Probably the best-researched terrorist attack has been 9/11. In a telephone survey of 3,512 persons from New York state, New Jersey and Connecticut, 75% reported problems related to the attacks, and 12% had sought help for these problems (Melnik et al. 2002). Not that these findings indicate high rates of mental illness; most of the help was given by family, friends or neighbours, and the 'problems' seem to have been no worse than anger (48%), worries (37%) and nervousness (24%). There was an increase in smoking (in 22%) and a slight increase in alcohol consumption (in 3.2%).

In New York state, Project Liberty, a counselling service for people affected by the attacks, was set up and funded by the Federal Emergency Management Agency.

> Nearly half (72 persons, or 48 percent) of 149 crisis counselling service recipients who participated in a telephone interview more than a year after the attacks indicated that they knew someone killed as a result of September 11. Among individuals who knew someone who died in the World Trade Center attacks, a substantial subgroup (44 percent) screened positive for complicated grief [such as protracted grief that is so severe that it impairs social, occupational and other functions].
>
> (Shear, Jackson, Essock, Donahue & Felton 2006)

Other conditions that often coexisted with complicated grief were major depression and PTSD, which, together, affected nearly two-thirds of the bereaved respondents. This is a much higher proportion than are reported by most bereaved people, but similar to the proportions found in those bereaved by the Oklahoma bombing (Pfefferbaum et al. 2001).

As was to be expected, after 9/11, those with the greatest direct exposure, such as witnesses to the attacks, experienced a six times higher incidence of PTSD, a 2.5 times greater incidence of anxiety disorder and twice the incidence of any mental disorder than those who were less exposed (Henriksen et al. 2010).

The main conclusion to be drawn from these studies is that, while many of those who witnessed the 9/11 attacks directly, or were closely involved in responding to them, suffered traumatic stress reactions, and many of those who were suddenly, unexpectedly and violently bereaved were at increased risk of complicated grief, the majority of American citizens showed no more than an increase in anger, tension and anxiety, along with a greater willingness to turn to each other. The social cohesion that is a regular consequence of communal threat drew people closer together and opened the doors of communication.

Police and military responses

Although this book is not primarily concerned with rescue operations and other organisational responses to terrorist attacks, which are not greatly different from responses to other civil disturbances, critical incidents and disasters, a few psychosocial differences deserve comment. Perhaps the most important is the potentially conflicting roles of the police. Their traditional roles of preventing and investigating crime may conflict with other roles such as providing information and support to those affected by an attack. This is most obvious when they are called upon to control angry crowds or individuals whose anger is being directed against them and others. If they meet anger with anger, the situation is likely to escalate and may get out of control. If, on the other hand, they recognise that the anger is an expression of grief and respond with sympathy, understanding and, most important, information, in a calm and non-judgemental way, they are more likely to prevent escalation. Like good parents, they may have to set limits, but should beware of overreacting.

Likewise, members of armed forces who are operating in countries where terrorism is rife often find that their traditional role of fighting terrorists conflict with their duty to protect and support the victims of terrorism. Since it may not be easy to tell the difference between a victim and a terrorist, they are bound to make mistakes, which may well be fatal. Again, they are most likely to succeed, and to survive, if they can find the right balance between these roles.

Problems are likely to arise when a fellow soldier has been killed. An entire unit may then become psychological victims. In that event, the natural fear, grief and rage which emerge are most likely to impair the judgement of those in the front line. Cruel or punitive treatment of suspects or overreactions which give rise to excessive deaths of non-combatants (overkill) may erupt.

The response of people who are sympathetic to the terrorist cause

If they see the attack as a triumph of good over evil, or a victory of the weak over the strong, they may celebrate their triumph by parading the streets waving placards hostile to the other side. Recruitment to the terrorist cause may even turn an act of terrorism into an insurrection. But, as we shall see in chapter 14 the opposite may occur if the terrorists have misjudged their support or lack support from the media. Many terrorists tread a fine line which attracts some supporters and repels others.

4. Legitimising authorities

Legitimising authorities are the leaders with the power to determine or sanction the response to a violent event or threat within a population. It is a natural response to danger to turn to those in authority for leadership; that is what leaders are for. As we saw earlier, *groups under attack* cohere around leaders. They may put pressure on those leaders to take action, to 'do something'. How the leaders respond can decide what happens next. Indeed, it is probably true to say that violence is unlikely to become cyclical unless actions which perpetuate it are authorised by leaders.

All leaders are human beings, who may themselves be traumatised by acts of deadly violence; they too may misperceive the attack and, like the rest of us, overreact, and yet they are expected to take on the quasi-parental roles of protecting and succouring their followers. It is a paradox that the people who are most in need of support when faced with enormous stress, the people at the top and bottom of the social hierarchy, are the ones least likely to get it. Those at the bottom of the hierarchy cannot afford, or do not know how to access, the help they need. Those at the top are looked up to and expected to save everybody else without the need for support for themselves.

Adulation is not support. Blaug (2012) has pointed out that *hubris* results from the interaction of followers who need someone to think for them and leaders who are seduced into overestimating their own wisdom. The follower who always agrees with the leader and assures them of their superiority is fostering hubris and spoiling the leader in much the same way that a parent who inverts the parental role, and fails to set limits, is spoiling the child.

Leaders may see it as a weakness to ask for help, and supporters may hesitate to give it because leaders cannot afford to be suspected of weakness. We shall see, in chapter 12, how politicians, and their families, can be given sophisticated help at times of national crisis.

Following a terrorist attack, the best action may be inaction – to wait until passions have subsided before taking important decisions. The response to the attack events may require some new thinking, and this too takes time. But it is difficult and politically hazardous for a politician to do nothing. Leaders who are seen to delay may lose support, but in today's world, the leader's orders can be transmitted within seconds, and it is politically dangerous for them to change their minds.

Problems are particularly likely to arise when leadership is already weak. In that event, it is likely that the incumbent leader will attempt to gain support by populist actions, even when these increase the risk of escalating the conflict. Indeed, one of the weaknesses of democracy is the need for leaders to be sensitively aware of and responsive to the wishes of the electorate, however irrational these may be.

Those who become leaders may do so because of their attachment to their God, tribe, race or state; indeed, they may be selected for that very reason. Faced with a terrorist attack, they may exhibit the same extreme reactions that were shown, in chapter 1, to lie at the roots of problematic anxiety and grief. They too may over-react; become fearful of separation and loss; and become enraged by, and behave aggressively towards, assumed attackers, and all those associated with them, while idealising the people, the state, and the God to whom they are attached, expecting others to be similarly infatuated. They may take extraordinary measures that defy ethical and social standards.

As an example, we can consider George Bush's reactions to 11 September terrorist attacks. My aim in listing these is not to pathologise or to belittle Bush, but to bring home the essential character of his reaction. Like other attachment relationships, it is essentially based on feelings rather than logic; although, like all feelings, it has its own logic. The fact that, in a huge and powerful nation like the United States, 19 men, armed only with box cutters, succeeded in killing nearly 3,000 people, is cause for horror, grief and surprise rather than alarm. Three thousand deaths in a country of nearly 300,000,000 is fewer than the number who die on the roads during one month, and many less than the number killed in the War on Terror which followed. It did not constitute a war.

George Bush's reaction is here illustrated by quotations from his speeches. Even allowing for the characteristic hyperbole of the political leader, his responses would seem to meet the criteria for a strong anxious attachment to a place, the United States as shown in chapter 1. The widespread public approval of his response suggests that many US citizens, and some leaders of America's allies, were similarly attached.

- *Stirred up by perception of danger.* ('Tonight we are a country awakened to danger and called to defend freedom …'.)
- *Their attachment becoming powerful.* ('On September the 11th, enemies of freedom committed an act of war against our country'), *exclusive* ('all who are not with us are against us') *and obsessive* ('Americans should not expect one battle, but a lengthy campaign, unlike any other we have ever seen'.)
- *Misperceiving and exaggerating the danger.* ('… Night fell on a different world, a world where freedom itself is under attack … what is at stake is not just America's freedom. This is the world's fight. This is civilization's fight. This is the fight of all who believe in progress and pluralism, tolerance and freedom'.)
- *Fearful of separation and loss.* ('Our government has taken unprecedented measures to defend the homeland'.)
- *Becoming enraged and aggressive.* ('Our grief has turned to anger … the only way to defeat terrorism as a threat to our way of life is to stop it, eliminate it, and destroy it where it grows'. And in a later speech: 'I vowed then that I would use all our power of Shock and Awe to win the War on Terror. And so I said we were going to stay on the offense (*sic*) two ways: one, hunt

down the enemy and bring them to justice, and take threats seriously; and two, bomb the hell out of them'.)

- *Idealising the people, state and/or God to whom they are attached.* ('America was targeted for attack because we're the brightest beacon for freedom and opportunity in the world. And no one will keep that light from shining'.)
- *Expecting others to be similarly infatuated.* ('This is a great country. It's a great country because we share the same values of respect and dignity and human worth. And it is my honour to be meeting with leaders who feel just the same way I do. They're outraged, they're sad. They love America just as much as I do'.)
- Gathering around them *supporters and allies who share their perceptions.* Mayor Giuliani: 'You're either with civilization or with terrorists ...We're right and they're wrong. It's as simple as that.' Tony Blair, prime minister, United Kingdom: 'This atrocity was an attack on us all, on people of all faiths and people of none.'
- *Defying social and moral standards* – Bush:

'... Some believe our military and intelligence personnel involved in capturing and questioning terrorists could now be at risk of prosecution under the War Crimes Act – simply for doing their jobs in a thorough and professional way. This is unacceptable. ... I'm asking that Congress make it clear that captured terrorists cannot use the Geneva Conventions as a basis to sue our personnel in courts – in US courts. The men and women who protect us should not have to fear lawsuits filed by terrorists because they're doing their jobs ...'

He later gave his approval to the torture of particular suspects by 'waterboarding' (ICRC 2007).

The fact that Bush's utterances were approved by a large section of the society from which he comes indicates that they are not outside cultural norms and should not, therefore, be regarded as 'pathological'. I would argue, however, that this is not the crucial issue. They may still be problematic.

If reactions of this kind can take place in wealthy and secure countries such as the United States, how much more likely are they in poor, insecure, ill-educated countries, in which day-to-day survival is already uncertain and people are desperately in need of protection. They are so much in need of leadership that they may cling to 'strong' individuals whose actions, in other circumstances, they would deplore.

Members of *resource-poor social units* cannot afford to relax. They must be constantly on the look out for the means of their survival and that of their family. Having little reason to trust their government to protect them, their family is their main source of security. Leaders of resource-poor social units remain insecure even when times improve. They may try to find security for themselves and their own family by taking more than their fair share of resources. This will evoke jealousy.

They may be tempted to remain in power by dynastic tyranny, whereby one tribe or family exerts a strict and ruthless control of resources, or claims a special relationship with God, who will give preferential treatment to their followers.

The Lord's Resistance Army is currently terrorising parts of the Southern Sudan, the Democratic Republic of the Congo, Central African Republic and Uganda. It originated as a rebellion against Museveni in Uganda, by members of the Acholi tribe who were led by a Christian fundamentalist, Alice Lakwena. She persuaded her followers that, thanks to a message from the Holy Spirit, they would be protected from bullets by God and by anointing their bodies with shea nut oil. This did not prevent their defeat, and Lakwena escaped to Kenya, being replaced by the current leader, Joseph Kony, who claims similar protective powers from God. In 2005, the International Criminal Court issued arrest warrants against him and four other leaders. They are charged with murder, rape, sexual slavery and enlisting children as combatants. In January 2013, he was still said to be at large (Heuler 2013).

The leader's declared love for the glorious family, God, nation and race that he endorses can easily switch to a kind of *narcissism*. By identifying himself with that superior authority, the extremist becomes glorious and can then justify anything that he does.

> I believe that I am acting in accordance with the will of the Almighty Creator: by defending myself against the Jew, I am fighting for the work of the Lord.
>
> Adolf Hitler, *Mein Kampf*

For leaders to be effective, it is advantageous for them to have the trust, charisma and respect that enables them to exert control. We saw in chapter 1 how patterns of attachment to God often echo attachments to parents. Attachments to leaders may similarly reflect earlier attachments; in fact, it is frequently the case that trust and respect for leaders is learned, or not learned, during childhood. In many societies, obedience is a predominant value, learning is by rote and children are discouraged from challenging their teachers. Leaders in these societies, like their own teachers, are often authoritarian and intolerant of opposition. In the West, the opposite is usually the case: children are encouraged to think for themselves and to question authorities. Leaders expect opposition; indeed, this may be built into the political system.

Both styles of leadership have their advantages and disadvantages at times of terrorist attack. Authoritarian leaders may have more control over their followers and, having no need for democratic debate, cope rapidly and effectively with emergencies (see the example of Rwanda in chapter 15). But they often ignore the opinion of others and surround themselves with cronies who seldom question the morality and decisions of their leader. When attacked, they tend to respond in their accustomed authoritarian manner and to be inclined to favour military action.

Democratic leaders may be less militaristic, but the greatest weakness of democratic systems of governance is their dependence on popular opinion and the media who influence it at times of crisis and may, as we have seen, be nationalistic and self-serving. Only the most secure politician can afford to ignore such pressures.

Parents must maintain a balance between keeping their child secure and setting limits to their freedom to explore; Buzan (1991) points out that this balance must also be maintained by states. In order to remain secure, it is necessary to limit the freedom of others. 'Nobody can be completely free or completely secure – balance is all.' In resource-poor countries, people may be prepared to trade off loss of freedom as a condition of greater security. Such considerations have caused many villagers in Afghanistan to accept the shackles of self-appointed war lords who will protect them, rather than vote for democratic leaders who cannot. See also the situation in Rwanda before the genocide (pp. 21–2).

The term *warlord* implies a leader who has seized power, but there are many countries in which military leaders have been elected to political leadership. Indeed, we shall see later why this may come about. At this point suffice it to point out that military leaders are well qualified to use military means to achieve their aims, they may be less well qualified to lead during times when non-military solutions are needed.

Turning now to the response of leaders to acts of terrorism arising within their own borders but *directed against members of other, more powerful, states*. Rightly or wrongly, they are likely to be held responsible and blamed by the victimised state. By the same token they will be held accountable, by their own citizens or pressure groups, for any actions which they take. It is not unusual to find such leaders playing a double game of promising much to the outsiders while taking very little action, or giving covert support to the terrorists. Either way, the cycle of violence will continue and may escalate to warfare.

In the context of the long conflict between India and Pakistan over parts of Kashmir, on 13 December, 2001, four gunmen and a suicide bomber attempted to gain access to the Indian Parliament in Delhi. A gunfight ensued in the course of which all five terrorists were killed along with five Indian policemen and two civilians. Immediately, the Indian government protested to the Pakistani government, demanding that immediate steps be taken against two Muslim extreme nationalist organisations. Pakistan responded by putting its troops on high alert. On 20 December, India mobilised half a million troops along the long-disputed 'line of control' in Kashmir. Pakistan also mobilised, and a ten-month standoff resulted between these two nuclear powers. Such tensions are still present and are rendered more dangerous by the necessity for the president of Pakistan to juggle 'opaque' strategies of tolerating popular Muslim extremists, controlling a militant army hostile to India, keeping the United States on his side and exercising secular capitalism in a predominantly religious country.

Finally, we must consider *the leadership of the terrorists*. As we have seen, they are often charismatic figures who will have played an important part in recruiting, inspiring and training the front line of attackers. They know that the terrorist attack is only a stepping stone towards the achievement of their long-term ends. Indeed, their own role may be crucial in determining what happens next. They will feed their own messages to the audiences they wish to influence, justifying the attack in ways that they hope will strengthen their influence and recruit others to their cause. They will also do their best to denigrate the responses made by their enemy to the attack, and draw attention to any excessive, cruel, illegal or irrational behaviour as evidence of depravity.

5. Polarisation

Acts of terrorism are unlikely to give rise to cycles of armed violence unless a substantial number of people take sides, and polarisation takes place. However, once polarisation is seen to have begun on one side, it may become dangerous for the other side not to follow the same course. This will only be the case following a terrorist attack if the terrorists manage to enlist widespread support.

Even so, when an act of terrorism is carried out by a small number of terrorists, who represent no substantial risk to a state or nation, escalation can still take place. The first step towards polarisation is the designation of a substantial number of people as the 'enemy'. By naming Iran, Iraq and North Korea as the 'axis of evil' and declaring war on 'terror', Bush was inviting polarisation. On the one hand, he attracted wide support in the United States, but on the other hand, he antagonised much of the Arab world.

What starts as suspicion of strangers or poorly understood categories of person soon turns into distrust and hostility. Dealing with absolutes of black and white is simpler than seeing threats as relative, ambiguous or justifiable. When leaders and friends identify attackers as an 'enemy', they are put into a category of 'Other', demonised, dehumanised and turned into prey or an object (target) to be attacked or killed.

> In today's wars, there are no morals. We believe the worst thieves in the world today and the worst terrorists are the Americans. We do not have to differentiate between military or civilian. As far as we are concerned, they are all targets.
>
> (Bin Laden interviewed for ABC News in 1998)

In the end, even former friends may become tainted by association with the enemy and turn away. They, in turn, will sense our distrust and withdrawal of affection; rejected and deeply hurt, they may become the very enemies that we imagined them to be. At the same time, both sides will attempt to attract allies to their cause. Friendship is tested and, as time passes, it becomes more and more difficult for people to hold the middle ground.

Following 9/11, there was much sympathy for the United States across the world, and even Arab leaders expressed their regrets. Sadly, this sympathy was soon dispelled, and any moral high ground lost after the establishment of Guantanamo and Abu Ghraib, where suspects were imprisoned without legal trial, mistreated, and some tortured. The troops who liberated Iraq and Afghanistan were surprised to discover that they were widely seen as invaders and are currently mired in conflicts that they cannot win.

On each side, friends and allies are identified and persuaded to declare commitment and to fight the supposed enemy; ambiguity is denied, and alternative explanations of events are ignored or prohibited; people are pressured to take sides; and preexisting myths are revived and new ones created.

Myth making is at the root of propaganda. Discourse is based on appeal to emotion and prejudice that extols the virtues of one side by comparison with the other, glosses over inconsistencies on 'our side', and invents or magnifies examples of evil on the other. Media can be controlled directly (e.g., by censorship, banning of critical organs, or exclusion of reporters) or indirectly (e.g., by smear campaigns, or giving publicity to one side only). Educational institutions can be controlled and syllabuses censored to ensure compliance. Secrecy becomes the order of the day, and 'national interest' is cited as justifying concealment of judicial processes, military operations, covert surveillance, and other restriction of human rights.

Polarisation is often supported by rewards for conformity and punishments for nonconformity.

> It is a duty now on every tribe in the Arab Peninsula to fight, Jihad, in the cause of Allah and to cleanse the land from those occupiers. Allah knows that their blood is permitted (to be spilled) and their wealth is a booty; their wealth is a booty to those who kill them.
>
> (Bin Laden interviewed for ABC News in 1998)

Those who maintain their support are rewarded with jobs, power and status; those who do not are penalised, lose power and status and are excluded from positions of leadership. Opposition is discouraged, even in purportedly democratic countries. Obstacles are often placed on freedom of communication and information. Polarisation drives people apart, but it can also unite disparate groups, forcing unlikely bedfellows to cling together for mutual support.

> The alliance negotiated in 2005 between bin Laden/Zawahiri and Zarqari's organisation in Iraq was an effective and strategic public relations move for both parties, breathing new life into the al-Qaeda movement at a time when its leaders were on the run, and providing legitimacy and fresh recruits for the insurgency in Iraq, with its opportunities to kill Americans and learn effective techniques to counter them.
>
> (Cronin 2009 p. 191)

6. Retaliation

Whereas in symmetrical conflicts, where the two sides are relatively evenly balanced, negotiation is often seen as a possible solution, this is seldom the case when the conflict is asymmetrical, as are most terrorist conflicts. Here, repression by military and/or police action and punishment by blockade or denial of resources are likely responses. To make matters worse, 'collateral damage' damages the attackers by undermining their moral standing, providing fuel for propaganda against them, evoking the rage of the bereaved and traumatised, and recruiting sympathy and support for the 'terrorists'.

Having closely analysed responses to terrorism in her scholarly book *How Terrorism Ends*, Cronin concludes that 'repression alone seldom ends terrorism because terrorist groups resort to strategies designed to turn a state's strength against itself' (Cronin 2009). The decision to retaliate is likely to have been made by leaders soon after the initial attack and, once taken, will develop a momentum that cannot easily be changed. All of the psychological forces described earlier will have made it easier for the attacked side to mobilise the resources to ensure that the damage done to the 'enemy' will far exceed the damage resulting from their attack.

Britain supported the Boers in a territorial dispute between Natal and the Zulus in 1869. When Zulu terrorists killed a small number of native Christians, this triggered unacceptable demands by the British High Commissioner of Natal for the Zulu army to disband. The demand was ignored, and an army was sent from Britain to enforce the ultimatum. The subsequent defeat and massacre of 1,300 British soldiers by Cetshawayo's Zulu army at Isandlwana gave rise to a monumental backlash in Britain. The British government rushed seven more regiments of reinforcements to Natal, along with two artillery batteries. Despite several attempts by Cetshawayo to negotiate, the Zulus were decisively defeated at the battle of Ulundi, and all prisoners and wounded Zulus were slaughtered. The memory of these events persists to this day and, in the years to come, Zulu demands for independence remained one of the biggest obstacles that Nelson Mandela had to overcome in persuading them to accept the peace process in South Africa. In the end, they were granted 'internal self-determination' in the renamed province of KwaZulu/Natal (Mandela 1994, p. 738).

Side A, having embarked on a military response to a terrorist attack by attacking side B, may then find that rising casualties and loss of the moral high ground undermines political support at home. This may then lead to a withdrawal of troops. Even if side A never intended a long occupation, their withdrawal will be seen as a victory by the terrorists. In Algeria (in 1962), Palestine (1948), Lebanon (2000), and against the Russians in Iraq (1988), weak states have been able to win sub-wars against a stronger power. In each case, the aim of the weaker side was to bring about the withdrawal of foreign troops from their homelands by persistent terrorism, subversion and denying them benefits from their victories.

Even the indirect punishment of 'the enemy' by denial of resources may be counterproductive if the suffering and resentment to which it gives rise improves recruitment to the terrorist cause. In Afghanistan, efforts to cut off funding for terrorists have encouraged illicit activities, notably narcotics trafficking, and, in Taliban-controlled areas, have seen terrorism escalate into insurgency.

Implications

It is a fundamental assumption of this Part that if we understand better why terrorist attacks can trigger cycles of violence, we shall be in a better position to prevent them. The saying 'forewarned is forearmed' comes to mind, but arms are only one of many alternatives. Everyone involved will be more likely to act in a rational way if we understand the risks of our own irrationality and that of others. Unfortunately, we all assume that our thoughts and behaviour are rational, that those we love are only slightly less rational, that the rest of the world is fallible, that our opponents are often irrational and that terrorists are plumb crazy. At the same time, we adopt a simplistic but similar scale of values, seeing ourselves as good, our loved ones pretty good, most other people untrustworthy, our opponents as bad and all terrorists as diabolical. Leaders, who share these assumptions, often assume that psychological knowledge is irrelevant to their own needs, although they may be willing to use it as a tool for political ends; they may employ psychologists to advise them how to influence the 'masses'. We even have schools of 'psychological warfare' that use (or misuse) their knowledge for purposes of propaganda.

Here, we give a central place to insight into the ways in which love, which we all know to be a virtue and a main source of happiness and security, and fear, which is an important indicator of threats to our security, can also give rise to unhappiness and insecurity.

Conclusions

Given the character of attachments, we cannot expect that they can easily be changed. As Peter Marris has shown, detribalisation and other social changes are like grief as communities slowly discover which aspects of the old assumptive world must be let go and which can be retained (Marris 1974). But it is the faith of the counsellor that such change is possible and that times of loss, when change is inevitable, are also times of opportunity. Many of the treasures of the past continue to be valued and remain valuable.

Our model of the psychological response to deadly violence provides us with a useful way of dissecting out the various factors that must be tackled if cycles of violence are to be prevented or broken. In the chapters that follow, we apply the model to look more closely at long-established cycles of violence in Northern Ireland and Rwanda, and we begin to see how and when responses to particular deadly attacks can lead either to perpetuation or to breaks in the cycle. We shall see that, at each point in the cycle of violence – anticipation, perception, response, leadership, polarisation and retaliation – change for the better *can* take place.

Although we may learn to prevent some attacks, deadly violence will happen from time to time in the best of worlds. How we anticipate and prepare for the next attack, how the attack is perceived, how we respond, how we influence our leaders and they us, whether we join or resist polarisation and whether or how we retaliate, can make or break the cycle. To respond to each of these challenges, we need to step outside the box of doing what comes naturally and, like a psycho-therapist or counsellor, assess and influence the emotions and cognitions to which the situation gives rise.

7

BLOODY SUNDAY IN NORTHERN IRELAND

Analysis of the response

Nora Gribbin and Rodney Turtle

In war, truth is the first casualty.

Aeschylus, 525 BCE–456 BCE

We have chosen Bloody Sunday for our analysis of an event that aggravated the cycle of violence because the incident had a profound, if unintended, impact on the escalation of the Troubles, and its effects were long lasting. It was seen, by the Catholics, as an act of terrorism by British soldiers rather than by nationalist or loyalist extremists. Up to this event, the IRA had been targeting police and army, while the loyalists had been targeting Catholics. Alongside the killings, intimidation and persecution were manifest at every level in neighbourhoods where 'the other side' were not welcome to the point of 'burning them out' of their homes. Sectarian and polarised communities resulted, in an already divided society. These strongholds were havens for vigilantes and paramilitaries who policed them and extracted protection money from businesses. The British army had been called in to provide security to both sides in the conflict. The fact that they failed deserves all the scrutiny that it eventually received, and this in turn provided much of the data that facilitated our analysis.

The Situation in Derry – February 1972

As we saw in chapter 4, in January 1972 the situation in Northern Ireland deteriorated greatly.

> By this stage the nationalist community had largely turned against the soldiers, many believing that the army, as well as the RUC, were agents of an oppressive regime. Parts of the city to the west of the Foyle lay in ruins, as the result of the activities of the IRA and of rioting young men (some members of the IRA or its junior wing, the Fianna), known to

101

soldiers and some others as the 'Derry Young Hooligans'. A large part of the nationalist area of the city was a 'no-go' area, which was dominated by the IRA, where ordinary policing could not be conducted and where even the Army ventured only by using large numbers of soldiers.

(Saville, Hoyt & Toohey 2010, vol. 1 ch. 2, para. 2.6)

Strategy was discussed at a high government level. 'No-go' areas operated where the IRA had a safe enclave, and were a constant embarrassment. Compensation claims by Derry businesses for terrorist attacks were expected to exceed 4 million pounds in six months. 'A community of some 33,000 citizens of the UK will be allowed to remain in a state of anarchy and revolt' (Rucker 2002, p. 118).

On 4 October, 1971, General Carver, the Chief of General Staff, had said:

The history of all previous campaigns against terrorists – and few of them have been wholly successful – proves that a purely military solution is most unlikely to succeed, and that whether it is achieved by military or political means or both, the isolation of the terrorist from the population is a *sine qua non* of success.

(Saville, Hoyt & Toohey 2010, vol. 1, para.8.78)

Nevertheless, two days later Prime Minister Edward Heath added: '... The first priority should be the defeat of the gunmen, using military means, and that in achieving this we should have to accept whatever political penalties were inevitable' (Saville, Hoyt & Toohey 2010, 8.8.89). On the following day, Heath met Brian Faulkner, the prime minister of Northern Ireland, who welcomed Heath's proposal to adopt tougher security measures and strengthen the British forces (but rejected his proposal to give republicans a voice in his government). In keeping with Heath's priority, General Ford, Commander of Land Forces in Northern Ireland, ordered on 26 October that the army must 'progressively impose the rule of law on the Creggan and Bogside. Hooligan fringe activity is to be vigorously countered: arrest operations are to continue to be mounted: and normal patrols through IRA-dominated areas are to be restarted when considered practicable'. He added: 'We should not hesitate to fire whenever events demand it and the law permits ...' (Saville, Hoyt & Toohey 2010, 1, §8.103–104).

Despite this aggressive stance, the soldiers were not given permission to ignore the instructions given on their Yellow Card, which was clearly intended to prevent just such abuses as took place on Bloody Sunday. These included the instruction that the soldier should 'never use more force than the minimum necessary to enable you to carry out your duties'. 'A warning should be given before you open fire ... unless either when hostile firing is taking place in your area, and a warning is impracticable, or when any delay could lead to death or serious injury to people whom it is your duty to protect or to yourself; and then only: a. against a person using a firearm (here used to include a grenade, nail bomb or gelignite-type bomb) against members of the security forces or people whom it is your duty to protect

102

or b. against a person carrying a firearm if you have reason to think he is about to use it for offensive purposes.'

By 14 December, 1971, General Ford was forced to admit 'the stalemate continues'. He added: 'The hate, fear and distrust felt by the Catholic community for the security forces is deeper now than at any time during the current campaign' (Saville, Hoyt & Toohey 2010, 1, §8.151 & 153). On the same day, General Carver warned the Home Secretary, Reginald Maudling, that any attempt to eliminate the 'no-go' area would 'involve, at some stage, shooting at unarmed civilians' or (according to another note) 'almost certainly' doing so. Saville concluded that, while a 'shoot-to-kill' policy was considered and widely discussed at this time, it was never adopted (Saville, Hoyt & Toohey 2010, §8.166 and §8.162 and 166).

This gives an important insight into the frame of mind of the military at the time of Bloody Sunday. Given that soldiers may sense that there is an invisible gradation between the 'official' orders and an implicit message that exceptions to the rules of engagement will be ignored or even encouraged, it is not far-fetched to suspect that those subsequently representing the bereaved families probably had good reason to suggest that 'within both the military and political establishment there was a lack of respect for human life. The use of lethal force against unarmed civilians was an option considered and discussed with increasing frequency as a legitimate method of law enforcement' (Saville, Hoyt & Toohey 2010, 1, §8.166).

The civil rights march

The Bloody Sunday attack occurred during a civil rights march involving about 15,000 people protesting against internment. It was organised by Derry Civil Rights in association with the Northern Ireland Civil Rights Association (NICRA) in the city of Derry, Northern Ireland's second city.

Keen to avoid a repeat of the violence on 22 January, 1972, at Magilligan Strand (see p. 61, NICRA placed 'special emphasis on the necessity for a peaceful incident-free day' at the march on 30 January, 1972 (*Irish News*, 28 January, 1972). A notice in the local Catholic newspaper, *The Derry Journal*, read 'Organisers Want Big Derry Rally Incident-Free' going on to say 'violence can only set back the civil rights cause'.

Army plan

On the day of the march, the British army rather than the RUC was in charge of security. Extra troops were brought in from their barracks 60 miles away to support Brigadier Patrick MacLlellan, Commander of the 8th Infantry Brigade. There was communication between General Ford, Brigadier Commander MacLlellan and Lieutenant Colonel Wilford – commanding the 1st Battalion of the Parachute Regiment (1 PARA) – and the RUC Chief, Superintendent Lagan. A decision was made to let the march proceed, but to enforce an alternate end point meeting place, rather than the Guildhall. Although General Ford realised that there was no way that he could stop the march, he saw it as an opportunity to arrest a large number of the 'hooligans' whom he anticipated would make use of the march to start a riot.

The Parachute Regiment was conceived during World War II as an elite advance force that could be dropped behind enemy lines. Through its years of administering colonies from east and central Africa to the Far East, the military developed tactics in counterinsurgency to win hearts and minds while defeating the enemy, tactics known as 'internal security'. Brigadier Kitson had written a paper on it called 'Low Level Operations' based on his experience, before coming to Northern Ireland to command the Thirty-Ninth Brigade in Belfast (Rucker 2002, p. 117). Rucker elaborates the operations and reputation of the Paras and how they were used as a reserve force in serious incidents and were much feared by the terrorists. He describes their culture of elitism and allegiance to each other and lack of trust in others in a community where they could not identify the enemy, whether on or off duty. He describes the tolerance of unscrupulous methods and how outbursts were known as 'going ape' and 'beasting' and how there was feelings of omnipotence when carrying a weapon. 'Personally I do not consider myself an aggressive or violent person; however, I did things that I was ashamed of in Belfast.' Private 027 likens his Regiment to 'the Rottweiler of the British army'.

On the evening before, at their barracks in Belfast, the Parachute Regiment was briefed (i.e., primed – see pp. 32–3 informally, focusing on the 'no-go' areas overrun by the IRA and how they would get results, and the phrase 'get some kills' was used (Rucker 2002, p. 124). The brief for Operation Forecast anticipated that a hooligan element would accompany the marchers and stated that 'almost certainly snipers, petrol bombers and nail bombers will support the rioters'. Once the marchers and rioters were separated, an arrest force was to be 'launched in a scoop-up operation to arrest as many hooligans and rioters as possible'.

A coordinating meeting within the army chain of command took place before the march. 'The mood of the meeting was one of complete determination that this really big arrest operation should go through. The risk of firing was discussed and quite clearly accepted' (Saville, Hoyt & Toohey 2010, 9, §9.621). The troops expected, from experience, that they would be attacked, and their orders permitted them to use 'necessary violence' in response. Immediately after the coordinating meeting, Lieutenant Colonel Peter Welsh, in charge of the 2nd Royal Green Jackets (RGJ) Brigade, expressed misgivings about the choice of 1 PARA to act as the snatch squad. 'I told Brigadier MacClellan that 1 PARA should not be used in Londonderry: they did not know the area and would go in blind. I said that I (2nd RGJs) should be given the role of 1 PARA.' Saville subsequently concluded that the misgivings also arose because of 'the reputation of 1 PARA as a hard force; the difference in Army tactics between Londonderry and Belfast; the altercation involving the C Company of 1 PARA the previous week at Magilligan Strand (see pp. 60–61; the natural desire of the resident battalions to have the task; resentment that an outside force was being brought in; and, perhaps, the nomination of the arrest force by General Ford at HQ NI' (Saville, Hoyt & Toohey, 2010, 9, §9.658).

The Paras seem to have relished the possibility of a big operation, after the evening briefing meeting. Their views could be affected by a group assumption that those demonstrating were the enemy and the riotous Derry Young Hooligans were very much like those who hassled them in Belfast, and they drew little distinction between them and the IRA.

The Attack on 30 January, 1972

It is not our role to pass judgement on the conduct of the actors in this conflict. That has been ably done by Lord Saville and his colleagues. Judgement was delivered 40 years after 13 civilians were shot dead and 14 more injured on Bloody Sunday. The fatalities were all male aged between 17 and 41. Six were aged 17. Suffice it to say this was not an isolated act by a single soldier; we shall see that it was not only the IRA who were seen as the terrorists but, in this case, soldiers of the British Army, a group initially welcomed in Northern Ireland and from whom the highest standards of discipline were expected. For many, the deaths shook and questioned basic assumptions about this major source of security. Here, we shall give an outline of the crucial events and then describe how they were perceived and the response they brought both from the people present and the various relevant groups who were not there.

The army set up and manned three barriers on three streets to block the route to Guildhall Square (see the map on p. 106). Instead of going down William Street, which was blocked by Barrier 14, the march was rescheduled to turn, at Aggro Corner, down Rossville Street to conclude with speeches at Free Derry Corner. Although the organisers were aware of this change, it was not adequately conveyed to the marchers, and this caused confusion at the corner. A large body of marchers continued along William Street to Barrier 14, where some rioters threw stones. They were repelled by water cannon and baton rounds (rubber bullets). Rioting spread, and for approximately 30 minutes attacks were made on barriers 12 and 13, where tear gas was used. Saville is satisfied that the resident troops 'deployed no more than properly proportionate force in seeking to deal with it' (Saville, Hoyt & Toohey, § 2.01–2.32).

Apart from baton rounds, no shots were fired until after the main body of marchers had passed, but rioters were still active. The brigade's plan was to separate rioters from marchers in the 'snatch operation' and not to conduct a running battle down Rossville Street into the Bogside 'no-go' area. Away from the barriers, two Paras shot and injured two civilians. Two IRA snipers were present, and one is known to have fired at a soldier and struck a drainpipe. By this time, about 3.30 pm, most of the Paras '… had been sitting in their vehicles for hours with the tension and expectation building' (Rucker 2002, p. 125). At 4.07 pm, believing that the marchers had left the rioters behind them, General Ford ordered Colonel Wilford to 'get a move on and send in the Paras'. Ford's aim had been to encircle the rioters in order to arrest the 'hooligans', but this plan was defeated by Wilford's decision to send part of his force, in armoured personnel carriers, through the barriers and down Rossville Street. This forced the rioters to disperse and brought the 'snatch squads' to the tail end of the march.

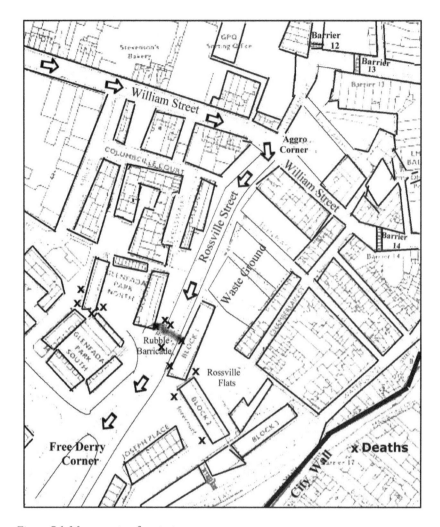

Figure 7.1 Map – route of protest.

Saville's Inquiry reports in great detail each soldier's account of his behaviour. It also includes notes by a journalist of an interview with an anonymous soldier and his comments on the behaviour of Lieutenant N. These capture something of their powerful feelings, and of the splitting into good and bad which Alderdice discussed on pp. 48–50.

'N officer, me in his pig [armoured vehicle]' cheering as we raced off, through the barricades, lads were shouting, "Get the fuckers", get the adrenalin going, snatch squad.

Waste ground below flats. Jump out, running away, thousands of them, screaming, shouting. Me with officer, loads of fuckers came around the corner at us.

Officer, firing, first, right by him, cartridges whistled past my head, he had lost it, hadn't he? Ran back to pigs to get our weapons, all did. Cover. See? Shooting started, not see anything, no targets, nothing …'.

(Saville, Hoyt & Toohey 30.64)

Saville '… concluded that the explanation for such firing by Support Company soldiers after they had gone into the Bogside was in most cases probably the mistaken belief among them that republican paramilitaries were responding in force to their arrival in the Bogside. This belief was initiated by the shots fired by Lieutenant N and reinforced by the further shots that followed soon after. In this belief, soldiers reacted by losing their self-control and firing themselves, forgetting or ignoring their instructions and training and failing to satisfy themselves that they had identified targets posing a threat of causing death or serious injury. In the case of those soldiers who fired in either the knowledge or belief that no one in the areas into which they fired was posing a threat of causing death or serious injury, or not caring whether or not anyone there was posing such a threat, it is at least possible that they did so in the indefensible belief that all the civilians they fired at were probably either members of the Provisional or Official IRA or were supporters of one or other of these paramilitary organisations; and so deserved to be shot notwithstanding that they were not armed or posing any threat of causing death or serious injury'.

(Saville, Hoyt & Toohey 2010, § 5.2)

These observations tally with the analysis on p. 32 et seq of the likely reactions of soldiers under fire, who were primed to expect attack and so misinterpreted the situation. Melaugh (1972) reports that, according to British army evidence, 21 soldiers fired their weapons on Bloody Sunday and shot 108 rounds between them. Two soldiers were responsible for firing a total of 35 live rounds.

Perceptions of the attack

As was to be expected, the attacked and the attackers had different perceptions of the same event, and little or no wish to understand the other's point of view. Those on each side of the sectarian divide had perspectives broadly aligned with their existing myths, outlook and bias. Other influences on interpretation would be linked to the experience of the event, if first hand, as a witness or indirectly by hearsay or reports.

For those 15,000 or so people on the march, who saw the paratroops, heard the firing, and saw people being killed and injured, this will inevitably have been a terrifying experience and one which, as we have seen in the previous chapters, was very likely to aggravate the cycle of violence that was already established.

John K, age 23 and married, took part in the march as did his sisters' husband and his 17-year-old brother Michael, who was shot dead that day. Michael, with three other victims, was taken by ambulance to Altnagelvin hospital. John was on the scene and travelled with the wounded in the ambulance, which he said held 13 in all. He recalls the vision of the hospital scene, his hearing the doctor's bad news, the injured, and dead, citizens, Paras and policemen, and seeing 10 bodies in the mortuary.

As the eldest of 12 with one remaining brother, his task was to go home and tell his mother. He describes her as devastated, subsequently unable to attend to or care for herself with no recovery for the next 5 years, visiting the grave daily, often vacantly, wandering, and on one occasion found carrying a blanket to the grave to keep her son warm on a winter night. She spent some time in the local mental asylum. The older married girls took it in turns to help the family, whose youngest was 6. His mother preserved Michael's clothes at home (which became evidence in the second enquiry), and later these were buried with her. John recalls a 30-year-old Mars bar preserved as well as the clothes Michael had worn on the day.

(Interview with John Kelly, who works in reception – brother of victim, Michael Kelly; MOFD 2012)

The local population heard the news from returning marchers, neighbours, community gatherings, radio and local newspapers. There was a heavy press presence which described how the first shots coincided with the start of Bernadette Devlin's speech, and how she and the others on the podium, including Lord Brockway (British Liberal Peer), dived for cover while individuals in the crowd scrambled away on all fours as the shooting started. There was a lull before it started again. Journalists reported to the newspapers, TV and radio, published in local Derry and Northern Irish newspapers, and the Irish, British and the international press. The stories of the events of that day were soon known around the world.

A statement issued soon after by army headquarters at Lisburn and published in the newspapers read as follows:

Fire was returned at seen gunmen and nail bombers … in all a total of well over 200 rounds was fired indiscriminately in the general direction of the soldiers. Fire continued to be returned only at identified targets.

The Saville Inquiry reported:

All the soldiers who were responsible for the casualties on Bloody Sunday, sought to justify their shooting on the grounds that they were sure when they fired that they had targeted and hit someone who was armed with a firearm or a nail or petrol bomb and who was posing or about to pose a threat of causing death or serious injury.

This was widely believed despite no guns having been captured or found on the streets of Derry that day and the absence of any injury to the armed forces (Saville, Hoyt & Toohey § 5 pp. 1–5).

Each side looked to their favoured newspaper to provide news that confirmed and expanded their existing 'myths'. *The Belfast Telegraph* claimed that 'four of Derry's dead, [were] said to be on "wanted list" as IRA men' (1 February, 1972, p. 4). This assertion was later investigated and 'could not be substantiated' (Saville, Hoyt & Toohey 2010, § 178.57). In Derry, the Nationalist *Derry Journal* reported eyewitness' stories with subheadings 'Simple Massacre', 'Completely Indiscriminate', 'Fired in All Directions' (4 February, 1972, p. 2). Its Friday edition had front-page coverage of the funeral and up to 14 pages on Bloody Sunday, including reports from the Bloody Sunday's injured and reports of sympathy from Scotland, Manchester and Oxford. Headlines included 'IT WAS WILFUL MURDER, SAY PRIESTS', 'SHUT-DOWN AS DERRY MOURNS ITS DEAD', and 'TEACHERS STRIKE AGAINST BUTCHERY OF THE INNOCENT'.

The Irish Independent in Dublin chose to print the following text in bold and in slightly bigger font size than the rest of the text – 'Mass Murder', 'Real Terrorists', 'Bloody Butchery', 'No Return', 'White Flag', 'No Provocation', and 'War Criminals'.

The Guardian adopted a less emotional tone under the headline '13 KILLED AS PARATROOPS BREAK RIOT', suggesting that rioters were to blame for the deaths. The BBC News included opinions from both sides in the conflict. According to bystanders, '… the troops opened fire on unarmed men – including one who had his arms up in surrender' (a rumour that was not later confirmed – Saville). They went on to report a statement by Major General Ford that 'there is absolutely no doubt at all that the Parachute battalion did not open up until they had been fired at'. *The Irish Times,* in its lead story, expressed extreme scepticism about this contention, writing that 'eyewitness reports claimed that the paratroopers opened fire first and fired indiscriminately into the large crowd'.

Most unionists held the view that the NICRA and the march were a threat to their security in their Northern Ireland state and the response by the British Army was entirely justified. This was to become the 'official' British government view and to be supported by Lord Widgery's ill-thought-out, hastily produced report. It took another 40 years for Lord Saville's exhaustive inquiry to reach a different conclusion.

To the many witnesses, a clear disjunction arose between the 'official' view and the truth. Local artist Willie Doherty, as a 12-year-old boy, witnessed the day:

> After Bloody Sunday, it became clear to me that what I had seen on TV and what I had read in the newspapers didn't in fact bear any relationship to what I had seen happen myself. So it was an experience that politicised me to some extent about how what was happening around me was being managed.
>
> (Rothfuss 1997, p. 42)

Another witness and journalist, Eamonn McCann:

> It seemed ludicrous that the British army were actually killing people, because absolutely nothing had happened that day to justify this in any terms whatsoever. There was the makings of a standard issue Derry riot, of which we had seen dozens in the previous couple of years, but the idea that they were actually prepared to shoot people and kill them seemed too weird to take seriously ... I actually saw a couple of people being shot outside Rossville flats, and at the time it simply didn't occur to me that what was happening was that these people were being killed. So I was numbed by the sheer awesome extent of the British army's violence for a time.
>
> (Kerr 1996, p. 97)

On the other hand:

> Apart from Private T (who claimed to have fired at someone throwing down acid bombs from the Rossville Flats), all the soldiers who in our view were responsible for the casualties on Bloody Sunday sought to justify their shooting on the grounds that they were sure when they fired that they had targeted and hit someone who was armed with a firearm or a nail or petrol bomb and who was posing or about to pose a threat of causing death or serious injury
>
> (Saville, Hoyt & Toohey 2010, § 3.77)

This position was maintained over some 30 years and through the two major enquiries (Widgery 1972; Saville, Hoyt & Toohey 2010), despite no army injuries and no ammunition or weapons being recovered from the scene. There have been no prosecutions, and the Paras were granted anonymity.

Response to the attack

Given these perceptions of the attack, it is hardly surprising that some of the Catholic population of both Northern and Southern Ireland responded with rage and violence. Father Daly (later Bishop of Derry), who is indelibly linked with the day, said:

> A lot of the younger people in Derry who may have been more pacifist became quite militant as a result of it. People who were there on that day and who saw what happened were absolutely enraged by it and just wanted to seek some kind of revenge for it ...
>
> (Mc Kittrick & Mc Vea 2001, p. 77)

Security forces stayed clear of the area, the police profile was low, and a meeting of the relatives and friends of the dead was held. In the Republic of Ireland, there was an outpouring of rage and protest which manifested itself in trade union walkouts and strikes across the country. The Irish government, sensing the mood, declared a day of mourning, and a cavalcade of limousines carried senior politicians and dignitaries across the border to the funerals at St Mary's church in the Creggan. About 25,000 stood silently outside. Among the mourners were clergy, politicians from North and South, as well as thousands of friends and neighbours. Twelve of the victims were interred in the city cemetery three days after the attack. The world's media were in attendance. Prayer services were held across Ireland to coincide with the funerals. The demonstration in Dublin was the largest for a generation where a 100,000-strong crowd gathered, held aloft 13 coffins and marched to the British Embassy, which was later razed to the ground.

> Acres of paper may be used to explain it away; but thirteen dead young men tell the only story that the majority of Irishmen will remember.
>
> (editor of *The Irish Times,* 31 January, 1972)

Some Protestant children were inclined to gloat: Colin Shaw, a Protestant Belfast architect, recalls at age 13 the local chant in his estate:

> We shat one, we shat two, we shat thirteen more than you, with a nick nack Paddy wack, give a Prod a gun, Paras thirteen, Bogside none.

Legitimising authorities

In Northern Ireland prior to Bloody Sunday, with the exception of Free Derry, the Northern Ireland Parliament at Stormont supported by Her Majesty's Government in Westminster was the legitimising authority. Following Bloody Sunday, that legitimacy was even further undermined in the eyes of the Catholic population. In Derry City, a three-day strike was called after Bloody Sunday, and most businesses to the west of the Foyle were closed.

At a press conference, seven Catholic priests accused Colonel Wilford of the Parachute Regiment of 'wilful murder' and General Ford, Commander of Land Forces, of being an accessory before the fact:

> We accuse the soldiers of shooting indiscriminately into a fleeing crowd, of gloating over casualties and of preventing medical and spiritual aid from reaching some of the dying, they said. The priests called the paratroopers 'trained criminals who differ from terrorists only in the air of respectability that a uniform gives them'.
>
> (Hoggart, S. 1972)

Thrown on the defensive, both the army authorities and the government took steps to bolster their position, which became more entrenched in the process. The incident was discussed in Parliament in London and Belfast, where a predominant view was forming to support the army's version of events.

Unionist MPs at Westminster, initially shocked by the death toll and injury list, reacted later by criticising the organisers of the Civil Rights
march, alleging that the extreme republican elements had intended to
cash in on the occasion for an assault on the army and had no regard for
human life. (*Newsletter*, 31 January, 1972, p. 2 – Northern Irish Newsletter with a Protestant readership)

   Yesterdays debate on the "tragedy of Derry" was unique in that for the
first time in recent months there was almost total unanimity on all sides
of the Commons in condemning those who organised the illegal parade
in Derry on Sunday.

(*Newsletter*, v.s. 2 Feb, 2012)

The British Government's response came in a statement from the Home Secretary
to the House of Commons the following day:

   The army returned the fire directed at them with aimed shots and inflicted
   a number of casualties on those who were attacking them with firearms
   and with bombs.

The Minister of State for Defence, Lord Carrington, gave the official version of
events and went on to say:

   We must also recognise that the IRA is waging a war, not only of bullets
   and bombs but of words ... If the IRA is allowed to win this war, I shudder
   to think what will be the future of the people living in Northern Ireland.

Edward Heath, the British prime minister, appointed Lord Chief Justice Lord
Widgery to conduct an inquiry. Heath told him he wanted a quick inquiry and that
a military and propaganda war was being fought in Northern Ireland. There was
much alarm in Derry at the suitability of United Kingdom's highest judge to
examine the actions of the United Kingdom's armed forces.

   On 21 February, 1972, the Widgery Inquiry opened in Coleraine, 30 miles from
Derry, and in two weeks it held 17 sessions and took evidence from 117 witnesses.
Despite their suspicions, and the possibility of a boycott, most witnesses were persuaded to give evidence. Widgery's report was published on 18 April, 1972. It caused
immediate outrage in the Catholic community and confirmed its suspicions so much
that it became known as the 'Widgery Whitewash', a cover-up. (Walsh D. 2012)

   I have heard even the relatives of the victims on Bloody Sunday saying
   that Bloody Sunday was bad but the day the Widgery Report was published was worse.

(Kerr 1996, p. 112)

Bishop Daly devoted a chapter – 'Widgery: The Second Atrocity' – to the perceived betrayal by this tribunal, in his book *Mister, Are You a Priest?* (Daly 2000).

The attorney general, in answer to a parliamentary question about the RUC Bloody Sunday File, reported: 'The conclusion was that there would be no prosecution of any member of the security forces as a result of the killings on 30 January, 1972. Charges in respect of riotous behaviour against some civilians were also dropped.' (*Hansard*, 1 August, 1972)

> Our overall conclusion is that there was a serious and widespread loss of
> fire discipline among the soldiers of Support Company.
>
> (Saville, Hoyt & Toohey 2010, § 5.4)

Within a year of his involvement in the attack, Lieutenant Colonel Wilford, the Commanding Officer of the First Parachute Regiment on Bloody Sunday, was made an OBE in the New Year's Honours List.

Although in possession of the findings of the Widgery Report, on 31 August, 1973, Major Hubert O'Neill, Her Majesty's Coroner at the inquest into the deaths on Bloody Sunday, issued the following statement:

> This Sunday became known as Bloody Sunday and bloody it was. It was
> quite unnecessary. It strikes me that the army ran amok that day and shot
> without thinking what they were doing. They were shooting innocent
> people. These people may have been taking part in a march that was
> banned but that does not justify the troops coming in and firing live
> rounds indiscriminately. I would say without hesitation that it was sheer,
> unadulterated murder. It was murder.

Polarisation

In chapter 12, Alderdice explains how the psychological process of splitting, as demonstrated here, can exacerbate polarisation.

> The incident had enormous ramifications, taking a place in Irish history
> as a formative moment which not only claimed fourteen lives but also
> hardened attitudes, increased paramilitary recruitment, helped generate
> more violence and convulsed Anglo-Irish relations.
>
> (Mc Kittrick & Mc Vea 2001, p. 76)

Brian Faulkner, who a year before (March 1971) had become the sixth prime minister of Northern Island in its 50 years, had presided over the implementation of internment, and now wanted even stronger security measures after Bloody Sunday. His unionist government, whose Catholic Social Democratic and Labour Party (SDLP) members had walked out five months earlier, was reluctant to give nationalists a voice. This left the British prime minister, Edward Heath, with no alternative but to suspend the Stormont government in favour of Direct Rule from Westminster, which took over control of security, law and order and the judiciary.

Heath recognised that the problems were wider than Stormont, and he stripped local government of virtually all its powers. He created The Northern Ireland Office and appointed Willie Whitelaw as Secretary of State. Stormont's suspension and the introduction of Direct Rule by Westminster in March 1972 were viewed differently by the two camps in Derry; a triumph for Free Derry and a major setback for the unionists.

> Gregory Campbell: The fall of Stormont was one of the major events of the unionist community. A bastion against a united Ireland had been taken away, and by a government that six weeks before had indicated that there was no possibility of such an action. That was a blow to the Protestant psyche, the removal of such a bulwark.
>
> (Kerr 1996, p. 27)

Stormont's fall and clandestine meetings between Secretary of State Willie Whitelaw with paramilitary figures such as Martin Mc Guinness and Gerry Adams along with the escalation of violence raised insecurity in the Protestant population and sparked the rise of vigilante groups. By the end of 1972, loyalists had killed 120 Catholics (Mc Kittrick & Mc Vea 2000, p. 86).

Unionist politician William Craig responded to the demise of Stormont and the mounting threat from the IRA by forming the Ulster Vanguard movement, enlisting support from various loyalist groups. At his rallies, he made inflammatory speeches advocating gathering intelligence to liquidating the enemy if the politicians failed. These became known as 'shoot-to-kill' speeches.

> Jimmy Cadden: As a unionist and as a Protestant the day Stormont fell was a bad day. That was probably the beginning of the Protestant Uprising, which then gave expression in the UWC strike ... let's show that we can control the situation as well ... But I fully backed the strike.
>
> (Kerr 1996)

Newspaper reports saw the way that Bloody Sunday and its aftermath would harden the divide between the Protestant and Catholic communities.

> Lord Widgery, according to Ivan Cooper, has produced a mammoth whitewash. That view is widely shared in the Bogside. Fraser Agnew, a young unionist spokesman, says that Lord Widgery has completely upheld and vindicated the action of the paratroopers. No doubt, that too, is a widely held opinion. These reactions emphasise a basic difficulty to be overcome in the struggle to end Northern Ireland's agony: an inability or an unwillingness to see another person's point of view.
>
> (Dawson, 1972)

To those on the Catholic side of the sectarian divide, the murderous brutality dealt out to innocent people on Bloody Sunday was a strike against the community, and it reinforced the view of many that the army, as well as the police, were trying to subjugate and suppress them.

> Raymond McCartney: In the aftermath of Bloody Sunday, any doubts and fears I had about committing myself to the IRA disappeared. I remember expressing that thought to a very senior member of the IRA at that time, and he told me – obviously having experienced a lot of people at that particular time expressing the same wish to him – not to allow emotion to influence what was a very important decision. He asked me to go away and reflect on it, and take a couple of months before making up my mind. I did eventually make that decision, and I joined the IRA.
>
> (Kerr 1996, p. 112)

> Tony Crowe: '... what the Protestant working class perceived as their neglect and marginalisation. They were being passed over by British Ministers, and the attention directed to much of the civil rights campaign created a great feeling of being under siege, and of fear and the UWC strike was a manifestation of that.'
>
> (Kerr 1996, p. 37)

> William Temple: 'When civil unrest came onto the streets, Protestants felt threatened and they were nervous going through some of the barricades. It was only natural they would think about moving to a safer environment.'
>
> (Kerr 1996, p. 158)

> John McCourt: '15,000 people from City-side moved to the Waterside or up the country ... trying to bridge the gap, saying to people that while there is a river between us, that's not the barrier we have to cross. We are trying to get people to cross the barrier of the mind.'
>
> (Kerr 1996, p. 150)

> WT: 'Violence has done a great deal of harm by creating victims who find it hard to forgive, thus impacting on future political progress.'
>
> (Kerr 1996, p. 158)

Retaliation

In his memoirs, Gerry Adams wrote:

> Money, guns and recruits flooded into the IRA.
>
> (McKittrick & McVea 2001, p. 77)

If the soldiers were permitted to shoot civilians, the IRA targeted the police and the army while the loyalists targeted Catholics. Alongside killings, there was intimidation and persecution at every level in neighbourhoods where the other side were not welcome. Widespread army house searches concentrated on republican areas, and the associated abuses promoted more anger, motivating retaliation and recruitment to paramilitaries.

> John Hume: 'Bloody Sunday was a dreadful occasion, it was probably one of the worst days in my own life, and that of itself led to massive recruitment for the IRA; in other words, violence leading to violence ... Violence ... deepens the divisions and make the problem worse ... leads to retaliation and attacks from both sides, the doctrine "an eye for an eye", which as I often say, leaves everybody blind.'
>
> (Kerr 1996, p. 62)

In the three years prior to Bloody Sunday, 210 were killed in the Troubles. In the 11 months after Bloody Sunday, 445 people lost their lives. 1972 was the year with the highest death rate of the Troubles, and July 1972 had the highest deaths of any one month: 2,000 explosions 10,000 shooting incidents, almost 5,000 injured. Security almost doubled to 29,000 soldiers. Vigilante groups emerged from the Protestant population and arranged thousands strong UDA parades in semi-military uniform in Belfast. Republicans killed Protestants while loyalists claimed Catholic lives, often with particular savagery. (McKittrick & McVea 2001, p. 86).

The capture, conviction and imprisonment of republican and loyalist terrorists did little to improve matters. Even inside prison they continued their campaigns. It became impossible to manage prisons on an integrated basis because of violence between the two sides. Once separated, prisoners used the educational facilities to develop their political ideas and strategies, as well as continuing to protest against their conviction as criminals on charges relating to what they saw as freedom-fighting (weapons, bombings, murder, robbery, etc.). They insisted they were political prisoners whose 'crimes' were all in the cause of their political beliefs. The fact that after almost ten years of violence the IRA's terrorist campaign had not brought about the withdrawal of British forces led to a strategic rethink by the increasing numbers of IRA prisoners, especially those in HM Prison The Maze. Their struggle with the authorities resulted in a cycle of regressive self-abuse and dehumanisation. First, they refused to wear prison clothes since these would identify them as criminals rather than prisoners of war. In retaliation, the authorities refused to let them leave their cells to answer the calls of nature. Prisoners responded by taking faeces from their slop buckets and smearing themselves and their cell walls – the Dirty Protest. Alderdice refers to the group cohesion of terrorist prisoners and the regression that led to blood sacrifices and martyrdom on p. 53. The inhumanity of the circumstances for them and their jailers led the prison authorities to power-hose and disinfect the cells, and inevitably, physical abuse and fights ensued. The cold, unswerving and punitive approach taken by Prime Minister Margaret Thatcher sparked a hunger strike. Tension heightened when the leader of the hunger strike, Bobby Sands, was elected to Westminster as MP for Fermanagh and South Tyrone. He continued his fast and was, as he had planned, the first to die, but the strike brought few obvious short-term benefits. Ten men died, and the protest was abandoned without concessions when the families, especially the mothers, successfully requested resuscitative measures to be used on the unconscious hunger strikers. There was no purpose in continuing the hunger strike. But the ten hunger strikers who had died in 1981 became martyrs, in a remarkable and possibly deliberate repetition of the executions of the leaders in 1916 (Bobby Sands instead of Padraig Pearce). Theirs was seen as a 'blood sacrifice' and became the basis for the political rise of Sinn Fein at the expense of the so-called 'constitutional Nationalists' in the SDLP led by John Hume, a man who was committed to peaceful and democratic means to bring about change. Terrorism and violence seemed to be making the possibility of a peaceful outcome more and more remote. A weary and fearful, even palpable, despair descended on the community.

Conclusion

The Catholic minority population, who sought civil and human rights and representation in a unionist-dominated state, was shocked by the brutality of the security forces and government on its own citizens on Bloody Sunday on 31 January, 1972. Those in the Protestant majority population saw the minority's assertiveness as a threat to 50 years of dominance, and it rekindled their own insecurity in Catholic Ireland and their allegiance to Britain, which had helped establish Northern Ireland 50 years before. Against this fragile dynamic, the poor judgement on Bloody Sunday had a symbolism of oppression and injustice that further polarised communities and legitimised violence.

Bloody Sunday was seen as a 'terrorist' attack which had the opposite result from that intended by the perpetrator. An unintended outcome was the prorogation of the Stormont government. On Bloody Sunday, the plan to reduce terrorism by punishing some terrorists and deterring others ended by confirming the injustice and hostility of the British forces and fed support for the old myths. It directly led to recruitment and the growth of paramilitaries on both sides. It was perceived as unjust, and with its ensuing cover-up, fuelled mistrust, galvanised the Troubles, and led to extreme and entrenched positions.

The Troubles were to last 30 years. They resulted in grief and pain from over 3,500 deaths and 35,000 injuries and caused the destruction of Northern Irish society, politically, socially and economically. The Troubles achieved little.

The proposed model can bring a psychological perspective on how conflict can be triggered or be reactivated by an attack and how actions taken after, or in response to, an attack, can polarise and escalate into a vicious cycle which can spiral out of control and into war. It is suggested that a psychological understanding of the complexity of conflict situations could inform remedial inputs to prevent escalation or promote earlier resolution to achieve and maintain peace.

8

THE ASSASSINATION AND GENOCIDE IN RWANDA

Peter Hall and Colin Murray Parkes

In this chapter, we consider the genocidal terror that took place in Rwanda in 1994 and analyse the historical and psychological factors that go some way to explain it using the model expounded in chapter 6. The event that had triggered the genocide was a terrorist attack on a jet aircraft.

Factors maintaining the cycle of deadly violence

1. The attack: Assassination of the two presidents and their entourage

At around 8.20 pm on Wednesday, 6 April, 1994, the Falcon presidential jet given to Rwanda by the French Government began its doomed final approach towards Kigali airport. Inside was not only President Habyarimana of Rwanda but also the new Hutu President of Burundi, who had asked for a lift back to Bujumburu, and General Déogratias Nsabimana, Chief of Staff of the Rwandan Army, whom witnesses subsequently attested had opposed plans for genocide.

They were returning from a momentous regional summit at which Habyarimana had reluctantly agreed to implement the Arusha Accords over which he had been stalling for months. On approaching Kigali airport, the plane was struck by a surface-to-air missile and crashed into the grounds of the nearby Presidential Palace, killing everyone on board.

As we saw on page 84 the killing of two Hutu heads of state was bound to have a profound impact. The fact that they were returning from a summit formalising the end of more than three years of war, and the violent nature of their deaths by means of a military weapon at a time of extreme tension and anxiety, would be expected to give rise to widespread alarm. In other words, the terrorists were 'putting a whole target population in fear of their lives, by undermining the protective power of a government or authority'(p. 42).

2. Perceptions of the assassination

In Rwanda, most people learned of the assassinations by the radio, ownership of radios being high by African standards, and from the Hutu newspaper *Kangura*.

Radio Rwanda and RTLM repeatedly attributed the assassination to the RPF (Des Forges, 1999). RTLM reported a rumour that '... after they have killed the president, they will exterminate the Hutus'. But the weight of the evidence now shows that the missile that brought down the plane was fired by terrorists, a group of dissident Hutu soldiers who were opposed to the implementation of the Arusha Peace Accords (Schofield, 2012; United Nations Organisation, 1999).

In December 2003, the International Criminal Tribunal for Rwanda tried the founder of RTLM, the editor of *Kangura* and the founder of CDR (Coalition pour la Défense de la République) on the grounds that:

> the power of the media to create and destroy fundamental human values comes with great responsibility. Those who control such media are responsible for its consequences (para 8) ... If the downing of the president's plane was the trigger, then the RTLM, *Kangura* and CDR were the bullets in the gun. The trigger had such a deadly impact because the gun was loaded ... The killing of Tutsi civilians and Hutu political opponents can be said to have resulted, at least in part, from the message of ethnic targeting for death that was clearly and effectively disseminated by RTLM, *Kangura* and CDR before and after 6 April, 1994 (para 67).

They found that the publication of these sources conveyed contempt and hatred for the Tutsi ethnic group and called on listeners and readers to eliminate them. 'The newspaper and the radio explicitly, repeatedly, in fact relentlessly, targeted the Tutsi population for destruction' (para 72).

The Hutu population

In the circumstances, it is hardly surprising that the Hutu population was suspicious, fearful and angry with both the RPF, over whom they felt powerless, and their Tutsi neighbours, over whom they felt anything but powerless. Any urge to take action was most easily directed against the assumed enemy within.

> Pancrace: 'The Hutu always ... sees a threat in even the feeblest or kindest Tutsi. But it is suspicion, not hatred. The hatred came over us suddenly after our president's plane crashed. The intimidators shouted: "Just look at those cockroaches – we told you so", and we yelled, "Right, let's go hunting".'
>
> (Hatzfeld, 2003, p. 207).

The Tutsi population

On the other hand, the Tutsi had every reason to feel afraid, for previous experience had taught them to distrust Hutus, and they anticipated becoming the targets of their vengeance. Even so, the Arusha Accords had raised their hopes, and some people from both ethnic groups were opposed to tribalism and violence. Jean Hatzfeld's records of the immediate reaction indicates that the Tutsi expected massacres, but nothing as bad as what happened. Only when they witnessed the full impact, or lost close relatives, did the enormity of the situation hit home.

Troops and militias

As we have seen, the government troops, the Interahamwe and the Tutsi RPF were in a high state of readiness for armed conflict. Consequently, their response would have tended to be more focused on the observation of procedures and less driven by emotion than that of the general population. Even so, a member of the Interahamwe said: 'We'd been too afraid, it's true. We believed that the inkot-anye, once installed on the throne, would be especially oppressive' (Hatzfeld 2003, p. 95).

The rest of the world

The rest of the world appeared indifferent to the assassination of a minor ruler in a small, black, distant country, and the US media was preoccupied with the murder trial of a famous ex-football star.

In the introduction to his book *The Media and the Rwandan Genocide*, Thompson writes:

> By most accounts, there were only two foreign journalists in Rwanda on 6 April, when Habyarimana's plane was shot down ... Although a sig-nificant number arrived on the scene shortly after the killings began, most were there with instructions to cover the attempts to rescue foreign nationals. And all but a handful left with the evacuees in mid-April. There was virtually no real time news out of Rwanda for the first weeks of the genocide ...
>
> (Thompson, 2007, p. 5).

The Security Council

The delay in the Security Council's recognition of the significance of the events in Rwanda was, in no small part, owing to the influence of Rwanda's membership as a non-permanent member of the council since January 1994. This 'hampered the quality of the information available and the nature of the discussions of the Council' (United Nations Organisation, 1999). The Organisation of African Unity's report expressed it more bluntly: 'Now that Rwanda had duly taken its seat on the Council, Habyarimana and the akazu had a direct pipeline to the inner corridors of UN power.' They dismissed the killings as a continuation of a long-standing tribal conflict.

3. Early responses

Even if the terrorist attack on the president's plane had been brought about by the RPF, the rational response of the Rwandese people would have been to go ahead with the implementation of the Arusha Accords. They could reasonably have expected strong support from France, the UN and the rest of the world, who could soon have put a stop to any incursions by the RPF. The only ones who would have lost out were the akazu and their clique. But the akazu were, it seems, aware that the response would be irrational and did everything in their power to promote the emotional overreaction to the attack.

A small group of Habyarimana's close associates launched a planned insurrection. The Presidential Guard and other troops commanded by Colonel Bagosora and backed by Interahamwe set about murdering Hutu government officials and other leaders of the political opposition, so as to create a political vacuum 'that would allow' Colonel Bagosora and his supporters to take control.

Albert: 'Then the killings began very early. Anyone who expressed an opinion [was in danger].'

Paul Rusesabagina, manager of the Hotel Milles Collines ('Hotel Rwanda'), phoned people he knew at UNAMIR (the UN's military force) to ask for an escort to the hotel. 'They said, "No way. There are road blocks all over Kigali, and people are being killed in the roads" … This was one hour after the president was killed, just one hour!' (Gourevitch, 1998, p. 113).

Soldiers and Interahamwe began systematically slaughtering Tutsi. Within hours, military officers and administrators far from the capital dispatched soldiers and militia to kill Tutsi and listed Hutu opposition leaders in their local areas. After months of warnings, rumours and prior attacks, the violence struck panic among Rwandans and foreigners alike. The rapidity of the first killings gave the impression of large numbers of assailants, but in fact their impact resulted more from ruthlessness and organisation than from great numbers.

On the day after the assassinations, Agathe Uwilingyimana, the interim prime minister, a moderate Hutu who supported the Arusha Accords, was murdered by the Presidential Guard along with ten Belgian UN troops who had been sent to protect her. By noon ' … the moderate political leadership of Rwanda were dead or in hiding, the potential for a future moderate government was utterly lost'. (Dallaire, 2003, p. 232).

On the same day, General Kagame warned Dallaire that the RPF military contingent in Kigali were prepared to leave their compound and take over the city if the UN did not take action to secure it before sunset. The following day, they engaged with the Presidential Guard, who eventually repulsed their attack. At the same time, the main body of the RPF, based in northern Rwanda, launched a three-pronged attack. Although the western prong was halted at Ruhengiri, the central and eastern prongs made rapid progress and, by the 16 May (five weeks later), had virtually encircled Kigali and forced the Provisional Government to flee west to Gitarama. Dallaire describes Kagame as '... possibly one of the greatest practitioners of manoeuvre warfare in modern military history' (Dallaire, 2003, p. 288). But the RPF's success only increased fear in the genocidaires and intensified their rage against their victims.

4. Legitimising authorities

Albert: 'It (the genocide) was regulated by the authorities, including the religious.'

Valentin: (At Ntarama) 'The Interahamwe, manipulated by the government, organised it ... they brought people here in motor coaches! Five thousand died in one day. The killers started outside the church and worked their way inwards.'

Although the murder of most of the members of the transitional government left Rwanda without a leader, the coup d'etat was well planned, and new leaders were soon able to implement their plan to eliminate the Tutsi menace from within. The genocide was not a killing machine that rolled inexorably forward but rather a campaign to which participants were recruited over time by the use of threat and incentives. The early organisers included military and administrative officials as well as politicians, businessmen and others with no official posts.

Colonel Bagosora and his circle sought first to obtain the backing, or at least the acquiescence, of the majority of the military commanders. They began negotiating for this support even as troops under their command slaughtered civilians in the streets. Colonel Bagosora's first proposal, to take control in his own right, was rejected by a number of influential officers as well as by the ranking representative of the United Nations in Rwanda. But his next move, to install a regime of extremists masquerading as a legitimate government, was accepted by the soldiers, the UN representative and the international community. In the face of the RPF attack and the ensuing pressure for solidarity, officers opposed to Colonel Bagosora found it increasingly difficult to challenge his actions.

As the new leaders were consolidating control over military commanders, they profited enormously from international vacillation. UN troops, in Rwanda under the terms of the peace accords, tried for a few hours to keep the peace, then withdrew to their posts – as ordered by superiors in New York – leaving the local population at the mercy of the assailants. Officers opposed to Colonel Bagosora realised that a continuing foreign presence was essential to restricting the killing campaign and appealed to representatives of France, Belgium and the United States not to desert Rwanda. However, suspecting the horrors to come, the foreigners had already packed their bags.

The first impression of international indifference to the fate of Rwandans was confirmed, and as anticipated by the organisers of the massacre of the Belgian guard, the Belgian government did not want to risk any further casualties. On 9 April, an experienced and well-equipped force of French, Belgian and Italian troops rushed in to evacuate expatriates serving in Rwanda, and then departed. US Marines dispatched to the area stopped in neighbouring Burundi once it was clear that US citizens would be evacuated without their help.

> Adalbert (Interahamwe): 'Ever since the plane crash, the radio had hammered at us, "The foreigners are departing … This time around they are showing no interest in the fate of the Tutsis" … For the first time ever, we did not feel we were under the frowning supervision of whites.'
>
> (Hatzfeld, 2003, p. 85)

5. Polarisation

Initially many Tutsi joined with Hutus to prepare defences against the invaders (McDoom 2011) and most of the killings were carried out at night.

Albert: 'I got frightened when it became general. Previously there was always somewhere to escape to … The witnesses had gone and anything could be done. I had had a false sense of security. Nothing could be done in public. But once the control was off the hunts took place in the daytime.'

The policy to implicate as many people as possible in the killings was intended to maximise the numbers killed, dilute culpability and feelings of guilt, increase the numbers of those with an investment in suppressing the truth, and legitimise murderous behaviour through common practice. A subtler rationale was the prospect of reforging the Rwandese national identity through the shared endeavour of killing all Tutsis and those Hutu who opposed the government, with the objective of making Rwanda a nation wholly committed to the ideology of Hutu extremism.

Against the backdrop of Rwandan military cooperation and the foreign exodus, Colonel Bagosora and his circle moved to recruit administrators and political leaders for the killing campaign. They expected and received support from politicians, prefects and bourgmestres associated with the akazu, but to expand the killing campaign more broadly, they needed the collaboration of administrators and local leaders from the other parties also, particularly the ruling authorities in central and southern Rwanda.

Supporters of these parties, stunned by the murder of their Hutu colleagues in the first days, were planning to oppose soldiers and militia whom they believed to be fighting to restore exclusive control to the extremists. Rwanda's new authorities hurried to dispel these concerns at a meeting of prefects on April 11 and through radio appeals for Hutu unity broadcast by the minister of defence and other influential politicians on April 12. They stressed that partisan interests must be put aside in the battle against the common enemy, the Tutsi. On the same day, Kagame's troops reached the outskirts of Kigali, but Kagame delayed a direct attack on the city, perhaps fearing it might draw in the Belgians in opposition.

In the event, it turned out to be the day on which the Belgian government ordered the withdrawal of all their troops from Rwanda.

> The more the inkotanyi (RPF) pushed into the country, the more we [the Hutu death squads] would massacre their Tutsi brothers on the farms, to deter them and halt the advance. That's how we saw the situation.
>
> (Kinzer, 2008, p. 158)

By April 15, it was clear that the UN Security Council would not order the peace-keepers to try to stop the violence and might even withdraw them completely. By this time, the organisers of the genocide had expanded their ranks considerably and were strong enough to remove opponents and impose compliance with the killing campaign. On April 16 and 17, they replaced the military chief of the staff and the prefects known to be opposing the killings. One prefect was later imprisoned and executed, and another was murdered with his family. Three bourgmestres and a number of other officials who sought to stop the killings were also slain by mid-April or shortly thereafter. The leaders of the genocide held meetings in the centre and south of the country to persuade hesitant local administrators to collaborate. At the same time, they sent genocidaires from areas where slaughter was well under way into those central and southern communes where people had refused to kill, and they used the radio to ridicule and threaten administrators and local political leaders who had been preaching calm. '... Throughout the genocide RTLM urged the killers on to greater zeal and efficiency, even furnishing listeners with the names, addresses and automobile license plate numbers of those who still needed to be killed' (Chalk, 2007).

By April 20, two weeks after the plane crash, the organisers of the genocide had substantial, although not yet complete, control of the highly centralised state. The administration continued to function remarkably well despite the disruptions in communication and transport caused by the war. Orders from the new prime minister were handed down to prefects, who passed them on to the bourgmestres, who called local meetings throughout the communes, where they read the instructions to the population. The same language echoed from north to south and from east to west, calling for 'self-defence' against 'accomplices'. Slaughter was known as 'work', and machetes and firearms were described as 'tools'. Reports on the situation at the local level and minutes of meetings held by people out on the hills were handed back up through the administrative channels.

By appropriating the well-established hierarchies of the military, administrative and political systems, leaders of the genocide were able to exterminate Tutsi with astonishing speed and thoroughness. Soldiers, who might have been more effectively occupied in confronting the RPF; gendarmes; former soldiers; and communal police played a larger part in the slaughter than is generally realised (Des Forges, 1999). In addition to leading the first killings in the capital and in other urban centres, soldiers and gendarmes directed all the major massacres throughout the country. Although usually few in number at sites of massive killing, their

124

tactical knowledge and their use of the weapons of war, including grenades, machine guns and even mortars, contributed significantly to the death tolls in these massacres. It was mainly after the military had launched attacks with devastating effect on masses of unarmed Tutsi that civilian assailants, armed with such weapons as machetes, hammers and clubs, finished the slaughter. In addition, the military encouraged and, when faced with reluctance to act, compelled both ordinary citizens and local administrators to participate in attacks, even travelling the back roads and stopping at small marketplaces to deliver the message.

The administrators were charged with driving Tutsi from their homes and gathering them at places of slaughter, with assembling the masses of assailants, providing transportation and 'tools' for the 'work', arranging for the disposal of the corpses, and directing the division of looted property and confiscated land. A proportion of the loot was passed to the administrators and the Interahamwe towards the expenses and expansion of the genocide. They transformed administrative practices that were benign in themselves, such as obligatory labour for the common good (umuganda) or the use of security patrols, into mechanisms for executing the genocide. Mamdani (2001) concludes that as defeat disgraced the Rwandan government army, which considered itself a custodian of the national revolution, its zeal was re-energised by its role in confronting the 'enemy within'.

The urgency and importance of the objective was deemed to justify departures from usual bureaucratic practice. Zeal for killing took on more significance than formal rank: subordinates could prevail over their superiors, in both civilian and military spheres, if they showed greater commitment to the genocide. As we saw on p. 97 this reward encouraged ambition and initiative among those willing to trade human lives for personal advantage. Actors could also bypass the usual limits set by law or administrative practice, with politicians or soldiers speaking for government officials, militia approving candidates for administrative position, and medical assistants calling in military strikes.

The Hutu workhorses of the genocide

The matter-of-fact perpetrator and survivor testimony often used to describe the gruesome details of the individual crimes does not explain how ordinary people found the ability to commit murders of neighbours in such numbers. The wider population of Rwanda was primed to respond to these pressures for aggressive action for the reasons given on pages 32–34. Thus, most of the putative killers were young, male and trained for violence.

As with others, Mamdani views the categories Hutu and Tutsi as long-term facilitators, but not the main cause of the genocide. He concludes that the genocide resulted more from recent historical developments, especially the 1991 invasion by the RPF. Mamdani sees the war as a prerequisite for the genocide because it created the fear in the population that allowed them to kill. They were under attack, and many believed that their very existence was under threat. They saw killing as a solution to their predicament, to which there was no alternative, and they were under considerable social pressure to adopt the norms of the group, even to the point that anyone who refused to take part in the genocide would be seen as hostile and killed. This does not excuse their behaviour, particularly towards the large numbers of women, children and elderly Tutsis whom they killed, but it does go some way to helping us to understand the trigger to their behaviour. Once the natural prohibitions on killing had been crossed, the hunt seemed to escalate. Although many killed because the Interahamwe threatened them with their own death, far too many others killed willingly.

As most Rwandans lived on rural hills rather than in the capital, Fujii (2009) conducted a series of interviews designed to establish how ordinary Rwandans made sense of what happened in their communities between 1990 and 1994, at two rural locations and their central prisons. He analysed the information he collected over nine months in 2004, in his report 'Killing Neighbours – Webs of Violence in Rwanda'. Fujii's research suggests that experience, social ties, and other group dynamics, as described in chapters 2 and 3, were much more influential than ethnic hatred or fear at determining who, and to what extent, individuals participated in the genocide at the grassroots level.

Fujii found that belonging to the Interahamwe meant that individuals participated in a number of activities that they specifically would not carry out when they were alone – such as killing, torturing, raping or indeed watching others kill, torture and rape. Throughout the country, the Interahamwe worked in groups – often much larger groups than were required to kill the victims. The size of the group meant that many members watched while a handful performed the murder. After the first weeks, the majority of killings were public acts, taking place in broad daylight in full view of onlookers. Even killings carried out in remote areas were conducted in full public view of the local population, who were ordered to watch the murder. Killings were physically intimate. Killers killed up close, face to face. The instruments used were clubs, hoes, axes, masues (nail-studded clubs), hammers, spears, swords and machetes. Killings often featured theatrical elements such as chanting to announce they were about to kill someone.

An example of the apparent normalisation with which some members of the professional classes approached genocidal violence is the comment of a Hutu teacher to a French journalist in Butare:

> A lot of people got killed here. I myself killed some of the children ...
> We had 80 kids in the first year. There are 25 left. All the others, we killed
> them or they have run away.
>
> (Fujii, 2009, p. 228)

Fujii's main findings and conclusions confirm the theories and research findings described in the foregoing chapters. At the neighbourhood level, the mechanisms critical to the process of killing were local attachments and group dynamics which exerted powerful pressures on local Hutus to join in the violence, and powerful new identities for continuing. The most powerful actors were the local leaders who were chosen by bourgmestres or higher officials, and may well have been selected as a result of previous party connections. They were responsible for organising their communities for violence, and they enlisted dedicated lieutenants (collaborators).

It was the local leaders who decided what the dominant myth was. Ethnic claims amounted to accusations, the most common of which was that someone was a Tutsi, or looked like a Tutsi, or supported a Tutsi. All of these made that person a legitimate target for killing. Mostly, the targeted person was whatever the local leader said he was. It was the local leaders' interpretation that mattered. Those who joined in the killing ('Joiners') made decisions about how faithfully they would keep to the 'script' of the official myth. In coercive situations, such as when they were with the Interahamwe, they spoke their lines and observed the stage directions, but when alone they might choose to drop the script completely. Of those who became Joiners, nearly half claimed they were forced to join, otherwise they would have been killed; a quarter joined willingly out of a sincere belief they had to protect their communities; and a few others appear to have joined without making any clear decision to join do so. All three groups explained that situational exigencies, such as the assassination of the president, influenced their decision (Fujii, 2009, p. 155).

The process of descent into violence was both dynamic and self-reinforcing; each step taken created the momentum to take the next step. So a Joiner might start with night patrols, then move on steadily to pillaging and burning Tutsi homes, and then on to hunting and killing Tutsi. The process by which Joiners first joined in the violence was shaped by group dynamics; this dynamic generated group ties, and group ties, in turn, strengthened these dynamics. Once initial inhibitions against killing had been overcome, it got easier. As genocidaires interviewed by Hatzfeld put it:

> Ignace: 'We'd gather in a crowd of about a thousand on the soccer field, head out into the bush ... all led by two or three gentlemen with guns, soldiers and intimidators ...You had to hunt and kill until the last whistle.'
>
> (Hatzfeld, 2003, p. 11)

The first day was the worst.

> Fulgence: 'I saw a gush of blood begin before my eyes ... I sensed it came from my machete. I looked at the blade, and it was wet. I took fright and wormed my way along to get out ... anxious to go home – I had done enough. That person I had just struck – it was a Mama, and I felt too sick even in the poor light, to finish her off.'
>
> (Hatzfeld, 2003, p. 18)

Adalbert, used a gun, for the first time, to kill two children:

Adalbert: 'Now, too often, I am seized by the memory of those children, shot, straight out, like a joke.' (Hatzfeld, 2003, p. 22)
Ignace: 'At the beginning we were too fired up to think. Later on we got used to it … it meant nothing to us thinking that we were busy cutting our neighbours down to the last one … They had become people to throw away, so to speak.' (Hatzfeld, 2003, p. 42)

This revealing statement may give us a clue to the biological roots of the hunting. It seems that they discovered some deep-seated ability to kill or to survive that reflects the fact that, in the environment of evolution, man developed the situational skills of either predator or elusive prey. Although aggression and hunting are two entirely different constructs, aggression being normally directed against members of the same species while hunting is directed against other species who are perceived as prey; hunting members of ones own species can take place when the individuals to be hunted are no longer perceived as human (Lorenz 1966). By denigrating Tutsis to the status of cockroaches, they could be treated as prey. It is this that Alderdice describes as 'splitting' on pp. 48–50.

In addition, some of the killing was carried out in particularly cruel ways; sometimes the victims were tortured to reveal where they had hidden supposed wealth or possessions, sometimes they were raped, bodies were mutilated, and some torturers seemed to be playing a cruel game for their own amusement. It is as if the aggressors were not only seeing their prey as different but were seeing themselves as different from their normal selves.

> Pio: 'We no longer saw a human being when we turned up a Tutsi in the swamps … The hunt was savage, the hunters were savage, the prey was savage – savagery took over the mind … .'
>
> (Hatzfeld, 2003, p. 42)

Once perceived as prey, captives could be played with, much as a kitten or cat will play with a mouse. But the cat's cruel play can at least be seen as a means as honing its skills; here there was more to it than that. Having set aside one set of prohibitions, against killing, the captors found themselves abandoning all inhibitions, against greed for money, against sexual gratification, against punishing the innocent for the supposed sins of their race, against the obscene celebration of triumph. And all of this took place in public. Like unruly children who, deserted by their parents, were ready to wreck the place, the genocidaires seem to have felt relieved of moral constraints. Having abandoned learned 'good' behaviour, they seemed to revel in being 'bad'. When they looked back at their behaviour, they saw themselves as having become as degraded as their victims.

Pio: 'We had become a ferocious species in a barbarous world ... Our daily life was unnatural and bloody, *and that suited us*'. (Hatzfeld, 2003, p. 43)

Ignace: 'I did not hear many [Hutu] women protesting against Tutsis being raped. They knew this work of killing fiercely heated up the men in the marshes ... except, of course, if the men did their dirty work near the houses'. (Hatzfeld, 2003, p. 103)

It is almost as if dutiful, God-loving children had thrown off all hope of achieving their parent's approval and were being as bad as possible. This is what Alderdice means by 'dissolution and regression' (p. 48 et seq.).

The avenging army was approaching, their time was running out, so they might as well wreak havoc while they could, 'fuck' the enemy, celebrate their triumph while they still could, cock a snook at God and Man. As one survivor put it to CMP (Colin Murray Parkes): 'Those of us who survived are all murderers'. While this was not strictly true, it is how some felt.

Once Joiners had become Interahamwe, they tended to continue to be an Interahamwe despite apparently having nothing to gain from continuing. Fujii (2009, p. 179) suggests that outside the group, an individual was no longer an Interahamwe, because Interahamwe activities are only performed within the group. Through interacting and killing in groups, Joiners were able to create order out of disorder, certainty out of uncertainty and power out of powerlessness. Killing in groups created new identities and new forms of power. The constitutive power of killing in groups turned a loose collections of friends and neighbours into tightly bound social actors.

The Tutsi victims of the genocide

Although some Tutsis attempted to defend themselves, they had little success against the overwhelming forces pitted against them.

> Angelique: 'When the Interahamwe encircled the fencing [around the church in Ntarama], men began letting stones fly so as to slow down their advance. The women gathered the stones, because they did not want to die any old way. But our resistance did not have much vigour behind it'.
> (Kigali Memorial Archive)

Others attempted to escape to the surrounding countries, only to be slaughtered at the numerous road blocks. A few tried to pass themselves off as Hutu.

> Ngoga: 'We had recently moved into this area, and most did not know that we were Tutsis. ... my Mum didn't possess an ID card that identified her as a Tutsi. Sometimes when Interahamwe came at home she tried to persuade them that she was not a Tutsi. But others did know and gave

information. On 7 May they came and killed my Mum and they cut my sister's arms off and hit her head. I don't know why I survived'.

Others, mostly adolescents and young adults, survived by hiding in the forests or marshes, and dodging their captors.

> Angelique: 'I raced down the slope, I ran so fast I forgot about breathing for an hour, then dived into the marsh urunfunzo [papyrus bushes], which I knew by reputation. At this moment, I did not of course have any idea that for the next month I was going to spend my days in the mud, covered from head to toe, under the tyranny of the mosquitoes' (Kigali Memorial Archives).
>
> Eugenie (not Eugenie Mukanohele): 'You found yourself doing unbelievable things you couldn't explain to anyone. Not even to yourself ... like tripping over a stump, rolling through three somersaults, then blasting off in a zigzaggy sprint to escape for one last instant from the hiss of the machete swiping at your back ... and when the killers seemed to be upon us, we'd scatter in all directions to give everyone a chance: basically, we adopted the antelope's strategy'.
>
> (Hatzfeld, 2007, p. 38)

Javan was one of five children who hid together in the forest and, when they were discovered, ran as hard as they could to escape. CMP asked how many times that happened, and he replied: 'Many, many times'. CMP told him about Hatzfeld's comparing the youngsters to gazelles whose survival depends on their ability to run and zigzag to escape a lion. 'Yes, it was just like that'. Three of the five survived. It seems that these youngsters had discovered some deep-seated ability to escape that reflects the fact that, in the environment of evolution, man developed the skills to avoid becoming prey.

6. Retaliation

Given the numerical superiority of the Hutu army, it is reasonable to ask how the RPF succeeded so rapidly in conquering them. Five possibilities may have contributed: (1) The temporary loss of leadership that resulted from the assassination of the army chief of staff, and the destruction of the interim government and its supporters. In the first three months, the Rwandese army changed commanders three times. (2) The lack of the support from French and other troops on which the Hutu had relied in the past. (3) The low morale of poorly trained men when confronted with the tough, experienced and disciplined warriors of the RPF. (4) The able tactical leadership of General Kagame. (5) The failure of both army commanders and government troops to admit the urgency of the military situation (Anyidoho, 1997). Just as Hitler failed to admit the fact that the tide of the war was turning against him in 1942, and devoted his speeches to escalating his attacks on the Jewish 'enemy within', so large numbers of Hutu soldiers, including the better-trained and equipped Presidential Guard, opted to murder vulnerable civilians and steal their goods rather than face the real threat (Morris, 2012).

As the conquest advanced, the RPF were the only source of justice; yet they had arrived to find the evidence of genocide at every turn. It can be no surprise that there is clear evidence that the RPF itself committed massacres of Hutus in Rwanda when they took power. The number whom they killed will never be known. General Kagame confessed to Richard Grant that he was helpless: 'You can imagine trying to stand between people who are so seriously aggrieved, and having the desire to settle it because there was no justice infrastructure at that time' (Grant, 2010). He admits that the troops were difficult to restrain, especially the new recruits whose families had been raped and butchered. Even so, unlike the genocidal killings, these massacres were never authorised by the leadership who soon introduced strict punishments.

By mid-June, the RPF had captured Gitarama and were besieging Ruhengiri. Kigali held out until 4th July and, on the 18th, General Kagame had ordered a ceasefire. By this time, the Security Council had approved a sixty-day French mission to set up a conflict-free Turquoise Zone covering a fifth of Rwanda, on the border with Zaire and Burundi, provided that they kept to their promise to withdraw two months later. The French contingent were greeted with flags and jubilation by the beleaguered Hutus.

The ceasefire brought the war in Rwanda to a close but also enabled the defeated Hutu army to escape to the surrounding countries, notably Zaire (DRC), where the conflict was to continue with more massacres on both sides and occasional attacks across the border into Rwanda. It played a major part in what has been termed The Great War of Africa (Grant, 2010). But in Rwanda, a peace process was to ensue. This will be examined in chapter 15.

Conclusions

In an impoverished population, prejudiced by lifelong exposure to tribal myths, desensitised by decades of cruelty and reprisal massacres of Tutsis, and harassed by international demands to adopt a peace process that threatened familiar leaders, there existed a highly unstable political situation and general anxiety. These are the kinds of factors that, as shown in chapters 1 and 6, were likely to make the population of Rwanda particularly susceptible to extremism.

Although it is likely that the implementation of the Arusha Accords would have broken down without the terrorist attack on the president's plane, and that some massacres would have occurred, as they had in the past, it is improbable that the violence would have escalated and obtained the public support that turned massacres into genocide. As predicted by the terrorists, the assassination triggered alarm among Hutus and Tutsis, both resident and abroad. Overreaction was inevitable and was fuelled by the RPF invasion, the insurrectionist leadership, and the media. Led by soldiers and trained Interahamwe many of whom had been 'hardened' in previous massacres, a process of rapid escalation was spread by propaganda and ruthless leaders. Once massacres of Tutsis became socially expected, and often compulsory, deep-seated brutality was unleashed and Tutsi people were degraded to non-people, treated as enemies and prey, to be hunted and killed.

By the time the genocide was brought to an end by the ceasefire the majority of survivors were deeply traumatised, both armies were still large and mutual hatred was deep-seated. There seemed little hope that the long-standing cycle of violence could be broken.

Part III

BREAKING THE CYCLE

9

COUNTERING VIOLENCE

The role of the school

Jenny Parkes

Melissa: Chantal said that you mustn't listen to them [pointing to Feriel and Faiza].
Chantal: I said you mustn't listen to the Muslims.
Jenny: Feriel, what do you want to say to that?
Feriel: But me and Faiza is not killing people.

This extract is from a discussion that took place in a primary school in Cape Town, South Africa, a month after the bombing of the Twin Towers on 11 September, 2001. The school was located in a working-class district built during the apartheid era for the forcible resettlement of those people designated 'coloured' – both Christians and Muslims whose skin colour was deemed to fall outside the categories of 'white' or 'black'. By 2001, several years after the first democratic elections marked the end of apartheid, the neighbourhood was facing rising levels of unemployment, with disillusioned young men increasingly attracted to gang activity. While media attention across the globe was focused on the aftermath of 9/11, largely ignored by the international media was a series of bombings in Cape Town which were attributed to PAGAD (People Against Gangsterism and Drugs), a predominantly Muslim group formed in 1995, initially viewed as a popular anti-crime movement but by the time of this discussion, increasingly perceived by the state as an urban terror group (Dixon & Johns, 2001). The association of Islam and terrorism in the international media at that time, together with the alleged link between PAGAD and bombings in Cape Town, produced a toxic discourse associating Islam with extreme violence.

It is not surprising that these local and international events preoccupied the six 10-year-old girls who were participating in a research study on how young people understood and coped with violence in their community (Parkes, J, 2007). I had not been prepared, however, for the conflict that erupted in this group of friends, and in particular for Chantal's wounding words, as she first reported that her mother said all Muslims are PAGAD, and then whispered to Melissa that 'you mustn't listen to them'. For Feriel and Faiza, the two Muslim girls in the group, these words evoked a strong defence, and Feriel's response shows how she heard Chantal's words as an accusation that she too was a terrorist.

I open this chapter with this extract because it illustrates some of the educational challenges relating to violence and extremism. First, it shows some of the complexity of the ways young people learn about violence. We can see how their identities and relationships in school are complexly interwoven with events of the past and present, near and far – with images from the international media, local news stories and conversations overheard with their mothers. While schools are often perceived as safe havens in times of conflict, we see how in this case the discussion provided a forum for the expression of nationalistic and religious divides, alienating and causing distress, with the injury barely concealed behind the whisper. Many studies point to the ways in which, all too often, schools perpetuate and even exacerbate forms of violence and conflict (Harber, 2004). Others question whether it is ever possible for schools to promote peace in contexts of inequality, violence and conflict. Jason Hart, for example, questions the value of peace education for young Palestinians in the West Bank and East Jerusalem, faced with daily experiences of harassment and delays at police checkpoints on their journey to school (Hart, 2011, pp. 11–31). Peace education programmes, he argues, are frequently imposed from outside, paying little heed to the complexities of local contexts, and ignoring the perspectives of young people themselves. Often, they are based on understanding children as passive vessels to whom programmes can be 'delivered' rather than as active learners. Such approaches tend to ignore the social context and the complex and often unintended processes of learning that go on in and out of schools.

As the discussion between the girls in Cape Town illustrates, children's beliefs, practices and identities develop through a complex imbrication of relations in and out of school. Is it, therefore, too much to expect schools to make a difference, to influence the seepage of conflict and injustice across the sites of family, friends, neighbourhoods and nations? This chapter will address this question through considering first how young people learn about violence and extremism, and then through critically reflecting on the potential of schools to present alternatives. My analysis will draw on evidence from a range of studies, including my research with young people living with risk and violence in urban settings in South Africa and the United Kingdom, as well as other studies of youth, violence, extremism and conflict.

Learning violence and extremism

During a recent study of youth, risk and violence in London, young people participating in the research interviewed friends and family members on their views about youth and risk. Thirteen-year-old TJ, whose family had migrated from Colombia, decided to interview his brother's friend, who was a member of a local gang and deeply involved in violent crime (Parkes, J & Conolly, 2011; Parkes, J & Conolly, 2013). After the interview, he told the research group of the young man's response when he asked him why he had joined the gang:

TJ: 'Because he said that, he used to get bullied in primary, and he didn't like it, 'cause he didn't know how to speak English properly, because he's Colombian, as well. And then – and then, in secondary, he started beating up all the bullies that beat him up in primary, and then some boy told him that he was a member of the gang. And then – and then, he – he's got some little like scar here, because they, like, ripped his eye here, just to be able to join the gang.'

In TJ's view, he and his friends had joined the gang because they '*wanted respect and to be known*'.

This account illuminates some of the triggers echoed in the research literature on why young people, and particularly young men, join gangs and extremist groups. First, there is experience of alienation and trauma. For this young man, moving to the United Kingdom from Colombia when he was eight years old left him feeling isolated and lonely in an unfamiliar and unwelcoming school context. Second, unfamiliar with the English language, he found it difficult to access the school curriculum. Low levels of academic achievement and exclusion from school have frequently been associated with engagement in violent crime (Budd, Sharp & Mayhew, 2005). Third, he was excluded by his peers at primary school, and subjected to bullying. Fear, humiliation and frustration may have contributed to his own violent acts of retaliation when he reached secondary school. Fourth, his capacity to use force awarded him status within the peer group, in which tough masculinity demonstrated control.

The relationship between masculinity and violence is complex, and it is surprising how often it is ignored in analyses of youth violence, despite the fact that most violent crime is committed by young men. While most men and boys do not engage in violence, in contexts where there are high levels of socioeconomic inequality and community violence, acts of violence may be functional, providing material resources and social status. Researchers have explored how manliness comes to be associated with success, control and physicality (Connell, 1995). When men are denied access to socioeconomic success, violence may offer a way to exert control or it may arise from feelings of shame and humiliation about 'thwarted' masculinities (Moore, 1994). For the young man TJ interviewed, joining a gang awarded protection, gave him a sense of belonging, enabled him to demonstrate tough masculinity, as well possibly as channelling feelings of anger and shame into violent acts.

Despite their exposure to violent aggression, TJ and the other young men who participated in the London study rarely admitted to feeling fearful, perhaps because such emotions are associated with loss of control. Macho talk as well as aggression towards each other seemed at times to be a way of displacing emotions of fear and humiliation (Parkes & Conolly, 2013).

In a rare study of young women's involvement in violence and extremism, Atreyee Sen interviewed women who had participated in the aggressive rightwing Shiv Sena movement in India. For these women, harsh socioeconomic conditions combined with displacement and alienation, as they migrated to Bombay slums. Compelled to seek work, they were vulnerable to economic and sexual exploitation. For these women, in a context where girls and women were expected to be gentle and compliant, violence transgressed gender boundaries, but membership of the extremist movement provided collective solidarity, and violence was viewed as functional, and allowed women to gain a sense of control of their lives – as women, as workers and as violent 'warriors' (Sen, 2006, p. 8).

While it is important to avoid over-generalisation, there are some interesting parallels between my research on young men and gangs, and research on young men who join extremist groups. In her analysis of triggers to extremism, Lynn Davies also writes of experiences of trauma, alienation and isolation; emotions of humiliation, fear and frustration; and expectations about masculinity (Davies, 2008). In addition, she discusses the appeal of absolutism, of black-and-white truths, and of respect for authority among young men who join extremist groups.

This tendency towards binary thinking (e.g., Christianity as good versus Islam as evil) was also evident in the discussion between the girls in Cape Town, but it shifted in interesting directions in the course of the discussion. Soon after the extract discussed earlier in which Chantal constructed a Muslim–Christian binary, the girls began to speak critically about the retaliatory actions of the United States in Afghanistan and of what they saw as US global domination and aggression:

Shanelle: 'The whole America's country is a gangster.'
Simone: 'America's country is against us.'
Faiza: 'Some people only have stones to throw and the Americans have the big cannons and guns ...'

The United States is constructed as a powerful bully, wielding its might over the weak, including South Africans and Muslims. The binary shifts from religion to nation. But whereas Davies' analysis stresses the ways in which binary thinking closes off alternative vantage points, leading towards authoritarianism, in this discussion the shift towards a different form of binary opposition served to deflect the conflict within the group, by constructing a powerful enemy outside they could all agree on. Cockburn (2007) observed that racist attitudes of young men in extreme right groups in the United Kingdom seemed to become more acute when they felt ostracised from the political system. For the girls in Cape Town, identifying collectively as South Africans overcomes the Muslim–Christian binary and seems to signal fluidity rather than absolutism in their perspectives.

Davies also emphasises how young men who join extremist groups are not always from poorer backgrounds, but may be middle-class, educated students, coming from 'unremarkable' backgrounds, with ordinary jobs and ordinary lives. Feelings of alienation, discrimination and disadvantage generate self-identification with radical groups, with young men drawn to visions of honour, bravery and sacrifice in a noble cause, often conveyed via the Internet. In her analysis, the process of radicalisation entails both self-identification and indoctrination by dedicated, committed leaders, in which isolation, brainwashing and cognitive restructuring concerning the moral value of killing are used to radicalise young men.

The role for schools

Since schools are key sites for learning, there is a strong case for examining how schools can help young people learn to counter violence and extremism. A challenge in discussing the role of the school, however, is the risk of proposing a 'one-size-fits-all' solution that ignores the specificity of local contexts and the meaning systems of young people within these contexts. In trying to establish some ways forward for schools, I will focus first on the importance of schools as safe spaces for learning; second on the establishment of a school ethos that emphasises rights, responsibility and respect; and finally on the possibilities for creating dialogues and spaces for challenge.

A safe space

For children to begin to think and learn about alternatives to violence, they need to feel safe. This means considering safety in the school itself, and in the relationships between school and community. Education has often been neglected in peace-building initiatives, which tend to focus on stabilising societies in the immediate aftermath of conflict (United Nations Educational, Social and Cultural Organisation, UNESCO, 2011). Where attention is focused on education, it is often concerned with increasing children's access to schools, keeping schools open, and providing children with routines in times of crisis. Many children are denied access to school, particularly in times of war and conflict. Yet schools are not always safe spaces for children to learn. In Nepal and Sri Lanka, during times of conflict, for example, they have been recruiting grounds for child soldiers, or the school buildings themselves may become military targets (Bush, 2000). Classrooms themselves have become ideological battlegrounds, reinforcing prejudice and intolerance (UNESCO, 2011). Children at the primary school in Cape Town were anxious about going to secondary school because they knew it to be a recruiting ground for gangs. Safe school initiatives around the world have laid emphasis on trying to create safe learning environments for children both in school and on the journey home (Management Systems International, MSI, 2008).

A recent review carried out by the United Nations Childrens Fund, UNICEF in Lebanon, Sierra Leone and Nepal concluded that education has a key role to play, both in providing protection, psychosocial support and helping to restore normality during and immediately after a conflict, and in the medium term to contribute to structural changes that address the social injustices that may cause violence (Novelli and Smith, 2011). Within education systems, for example, policies may redress inequalities (geographic, ethnic, political, and gender) in access to school, or language of instruction. Education initiatives can impact a range of areas, including providing skills to support economic regeneration, changing behaviours and attitudes to violence, social relations between groups and understandings of and engagement with political systems. Weak, inequitable and segregated school systems can be drivers of conflict. In Lebanon, for example, the highly segregated education system reinforces socioeconomic inequality and may contribute to ongoing tensions (Novelli and Smith, 2011).

Schools segregated by religion or ethnicity have been viewed on the one hand as providing choice and diversity in a pluralist society, and on the other as perpetuating division and sectarianism through hindering the increased contact or integration that will promote peace and social cohesion. In Northern Ireland, still only 6% of schools are integrated, with the vast majority of children attending either Catholic or Protestant schools. In one study, ethnic isolation of young people in a Protestant school was associated with a strong 'own' group bias and negative stereotyping and prejudice towards Catholics (Hughes, 2011). While some have criticised the government for the slow pace of change, others have argued that imposition of change from above may be counterproductive and that integration depends on community commitment (Smith, 2008). At the same time, just having mixed schools does not solve binary divisions, stereotyping and exclusion, as we have seen from the young people's talk in Cape Town and London. A study of integrated schooling in Bosnia-Herzegovina explored student protests following the policy of ethno-national integration, and found that students talked of feeling unsafe when they had to travel through neighbourhoods and to share classrooms with pupils from the opposing group (Jones, 2011, pp. 81–102). Integration attempts need to be carefully planned, taking into account the specific local contexts, in order to reduce inter-group anxiety and promote trust, leading eventually to greater mutual understanding. Possible initiatives for cross-community contact could include co-teaching between teachers of different faiths, or opportunities for children in different schools to learn side by side in curricular or extracurricular activities, working towards common goals (Hughes, 2011). But it may be naïve to assume that merely providing contact is sufficient to disrupt racist attitudes or long-held conflicts, without addressing underlying inequalities, ostracism and alienation (Cockburn, 2007).

Reviewing the evidence on education in conflict and post-conflict settings, the 2011 Education For All Global Monitoring Report identifies key areas for education policy makers to consider, including the language of instruction, curriculum and education governance (UNESCO, 2011). A single language of instruction can foster a sense of national identity, as in the case of Tanzania, but it can also fuel violence, leading to a need for bilingual and intercultural education, as in Guatemala. Rethinking the teaching of history and religion can foster critical thinking and respect for other faiths and beliefs, while the curriculum can also promote peace and citizenship. Devolution of education governance can increase accountability, but it can also hamper national peace-building initiatives.

Rights, responsibilities and respect

While lessons in citizenship education, life skills or peace building may be valuable, on their own they can do little to address the triggers discussed earlier, such as alienation, difficulties with learning, bullying and exclusion and the dominance of tough masculinities. Disciplinary systems in school frequently employ physical punishment, and even where laws prohibit corporal punishment, in many contexts around the globe, practices persist, sending a clear message about the acceptability of imposing power through force, or might is right (Parkes, J and Heslop, 2011; Rojas, 2011). Tackling these issues requires a whole school approach, in which relationships across school – between children, and between teachers and children, as well as parents – are considered.

Based on the UN Convention on the Rights of the Child, UNICEF's Rights Respecting Schools ensure that teachers, children, parents and ancillary staff learn about the convention, employ commensurate teaching styles and engage children in decision making throughout the school, in, for example, school councils. The emphasis is not just on teaching about children's rights, but on modelling rights and respect in all its relationships. Research on these schools signals positive effects on self-esteem, positive attitudes to diversity and less adversarial approaches to conflict resolution, with rights-based explanations leading to children taking more responsibility for their behaviour (Davies, 2008; Sebba and Robinson, 2010). Through the curriculum and teaching approaches, there needs to be an emphasis on tolerance of difference, as well as highlighting commonalities, which can create a sense of belonging for all. Disciplinary systems which emphasise restorative justice rather than punishment may look at the underlying reasons for violent acts, encouraging protagonists to take responsibility and make reparations. Peer mediation gives students responsibility for conflict resolution between students, and between teachers and students.

Creating dialogue: Challenging inequality and injustice

One reason for the success of UNICEF's approach may be the emphasis on young people's perspectives, and it is important to ensure that such rights-based approaches engage with girls' and boys' meaning systems in specific local contexts. Hart questions the 'lack of fit' between education initiatives and lived experience and conditions of children's lives, and concludes:

> The most important quality of teachers may be the humility to listen without passing judgement and the patience to work at a pace that suits each group rather than dictated by a handbook.
>
> (Hart, 2011, p. 26)

These are wise words, but as well as listening, teachers have a role in presenting alternatives, so that young people learn to question and critique. In considering the role of schools in challenging extremism, Davies (2008) argues that schools should foster critical thinking, with three main aims, to which I have added a fourth:

1. How to prevent intolerance.
2. How to prevent people joining extremist/violent movements.
3. How to enable people to challenge extremist/violent movements.
4. How to prevent people using violence to communicate.

It is easy to propose approaches such as dialogue as a pedagogy, but much more difficult to put them into practice in a classroom. Democratic principles, such as encouraging children to freely express their views and to participate in decisions which affect them, do not automatically solve conflict. Many teachers will understandably prefer to deflect conflict, avoiding sensitive, controversial and politically contentious areas. Training and support for teachers is crucial. They may need support themselves to cope with their own painful memories, or their own prejudicial attitudes and to gain skills in facilitating critical reflection with pupils. The extract at the start of this chapter from the girls in South Africa illustrates the emotional harm that may be incurred by such discussions. How then should a teacher deal with such moments?

Davies proposes *interruptive democracy*, in which injustice is actively challenged. While extremism seeks absolutes and simple dualisms (good and evil), the role of education is to question and critique, and to be comfortable with doubts and ambiguity. In the group discussion with the girls in South Africa, my approach was to encourage free speech, and when that entailed an offensive remark, I tried to ensure that the girls who had been offended were able to respond. As a researcher, I had planned to listen, not to judge or confront, and their articulate riposte made my work easier. But since then, mindful of the potential for harm to arise in group discussions, I have reconsidered my role as a researcher, and intentionally taken a position that includes occasionally actively challenging perspectives. In our discussions on gangs, for example, I have disagreed when TJ and his friends have advocated revenge or denigrated others, though I'm not convinced that this has had any impact. Perhaps more effective has been the creation of discussions which have stimulated debate and critical reflection between young people. For example, when I shared extracts of children talking about risk from earlier interviews and invited the group to analyse them, this generated lively discussions about fear, bravado and tough talk. For young men in particular, the strategy of talking about perspectives through the eyes of another enabled them to express emotions without exposing their vulnerabilities or risking losing face among the peer group. Using humour, role play, art and photography have also stimulated discussions on sensitive themes.

As well as teachers, mentors could be well placed to encourage such discussions. Their task is challenging. They need to be active listeners, gradually over time building trust, warmth and empathy. They need to be sensitive to the adult–child power dynamics, and to the power dynamics within groups, as they articulate tentativeness, doubts and sometimes disagree. And they need to be creative in planning and managing activities that spark interest, debate and critical reflection.

Conclusion

For the young gang member TJ interviewed, it is difficult to be optimistic about his prospects for the future. He has dropped out of school, been kicked out of home by his parents because of his drug habit, and has already committed acts of extreme violence himself. For TJ and his friends, and for Chantal, Faiza and their friends, however, the prospects seem much better. For them, many factors that may make a difference lie outside school – employment opportunities, parental support and safe neighbourhoods. But education also has a part to play, not just in increasing their academic prospects, but also in helping them to learn about and build relationships characterised by rights, respect and responsibility. School can provide a space for young people to question and critique in a context where they feel safe to take the risks to learn. The discussion with the South African girls, which had begun with the wounding association of Islam and terrorism, and then shifted to a critique of US foreign policy, ended with their proposals for what should be done in the aftermath of the bombing of the Twin Towers:

Shanelle:	'They must build the building'.
Jenny:	'What do you think?'
Melissa:	'They must stop the war ...'
Jenny:	'Stop the war.'
Faiza:	'... and make friends.'
Jenny:	'And what do you think, Chantal'?
Chantal:	'I say they must make it exactly the same like it were ...'
Jenny:	'Build it up again?'
Chantal:	'Yes. And then it mustn't be and they must stop the war also fighting and they must sort things out and ...'
Shanelle:	'They must build it again, because that's the only world we live in.'

In contrast to their earlier dispute, their words metaphorically signify the rebuilding of relationships built on tolerance and justice, and it seems to me that we have much to learn from them.

10

ISLAMIST TERRORISM AND BRITISH UNIVERSITIES

Anthony Glees

> More than 30% of people convicted for al-Qaeda-associated terror-
> ist offences in the UK between 1999 and 2009 are known to have
> attended university or a higher education institution. Another 15%
> studied or achieved a vocational or further education qualification.
> About 10% of the sample were students at the time when they were
> charged or convicted ...
>
> We believe there is unambiguous evidence to indicate that some
> extremist organisations, notably Hizb-ut-Tahrir, target specific uni-
> versities and colleges (notably those with a large number of Muslim
> students) with the objective of radicalising and recruiting students
>
> (Home Affairs Committee, 2012)

In this chapter, the term *Islamism* is defined as the use, for political purposes, of a
perverted interpretation of Islam to justify the use of violence against its supposed
political enemies. I realise, of course, that for many Muslims, the use of the term
can be offensive (as is sometimes the linking of 'extremism' with 'violence') on
the grounds that Islam has political and legal applications and that an 'extreme'
desire to promote Islam in the modern world should not be equated either with
'terrorism,' which the vast majority of the world's 1.5 billion Muslims self-evidently reject in its totality. However, this term has entered the realm of public
understanding, and its use is today justified.

The higher education stream of Islamism in the United Kingdom is by no means
the only source of Islamist terrorist plots. However, it is an important one for
academics in particular to reflect upon. This is not because universities and colleges in any way teach or encourage extremism, let alone violence. Rather, it is
because our campuses may be visited by extremist radicalisers able to recruit
students in this way. It is also because every graduate who turns towards violence
(and away from civilised values) represents a signal failure of British higher education. Extremists are not born, they are made. If they are made, they can, in
theory at any rate, also be unmade. But this can only happen if their teachers
recognise the danger signs and engage fully with those of their students who are

at risk and are able to convince them that in a democracy violence is not just wrong but also counterproductive.

What we are dealing with here are 'sins of omission' on the part of our universities and colleges, not 'sins of commission'. Those responsible for training terrorists from whatever stream they emanate are al-Qaeda-inspired Islamist radicalisers and not academics (although it needs to be added that increasingly we believe we are witnessing 'self-radicalisation' of terrorists via the Internet). That these 'sins' continue to be a focus of government attention can be seen in the decision, announced in April 2013, to establish ten regional counter-extremism experts to advise the higher education institutions in each of these regions how to spot extremist activity and act against it. Aspects of recent terrorist activity both in Boston and the United Kingdom demonstrate that campuses are still sites connected with violent extremism. Although it can be argued that since some 40% of an age cohort are participants in higher or further education, that 45% (or even 55%, depending on the meaning of the word 'sample' in the Parliamentary report cited at the start of this chapter) of convicted terrorists should be students or graduates is regrettable but not remarkable. However, to make this point is to ignore that students are, by their nature, in a different position from others in society. They are learners and recipients of teaching. If higher and further education were effective, it ought to mean that students and graduates would be strongly *under- represented* in terrorist streams, not the reverse.

It is indeed a bitter truth that since 2005 many major British terror attacks have involved students or recent graduates, often in leading roles (Simcox et al., 2010). The well-known list of universities they came from makes sombre reading. That this was so was realised only slowly by universities, and some remain passive about it even today. Yet British universities, like other universities throughout the Western world, have for more than one hundred years frequently been sites of extreme (if non-violent) political activity. Why would militant Islam be an exception? What is more, there was evidence to support the argument. In 2004, when I first took a serious interest in Islamism, it was already clear that a significant number of those convicted of Islamist terrorist activity, or those killed in the execution of such activity, had been university or college students. Indeed, many of the universities of Europe have had a long history of generating political extremism. In the 1930s, they were places where both fascism and communism flourished and where groups of young students were radicalised and then turned into active fighters for their particular causes. In a book published in 2003, I had noted how the East German intelligence service ('the Stasi') had worked on some British campuses to recruit agents in order to work for what was undoubtedly an odious Communist police state (Glees, 2003).

Why, then, do such quintessentially liberal and open institutions harbour people who can, with apparent ease, be transformed into those who wish to destroy them? Why has contemporary higher education proved unable to combat illiberal and anti-democratic thinking?

It is worth recalling that what we might term the contract between the taxpayer, the state and the higher education institution (HEI) was set out in the Dearing Report (Dearing, 1997):

- 'to inspire and enable individuals to develop their capabilities to the highest potential levels throughout life, so that they grow intellectually, are well equipped for work, can contribute effectively to society and achieve personal fulfilment;
- to increase knowledge and understanding for their own sake and to foster their application to the benefit of the economy and society;
- to serve the needs of an adaptable, sustainable, knowledge-based economy at local, regional and national levels;
- to play a major role in shaping a democratic, civilised, inclusive society.'

Dearing's final aim is especially trenchant because Islamist terrorism plainly seeks to destroy the very idea and practice of Western democracy. It was not 'civilised' nor is it 'inclusive' because the very concept of a worldwide caliphate to replace democracy would set the ideas and rights of Muslims much higher than those of non-Muslims. Rather than being tolerated or allowed, it ought to have been obvious to our universities that Islamism was a serious threat to our society and incompatible with the basic contract between state and university. Instead, universities, which on the whole were (and are) unpoliced, were being used by Islamist people to conceal from public gaze activities which could undermine democratic practice. This needed (and in April 2013 continued to need) investigation which might lead to remedies.

Serious thinking on this subject required not just a description of significant sites of extremist activity (in this case, on our campuses) as I had argued in 2005 but also, today, an answer to the question why sites of higher education in particular had become places of interest to Islamist recruiters and what, if anything, might be done to prevent what might have been perfectly decent, gifted and clever young Muslim men and women from turning to terror as the answer to their political aims. As Lord Carlile, Queen's Council, observes, radicalisation is not an 'event' but a 'process'. He adds that the government is right to argue that the line between extremism and terrorism is often blurred and that what appear at first to be non-violent extremist ideologies are drawn up by terrorists to justify violence'. It is precisely at this critical interface that thoughtful pedagogy could produce real results by preventing with intellectual ground rules and moral support the slide into terrorism, whether through their student Islamic Societies, or as guest preachers at Friday prayers, or through visits to certain mosques. Such rules should apply not just to the time spent on campus but as a guiding principle for later life. After all, higher education is intended to be a lifetime asset.

Some might think the existence of a higher education stream of Islamism is a matter for the Security Service, MI5, not academics. But it is my view that MI5 regards its duties as 'fire fighting' rather than 'fire prevention'; that is to say, it will intervene with every weapon in its lawful armoury once it discovers that a terror-ist act is under way but it will not do anything to stop potential terrorists from becoming violent at some later date.

One can legitimately criticize this view historically (on the grounds that it meant MI5 missed the Islamist radicalisation of the late 1990s which fed directly into a culture that spawned the 2005 and subsequent student-led terrorist plots detailed later). However, it is plain that, even before 2005, the *police* were begin-ning to take on the 'fire prevention' role, thinking about radicalisation and how it could be legitimately prevented from turning young people into violent terrorists and seeking to gain intelligence of their own about when, where and how this might be happening. The concerns of the police, in turn, fed into the work of higher education. This raised the question, hotly debated since 2005, of what, if anything, universities could do to work with the grain of the counter-radicalisa-tion policy being executed primarily if not exclusively by the police, including community police officers, and, indeed, whether ethically it would even be right for dons to do so. The problem was that academics preferred to let others deal with the problem, and some of them resisted the notion that tackling it was their respon-sibility, regarding it as a police matter, not a pedagogical one.

By 2007, however, government, at any rate, accepted that there was a higher education strand of Islamist terrorism and a policy, particularly a counter-radicali-sation policy, was developed to address it. In January 2008, for example, all UK universities received guidance on extremism and terrorism from the government's Office for Security and Counter-Terrorism (OSCT) and then, in February 2010, a letter from Lord Mandelson in which he looked at 39 institutions which OSCT had identified, on the basis of intelligence received from the Joint Terrorism Analysis Centre (JTAC), as being 'more vulnerable to violent extremism' than others. The 39 were then given a restricted JTAC briefing, and each university received £10,000 to 'improve capacity and capability' to combat violent extremism.

Whereas in 2005 there was little data on the actual extent of radical and extreme Islamist views in British higher education, the publication in 2008 of *Islam on Campus* provided the most comprehensive survey ever undertaken of Muslim student opinion in the United Kingdom (Thorne & Stuart, 2008). It was based on a specially commissioned YouGov sample of 1,400 students. It should go without saying that 'Muslim' is not the same as 'terrorist' (indeed worldwide, Muslims are the chief victims of Islamist terrorism). However, inasmuch as Islamist terrorists recruit from Muslim communities, it is not reassuring that the 2008 survey showed that of the 90,000 or so Muslim students in the United Kingdom, 40% supported the introduction of Sharia law in the United Kingdom, 33% wished to see a global caliphate established, 32% were prepared to see Muslims kill non-Muslims if they felt their religion was under attack, 25% expressed violent feelings towards gays, 46% wanted a separate Muslim political party in parliament, and 3% said they believed it was right to kill people to promote Islam. The publication of these find-ings gave rise to the development of policies to address the higher education stream of Islamism, yet the problem clearly persisted after 2008.

Ten of twelve Pakistanis arrested early in 2009 (but not charged with terrorism) were students. One of these (Abid Naseer) was extradited to the United States in January 2013. The other (Ahmed Faraz Khan) returned to Pakistan, although he was initially allowed to stay in the United Kingdom despite the judge in their case being satisfied that both were al-Qaeda (AQ) operatives, and that Naseer, who had been given and accepted a place at John Moore's University in Liverpool, 'was an AQ operative who posed and still poses a serious threat to the national security of the UK'. Roshonora Choudhry, 21, was a student of English at Kings College London (KCL) (Dodd, 2010). Given a life sentence for the attempted assassination of Stephen Timms MP, in May 2010, she said, significantly, that she did not recognise the jurisdiction of English courts. The Security Service, MI5, commented on 19 May, 2010, in respect of the 2009 Pakistani students' conspiracy, that their arrest had disrupted 'an AQ-directed plot aimed at carrying out a mass casualty attack in Britain. That terror threat is serious and ongoing'.

Before al-Qaeda can recruit them, potential terrorists must first be radicalised, and during that process they are not actual suicide bombers; the process is completed only after radicalisation and explosives training, which for the main part seems always to take place far beyond the shores of the United Kingdom. Yet MI5's dogged insistence that using intelligence to counter radicalisation ('fire prevention') was not its job (despite its not being anyone else's either) came within a hair's breadth of costing the lives of almost 300 people in the skies above Detroit in 2009 (and probably a similar number on the ground below) thanks to Umar Farouk Abdulmutallab. He had been a student at University College London from 2005 to 2008, and became president of the university's Islamic society. His case is of particular interest here because neither his university nor MI5 correctly identified him as a potential suicide bomber despite his known association with al-Qaeda's senior recruiter and motivator, Anwar al-Awlaki. If reaching out to al-Awlaki was not evidence of 'radicalisation', it is hard to know what is. After travelling to the Yemen for training, Abdulmutallab applied for a student visa to return to the United Kingdom, but was denied one because he had applied to a bogus college. It seems unlikely that he would have been permitted onto the plane to Detroit if his name had been on an international list of suspects, and he deserved to be because in London he was being transformed into a militant Islamist. Perfectly ordinary Muslim students do not become suicide bombers in an instant, yet the process by which this happened in Abdulmutallab's case was missed not only by the security service but also, of course, inadvertently, by his tutors and academic mentors.

This is not to say that MI5 and Britain's intelligence-led counter-terrorist police have not scored many notable successes in its fight against Islamist extremism after 2005. But everyone involved, from academics to the counter-terrorist police and the security service, must think constructively about how they can work together to mitigate the risk and if possible prevent young minds from turning to violent extremism.

In the past, some universities may have thought that the concept of free speech required them to let extremists speak on campus. But free speech is actually 'free speech within the law', and there are laws against incitement, conspiracy and discrimination whose writs run inside and well as outside universities and colleges. This was plainly not understood. Campuses deliberately allowed themselves to become 'safe spaces' for extremist radical thinking. This, unintentionally of course, gave violent extremists the space to recruit terrorists, whether on-site or off-site, hiding their tracks with spurious if vehement free-speech arguments.

It appears that universities and colleges still refuse to take even the most basic steps to protect their charges (at any rate, in the eyes of the government, for otherwise they would not have appointed new counter-radicalisation advisors to campuses in April 2013, as mentioned earlier). 'Clamping down on speakers', Nicola Dandridge of *Universities UK* insists, 'is just not the way forward' (*Daily Telegraph,* 27.05.11). The 'whole point of university', she added, is to 'listen to these things'. I myself would argue that a policy of 'clamping down' would certainly help some young people resist Islamism. But it ought also to be possible to debate and discuss difficult and complex issues in an objective and balanced manner. Academics should have the professional skills to teach students about violence and man's inhumanity to man in a dispassionate way. If they cannot do so, they are almost certainly doing the wrong job.

It is also conceivable that the search for external funding now required of universities may have made some of them reluctant to act against Islamist radicalisers and extremists on campus on the grounds that some funders might feel the important distinction between Islam and Islamism was being ignored and become reluctant to consider becoming donors (Glees, 2009). Equally, universities must be careful not to let funding from donors who might have a particularly radical view of the nature and purpose of Islam from impacting teaching and research or on the need to guard against extremist radicals visiting their campuses.

We know that the LSE had accepted £1.5 from Colonel Gaddafi (and awarded his son, Saif al Islam, a doctorate under circumstances recently investigated by Lord Woolf, 2011). Is it likely that a research project into human rights abuses by the Gaddafi regime would have received a grant from this Libyan fund? But even when funding does not dictate either the research questions academic ask or their conclusions, donors with specific political goals will always find academics who, deeply and genuinely, believe in viewpoints which may favour a particular regime.

In short, there is no shortage of evidence to support the idea that there exists a higher education strand of Islamist terrorism and that our higher education system would prefer not to confront this reality as fully as it might, or think carefully about the immediate and long-term benefits of doing all it can to prevent any extreme and violent thinking to spread among our students, whether Muslim or not. The case presented to the All Party Homeland Security Committee indicates the continuing necessity of monitoring what happens on our campuses (Lewin, 2011).

What should universities be doing? The answer is really simple: they should be doing what they are meant to do in honouring their contract with the state as set out by Lord Dearing. Their core duty is to teach their students in ways appropriate to civilised higher education by working with them, knowing them, guiding them and ensuring they keep to the basic values which have made this country a decent, mature democracy. Straightforward tutorial teaching and mentoring will do much to help students reject the call of Islamism. In addition, universities must exclude extremists and welcome with open arms the skills and experience of the counter-terrorist police and (if only it would agree) of the security service as well. Finally, instead of running universities as businesses, selling services and raising funds, they should meet the teaching and pastoral needs of the 21st century more thoughtfully. In working with young impressionable people (by definition 'impressionable', because that is why they are students), vice-chancellors need to remember they and their colleagues are not chief executive officers and business persons but teachers and ethical mentors.

The best means of ensuring the continuation of open Western democracy and all that is contained within it (a belief in secular society, in scientific rationalism, in lawfulness, and in gender and sex equality, etc.) in opposition to the sometimes violent wishes of its enemies is good intelligence-led security. This extends into the realm of higher education. We may recall what the Prime Minister, David Cameron, said in Munich on 5 February, 2011, (the italics are mine):

'The biggest threat to our security comes from terrorist attacks – some of which are sadly carried out by our own citizens ... *Many of those found guilty of terrorist offences in the UK and elsewhere have been graduates* This threat comes overwhelmingly from young men who follow a completely perverse and warped interpretation of Islam and who are prepared to blow themselves up and kill their fellow citizens ... Islam is a religion, observed peacefully and devoutly by over a billion people. Islamist extremism is a political ideology, supported by a minority ... *We must stop these groups from reaching people in universities. Some say this is not compatible with free speech and intellectual inquiry. I say: Would you take the same view if there were right-wing extremists on our campuses?* At the furthest end are those who back terrorism to promote their ultimate goal: an entire Islamist realm, governed by an interpretation of sharia ... We need to be clear: Islamist extremism and Islam are not the same thing.'

11

RESPONSES TO TERRORISM

The role of the media

Brian Rowan

> WB Yeats wrote that too long a sacrifice can make a stone of the heart. Republicans have endured many sacrifices indeed, but our hearts have never turned to stone. The war changed our lives, but not our humanity.

The foregoing words were spoken by Declan Kearney, the national chairman of Sinn Fein, at a republican commemoration in Belfast at Easter 2012. During the conflict in Northern Ireland or the north of Ireland, his party was often described as the political wing of the IRA, the Irish Republican Army, whose fight was against British occupation. It was a bloody and decades-long war, in which there were many killings and, as we shall see, many sides.

As the story has been told, the word *terrorist* is the one most often used to describe the IRA and its armed campaign or struggle, but in the quotation above, Kearney speaks of 'humanity'. He was talking to a community of which the IRA is a part, but also speaking out to a wider audience on the next issues for this peace process, the issues of reconciliation and trying to heal hurts. For many, it will be too great a mental challenge to think and believe that humanity can be found among the debris of bombs and bullets and death, but his words were and are important. They are a reminder to us all, and to journalists reporting conflict, that when the shooting stops, peace building enters a long process, in which for some the memories and scars of war will remain forever. John, Lord Alderdice described it when he said:

> Part of the wish to deal with the legacy of the Troubles is not simply a perfectly understandable and appropriate wish to move on and make a better future . . . but part of it is a wish to be able to resolve and heal and take away the horribleness of what happened on all sides and it isn't possible. It is not able to be done.

There is no magic wand to make things better, no magic potion to make people better, and reporting conflict, wherever it happens, must include this reality; that after the gunfire and the explosions there are broken people who cannot be fixed.

A war of words

Elsewhere in this book (pp. 85–86, Colin Parkes writes that in most instances terrorism will be witnessed and perceived through the eyes and ears of the media of communication. That one thought and sentence is a reminder of our responsibility, of how our words can influence responses and thinking, and trigger reactions; break or perpetuate a cycle of violence. So, it is a reminder also of the need to consider and measure every word, while at the same time not putting ourselves inside a kind of reporting straitjacket, being too frightened to explain what we see and express what we think.

I live and report in a divided society, in a place of many different sides and opinions. So, there is no one description of events, no one set of words, no one journalistic way of doing or not doing things. It is a working environment in which we correspondents can also be labelled because of what we say and how we say it; for example, the North rather than Northern Ireland or Derry instead of Londonderry, and the descriptive terms we apply to what we are witnessing and reporting on. I now call the conflict 'war' – a description that some will view as controversial because it steps outside the established reporting norms. Others are more comfortable setting or placing this conflict within the frame of a 'terrorist campaign', a breakdown in law and order with the British government, its security service MI5, the police and the army involved in a struggle against evil and to restore normality. This reporting narrative establishes good and bad; right and wrong. The sides are clear, and it puts the journalist on a side. It is much more difficult to think and report outside that box; to have and to use your own words and language; to look for deeper reasons, meaning and explanations; and to examine all sides. Conflict/war dehumanises all participants, and yet the 'terrorists' are meant to be the 'monsters' and 'psychopaths' on the battlefield, with their involvement in killing often presented as some kind of unthinking and uncaring blood lust. This is what those deemed 'terrorist' describe as 'demonisation'. It strips away any notion of cause or legitimate motivation for armed actions. Yet when we dig deep, when we explore, when we know and speak to some of those directly involved in the actions, we find people just like ourselves, but who made different life choices. This takes us beyond the normal and the safe media responses to terrorism; it takes us beyond the killing act to think about the person and people we call/label terrorist. It is not an easy journey to make, and much easier to do afterwards than in real time. In the actual moments of war/conflict, when the killing is happening, there is the danger of being misunderstood, to be accused of being some type of cheerleader or apologist for violence, a mouthpiece for the terrorists. Yet to try to understand is not to condone, but rather to know the person and the people who are labelled the 'enemy'. From that better-informed position, it is possible to report in a more analytical and in-depth way; exploring not just what happened, but, more importantly, why. This is a thinking challenge that goes beyond the responsibility of the journalist. It is a responsibility for all of us, and if it were to happen in real time rather than afterwards, then there could be speedier resolutions to violent conflict or what others call 'terrorist campaigns'. Lives could be saved.

Knowing the 'terrorist'

In any conflict and in every conflict, there are headline events; those moments that are remembered above others because of the numbers killed, or, to express it in colder terms, the body count. Our situation is no different. We have the Enniskillen, Shankill and Omagh bombs; the different shootings in Loughgall, Loughinisland and Kingsmill; Bloody Sunday; and Bloody Friday. It is a remembering process in which much is forgotten, those many other Bloody Days on which just one person was killed or someone was hurt. Parkes is right when he explains in this book that 'the intensity of the response is greatly influenced by both the number of the dead and the strength of our attachment to them' (p. 84).

Outside of those closest to them, few remember the 'terrorists', the people behind the label, and as part of the journey I described above of going beyond the act to find the person, I want to tell the story of Rosemary. In the mid-1970s, several years before I began my journalistic career, we worked in the same central Belfast office. She was eighteen and a few months older than me when she was killed, on one of those days I probably think more about now than I did then. At the time, the details relating to her death emerged in a scattered jigsaw of information pieces. She was a member of the IRA. A device had detonated prematurely while it was being assembled, and another IRA member was killed along with two civilians. The incident takes us back into the darkest decade of our wars, and into a city that was nothing like it is now.

If I remember correctly, it was the evening before the explosion that I stood chatting with Rosemary outside our workplace. I had no idea she was in the IRA, no inkling of anything that would suggest what was about to unfold. The 'terrorist' had not stood out as being different from the rest of us; as someone or something easily recognisable. As the news reached us of the bomb and Rosemary's death, I remember one of her friends in the office crying uncontrollably. I also remember a reserve member of the police – the then Royal Ulster Constabulary (RUC) – who also worked with us, sealing or taping her desk. They were two very different responses to the death of a colleague: tears remembering a friend, and the tape a routine police/security reaction to the 'terrorist'.

In the news of those events back in January 1976, what happened was described, but not why it happened; why this young woman had chosen this path, and how she died on the morning she received confirmation of being accepted to begin her teacher training. It is just one of our many unexplained and unexplored stories. In all the shock and disbelief of that moment, I am sure my own thoughts were very confused. Back then, I would not have been thinking about political and social contexts, about the complexity of conflict or about how someone's 'right' is another person's 'wrong'. Four people were dead, one of them a work friend, but why?

Correcting and disturbing the narrative

These many years later, after war, when the killing has stopped, and in the developing peace process, there is more time now to think, to properly analyse and to try to better understand. In real time, as we move from one violent incident to another, events and people are too easily and too quickly forgotten, except by their families and friends and local communities. A reminder of what they cannot and do not forget is found in a comment from a father whose son was killed in a gun attack in Belfast in 1992. 'Bullets', he said, 'do not only travel distance, but also through time'. In our reporting of the conflict, people were dead for several hours or days, before another bomb or bullet took our attention and the news elsewhere. There was not the time then to do the necessary thinking and analysis, the type of deep research excavation that has now become possible after war and in explorations of what we call 'the past'. It means the best we as journalists can do in the Northern Ireland or north of Ireland context is to correct the narrative; write in the missing context and admit/accept that a proper and detailed explanation/examination has had to wait until after the war.

It is possible to think differently and more clearly as peace develops, and in our search for more information and for explanation, we are challenged to stand in the shoes of others, to look through different eyes, and to try to think beyond our own narrow opinions and perspectives. As it develops, this exercise will deliver ugly truths, and news and reporting that in some quarters will be unwelcome and unwanted because it disturbs the narrative and thinks and writes outside the established template. The peace and political developments in Ireland have made it a visiting post for many people from other conflict zones. In conversations with our visitors, from the Basque region, from the Middle East, and elsewhere, I have argued that you cannot report a conflict by talking to one side or by taking sides. Yet the reporting words that journalists use, and I have used, will have conveyed/suggested the opposite, and the taking of sides. All of this is a learning process. It takes time, and I have now arrived at a point, through experience, of being confident enough to think and speak for myself, with words and language I am comfortable with, and that are not dictated to me or decided for me.

The politics of conflict

Calling the Northern Ireland conflict a war does not make everything right or better, does not put everything beyond question, scrutiny, criticism or condemnation. It is not meant to legitimise every action. What it does is ask for a more detailed examination of cause, motivation and actions by all sides; not just by those designated 'terrorist'. As our political and peace processes developed, prisoners were freed early from jail. It marked them out as different. When 'terrorist' weapons were decommissioned or 'put beyond use' by republican and loyalist organisations, there was no forensic testing; no attempt to gather evidence for prosecutions. When information was given to help recover bodies that had been 'disappeared', there was no pursuit of those who cooperated in that process and who provided the information.

Unionists entered government with Martin McGuinness of Sinn Fein, who for decades in another part of the republican movement, directed the IRA war. Deliberately or otherwise, consciously or subconsciously, these policies and decisions have confirmed the political nature of the conflict and it could be argued 'decriminalised' its 'terrorist' participants. This is not to say that the psychological journey has been made or completed by everyone. For many the 'terrorists' will always be 'terrorists'. This is a process of change. People are changing, closed minds are opening, and past enemies are talking to and working with each other.

These are significant and important developments that deserve and demand as much news attention as the events of war. The dead of the conflict may make better and bigger, dare I say it, more exciting or startling headlines, but, in our responses to a changing and different situation, there is a responsibility to report the peace with as much energy and interest.

In an international context, the great danger is that many now take war and its violent deaths for granted. Who really hears the news or the names of soldiers being killed in Iraq or Afghanistan, or of the death toll in the latest bombs in Baghdad? Was it not the same as the conflict in Northern Ireland developed, when the deaths of soldiers, police, republicans, loyalists and civilians were reported but not really heard? The abnormal becomes and became the normal, the way of life and death, and in our not listening, not caring and not paying enough attention, we all became part of the non-thinking and non-doing that meant the killing continued – that the cycle of violence was perpetuated. It is why real-time responses, real-time thinking and attention are so important, and this is one of the pieces of learning we should be exporting from post-conflict Northern Ireland.

Knowing the victim

Reporting on that conflict in such a confined geographical area meant there was always the possibility of being at the scene of a killing and knowing the victim. It happened to me in May 1991, and it is in those circumstances that you have to think and act outside the 'pre-programmed responses' that Colin Parkes described earlier (pp. 83 et seq). A police officer was killed in an IRA rocket attack in west Belfast on one of those streets that had become part of the battlefield, but it was not until after I left and had returned to the office that I was given the name of one of those inside the vehicle that had been targeted. Stephen Gillespie died within hours of that attack. Both of us had been runners, had competed for Willowfield Harriers in east Belfast, where in the 1970s some police cadets had come to train. His name and knowing him meant a reporting response that was different, more personal, that thought beyond the coldness of the latest death statistic. We had trained together, raced together, chatted on many occasions, had had a drink together. So, on this occasion, there was more than a police uniform and a killing to consider. There was a person, a name, a husband, a father. Over the telephone,

I interviewed Stephen's widow Norma for BBC radio output. She spoke to me about the weekend they had just spent with their children. I also remember Stephen's young son at cross-country races after his father's death. He was there with one of Stephen's police colleagues, brought along I suppose, to identify with and remember part of what his father did, part of his life outside his uniform. This, I imagine, was only part of the reason. It was also a demonstration of solidarity with the bereaved family, about remembering and caring, and about providing company and friendship to a young boy whose father had been killed in an action and a war that youngster will not have understood.

I was watching and seeing these very human responses, but when you report conflict, day after day, year after year, you have to try to lock yourself outside what is happening, try not to think too much or too deeply. It may sound selfish or uncaring, but it is necessary to try to protect your own mental well-being, and yet there are those moments, such as the one described, when knowing the person makes you think and remember in a very human way. These are moments when there is no hiding place, when the killing, the brutality of the violent act, reaches someone you know, and the reporting response goes beyond the usual of who, what, when and where.

The fog of war

Of course, it is not just about who, what, when and where. 'Why' is hugely important, but in the moment, when the killing is happening, there is not the necessary time for proper exploration, and yet there should be. I knew Stephen Gillespie, but those who killed him did not. They knew his uniform and identified it with the enemy, in the same way, and out of other eyes, the 'terrorists' – people with labels but no names – were the other enemy. Our responses as journalists should be to think beyond these labels.

In Northern Ireland, over a period of many years, pre-ceasefires and then into the peace process, I talked to the 'terrorists'; to those many organisations labelled such to put them on the wrong side, and bad side, of the moral line. Yet another part of my learning is that conflict is not that simple or straightforward. It is why we talk about the fog of war, about how truth is lost and about lines and trenches not always being what they seem. The usual telling of the Northern Ireland story suggests two warring tribes, republican (pro United Ireland) and loyalist (pro United Kingdom). The British government, the army, the police and MI5 are presented as a kind of referee in the middle. It feeds that notion or idea of goodies and baddies, of right and wrong, evil and good. It wraps everything up in a neat package. It is a one-version spin or description of events; the way the 'goodies' would have it told. Yet the story is very different, and the narrative is being disturbed and reworked as more information pieces emerge to make another more complicated picture, one that takes us inside the so-called 'dirty war'. This is the place of ugly truths and practices; intelligence places where operatives and agents have played God with lives, a protected dark side that hides behind the curtain of national security. As journalists, we are not meant to intrude here, not meant to delve into this world to ask how it works, and when we do, the barriers go up to shield its secrets and its ways.

When journalists trespass

At times I have trespassed in all sorts of sensitive areas of security and politics; inside the intelligence world and that so-called dirty war, inside the IRA, and inside the loyalist organisations. Source relationships carefully constructed over years have at times collapsed. Some can be repaired and rebuilt. Others cannot. There are examples of this on all sides of this conflict, and I will touch on these as this chapter evolves.

Trust is a huge part of the reporting process, but these source relationships should never become cosy. As journalists, we are not there to parrot, but rather to gather and analyse and test information. There are issues about who we speak to in reporting processes and the language and words we use to describe events and the participants or actors in our wars. I now believe that the use of the word *terrorism* as a description just to identify sides and to separate the good from the bad is much too simplistic. This also has been part of my learning. The conflict in Northern Ireland or the north is much more complex. Responsibility for some of the ugliest moments in this war takes us outside the republican and loyalist organisations; outside the groups that are labelled terrorist. The more we learn, the more information that emerges, the more we see how the puppets and strings become – and became – a tangled mess. It is the responsibility of the journalist to tell these stories, not to erase them from the record, no matter how unpalatable and uncomfortable the stories may be for those in government, politics, security and intelligence. To raise these issues is not to distort history, but to ask all the questions in an attempt to produce a more complete and accurate description and record of events.

In my writing, I have made clear that there is no point or purpose in a half-truth process. There is no point in a blame process that does not think outside the established telling and reporting of the Northern Ireland story. There was a political dominance and social context within which conflict occurred. The 'terrorists' were responsible for horrific actions; for the slaughter of civilians, for violent acts that should be dammed whether we call it war or something else, but the scrutiny and the questions should not, and cannot, stop there. We need an x-ray-type examination that looks not just on the surface for the usual and for the obvious, but that goes deeper in a search for the hidden.

As one example, take the case of an agent codenamed Stakeknife. He was part of the IRA internal security department tasked with the culling of informers. His job was interrogation/torture often leading to execution, and his story is one that criss-crosses those blurred lines of war. It is a journey from one side to the other. Republicans would call it betrayal, collaboration with the enemy, and it is an example of how the picture is disturbed as more and new information emerges.

We never have all the jigsaw pieces, and the bits we do have, often have to be adjusted or moved, creating a completely different scene on the stage which shows those plays and practices of war. This IRA disciplinarian was also in the pay of a covert Army unit, an agent operating inside a 'terrorist' organisation, someone who, to use the jargon of these battles, was either turned or turned himself. So, what is his label, how should he be described and how do we describe those who brought him across those war lines and handled him? These are matters that are often described as not being in the public interest. It is when arguments of national security are produced as reasons not to answer, and it is in that silence and evasion that the ugly truths of war are buried. One agent, in the pay of the state, presided over the deaths of other agents. What is the right and wrong in those actions; the good and the bad? Where should the terrorist label be applied? When we ask these questions, this is when we as journalists trespass in places we are not welcome, but the Stakeknife example is one illustration of the complexity of reporting conflict. Terrorism stretches from the 'bad' to the 'good' and the 'good' to the 'bad'. It is not the sole practice of one side, and in the Stakeknife case, the argument can be presented that the state, through one of its agents, presided over acts of unlawful violence. Others may describe them as acts of terrorism.

Living and reporting war

In this chapter, I also want to focus on the challenge of reporting to a divided society when you are part of that place and its people; part of its torn and deeply traumatised communities. I was not a war correspondent sent to some international conflict zone, to a place of no emotional attachment. Over several decades, I have reported on the war and peace of Northern Ireland, on events not many miles from my doorstep and my home. I tell people that I am stitched into the fabric of this place and its past and present. As a journalist, you can become a kind of thread able to weave through the different sides to present the many different opinions and disputed assessments. This is what I mean by trying to talk to all sides and not taking sides.

You do not come through this experience untouched or unscarred. Your memory becomes a swamp pulling you back into past events; killings you remember above others, interviews that rewind and replay inside your head, and the recall of moments when you got things wrong. There is no such thing as a perfect reporting record of conflict. Whether dealing with those deemed terrorist or governments, the police, the army or intelligence services, you are left to read between and behind the lines. In the decoding of spoken words, statements and silences, there is room for error, no matter how good your sources. Those involved in war/conflict also believe in what is termed 'permissible lies'. Add to this the tactic and practice of disinformation by all sides, and you get some appreciation of the complex maze and muddle of fact and fiction that the journalist has to find a way through. In all of this, there are false trails and blind alleys, and places where you get lost.

When you are part of a divided society and you are reporting in and to it, there is also a constant pressure, an invisible tug of war, not seen by others, but that is always pulling between your citizenship and your work. This has been my experience where I live and as the different ceasefires have bedded in and the peace and politics have developed. Governments, politicians and the so-called 'combatant groups' expect a propping up of the new dispensation, what could be described as 'good news' reporting. So, they view as unhelpful journalistic inspections of the blemishes; the dents and imperfections visible on what for a long time was described as an 'armed peace'. Political spin, exaggeration, becomes a feature in the telling of the progress within negotiations.

We hear of 'seismic shifts', when, in fact, movement has been much more limited and modest, and these big sells do long-term damage. They trip the process up when the overselling and spin are exposed. An example of this is found in 1999 in a negotiation designed to achieve the implementation of the new political institutions that were part of the 1998 Good Friday or Belfast Agreement, an agreement that was meant to confirm the peace. The stand-off in between was summarised in the phrase 'no guns, no government'. In other words, unionists would not enter government with republicans unless the IRA began to decommission or destroy its weapons, many of them Libyan supplied. I knew this was not the IRA's short-term intention, and my news commentary across BBC output fitted into those previously described categories of unhelpful and unwelcome. At a crucial time in the negotiations, the Northern Ireland Office was contacting me after each of my broadcasts. Peter Mandelson was secretary of state, and his spokesman was telling me that I had 'got it wrong', that I was being told 'downright lies', that I was 'overstating knowledge' and that I should 'suspend judgement'. The unionists entered a power-sharing government with republicans, but the IRA did not begin the decommissioning process and within weeks the political institutions were suspended. The importance of having a range of sources, speaking and operating outside the spin, was crucial to the accuracy of my reporting in this period. I was speaking to the IRA, to the 'terrorists', on a regular basis, but also to security, intelligence and political sources outside of government, and this information proved much more credible.

The government and unionists did not understand the 'terrorists'. How could they? For decades, their responses were 'pre-programmed'; routine political reactions, what some journalists came to describe as 'the usual' and fixed within the narrow boundaries of condemnation and criminalisation. There was no attempt to try to understand or to explore possible motivation. So, in this period of 1999, they applied too simple a political logic; that if the IRA wanted to sustain the political institutions, then it would meet the demand to decommission. It was thinking and a response that showed how little they understood the 'terrorist' or 'enemy' mindset.

What they failed to realise was that the politics of demand was the completely wrong approach. The advantage I had in this situation was being able to speak directly to the IRA, not just in this period, but over many years. Listening to and hearing that organisation, knowing the symbolic importance of weapons, knowing in their minds and in their thinking they were an 'undefeated army', knowing that they considered their armed campaign to be 'entirely legitimate', and knowing how they would translate the government/unionist demand into surrender brought me to introduce different thinking and a different predicted outcome.

I knew that in this relatively early phase of the peace process, there were issues/ matters to be considered that went beyond simple political logic. There were reasons why the 'undefeated army' would not engage in actual decommissioning at this time, one such reason being to protect the cohesion of its organisation. This is why I presented a different opinion/analysis. I knew it would have a damaging/ negative impact within the fledgling political institutions, because it was not the required 'good news' message. That invisible tug of war I described earlier had pulled me on this occasion, and I hope on all occasions, to say what was correct in terms of information that would stand up to scrutiny. The message here, the important learning, is that reporting conflict, then ceasefires, then developments in politics and peace is not about saying what some would describe as the 'right thing', but rather the 'correct thing'. In this example just outlined, the 'terrorist' information and guidance proved much more reliable than government and unionist political assessments.

Building relationships – breaking relationships

Earlier, I described the use of 'permissible lies' and how source relationships patiently built over years can crumble. This happened with the IRA in 2002, primarily as a result of my reporting of three developments: the theft of sensitive information from a Special Branch office in Belfast, revelations of alleged IRA weapons development/training in Colombia, and political intelligence gathering, including what was described as the 'penetration' of the Northern Ireland Office. The culmination of these and other events was instrumental in the collapse of Northern Ireland's power-sharing government, which then took almost five years to restore. In the developing events, the IRA, including in briefings with me, denied involvement in these intelligence-gathering operations and dismissed suggestions of weapons development, and while I could understand the reasons for their denials, I did not believe them. On this occasion, I trusted other information, and my reporting brought me into conflict with the IRA organisation and my sources within it, but the fallout went much wider.

Of interest and concern to others was how I got the detailed security and intelligence information which I relied on to make my assessments of IRA involvement in the foregoing activities. The British Security Service MI5 believed that in some of my reporting there was 'prima facie evidence that a breach of the Official Secrets Act may have taken place'. A senior Police Service of Northern Ireland (PSNI) Special Branch officer retired early from his position, and later claimed he had been 'forced out'. There was a Police Ombudsman investigation, and a leaks inquiry, and, several years later, as I further researched these events and that period of 2002 for publication in a book, I received letters from the Treasury Solicitors acting, I was told, on behalf of Her Majesty's Government. I was informed that there was concern 'that the book might contain information that could put lives in danger and be damaging to national security'. The correspondence continued: 'In these circumstances, I am writing to request pre-publication access to the manuscript to enable my client to make an assessment of its contents.' This was one of several letters, several attempts, I believe, to censor my book and my reporting of this period, and to curtail or shut down publication of information that would reveal the methodology used in counterterrorist intelligence operations. I refused to give pre-publication access to MI5.

Back in 2002, the IRA had closed down one information route – albeit a source which at that time I could not trust – and the security service was trying to shut down another. These are pressure moments in which just trying to think clearly is a challenge. In this period, I had been warned from inside the police of an application to eavesdrop on my telephone calls and to monitor e-mails. I was also later told that the application was refused. I have no way of knowing with any certainty the absolute accuracy of these events, but I was trying to protect my sources, defend journalistic ethics, report the developing story, and think even more than usual about every word I spoke. At the time I was the BBC's security editor in Belfast, a government was collapsing because of a lack of trust, and news reports were being listened to for every word. So, the onus on being right was even greater than usual, and trying to find a way through that maze of fact and fiction was particularly hazardous.

I mentioned earlier that there is no such thing as a perfect reporting record of conflict, especially when your journalism strays into these intelligence areas. You rely on trusted colleagues for guidance in trying to make the best and correct judgements, and you have to think about why certain pieces of information are being shared and others withheld. As I also mentioned earlier, you never have all the jigsaw pieces, and there are always gaps in the picture. In all the pressure of that period, there was a big piece of journalistic learning; that even as politics and peace are developing, the wars are not quite over.

This takes me back to the important examination of why; why the IRA after the declaration of two ceasefires and after republicans had helped negotiate the political agreement of 1998, why then would that organisation still be developing weaponry and gathering intelligence? The answer is found in what its 'enemy' was still doing, found in the activities of the Special Branch and MI5; found in the discovery of listening and tracking devices in cars, offices and homes. The 'war-war' was over in terms of violent actions and killing, but the intelligence war continued in both directions. Of course, the IRA was always going to deny this activity. It had to for the sake of the peace and political processes. This is my thinking that attempts to make sense of that chaotic period in 2002. My source/working relationship with the IRA was later restored without either of us changing our positions.

Asking all the questions

Journalists, including myself, had a front seat in the theatre of this war, a close-up view of the plays and practices, and yet there was much we did not see, on occasions because we failed to look and, at other times, because it was hidden, and remains so. Some of that fog is clearing, and as it does, it presents different scenes so, different words and thinking are needed to describe that changing landscape.

This is our task now; to colour in as much of the missing detail as possible. Along the way on my reporting journey, there have been comments, images and moments that have shaped my thinking, changed my thinking and made me think. I remember an interview with a loyalist, Billy Giles, jailed for life for killing a Catholic man, and who later told me he 'sleeps with the victims'. He meant he could not sleep with his conscience, and, later, he took his own life. Another loyalist, William Smith, was jailed in 1972 when he was a teenager. Twenty-two years later, in 1994, he chaired the Combined Loyalist Military Command (CLMC) news conference announcing details of their ceasefire, and more recently, said something to me that again made me think: 'When people say to me, how did you get involved in the Troubles [the conflict], I say I was born into them.' In the simplistic, unthinking, telling of our war story and conflicted society, Giles and Smith are labelled 'terrorists', and yet behind those labels I found people, as I have in many conversations with many republicans.

This is more of my learning; that it would be far too easy, too convenient, to blame only those who went to jail for our war and its many deaths. This ignores a political context, dismisses the causes of conflict, ignores the rousing speeches that cheered young people onto and into war, ignores the orders given and the hidden hands that pulled many strings. It allows those who created and acquiesced in all of this, who ignored and looked the other way, to escape the stage or leave the theatre without any blame or responsibility or guilt. This is, and these are, the missing pieces of the narrative, and what needs to be corrected. It is not about distorting history, not about condoning violence, not about supporting the 'terrorists', but about filling in the gaps; making all sides and the many sides accountable; asking all the questions, and not just some of them.

End thoughts

Covering this conflict was at times a deeply disturbing and frightening experience. On occasions, I felt I was walking the thinnest of lines. I struggled with the morality of my work, of talking to and reporting on the people behind the killing; struggling because of that narrow, restrictive and judgemental frame in which the conflict was set and reported on, 'good' and 'bad', 'right' and 'wrong'.

I want to give one last example of what that work entailed; one more example of talking to the 'terrorists'. In the summer of 1992, the IRA killed three of its own men; interrogated and executed them before their bodies were dumped on roads as a final humiliation for those deemed 'collaborators'.

With a small group of journalists, photographers and cameramen, I found two of those bodies, came across them in the dark of south Armagh. The next day, along with a journalist colleague, Eamonn Mallie, we were in a car with two other men we had never met. Our eyes were taped, and we were wearing thick black glasses. We were taken to a house, and searched before the tape was removed from our eyes; before us were two men in balaclavas, there to deliver the IRA statement on the executions. It was on toilet paper so that it could be disposed of easily if the security forces raided the house. Many years later, I transcribed the full note of that meeting, and within it there are many questions, not just for the IRA, but for the police Special Branch and army. It is one example of what was not reported in real time. I had become lost in my own experience of finding the bodies and then that journey to meet the IRA.

At the time, the BBC offered me some counselling, and I can remember feeling insulted, thinking that this offer in some way suggested weakness on my part. Many years later, I realise that the penny was beginning to drop in terms of what was being asked of those involved in the reporting of our conflict/war. I use that disputed term *war* because that is how it appeared to me. We had a battlefield on which there were thousands of soldiers and special forces, on which bombs and bullets were part of the daily routine and in which almost 4,000 people were killed and many thousands injured.

As I wrote earlier, the political nature of the conflict was also recognised in the Good Friday or Belfast Agreement of 1998, and in subsequent developments. We do not yet have a perfect peace, and we still have divided communities, with sectarianism a scratch beneath the surface. There is continuing violence by what are termed 'dissident' republicans, but on nothing like the scale that went before. An important part of our reporting response is to ensure that context is explained and that this residual threat is not exaggerated. There is also the unfinished business of answering the questions that linger after decades of war.

This is the hardest part of the journey out of conflict, the part that challenges us to double-back and to excavate and explore the past before declaring the new beginning. There are those who do not want to go there because of the ugly truths that could be shovelled onto the surface; truths that will take the blame beyond the prisoners, and beyond the 'terrorists'. Thirty years into my journalist career, with that accumulated experience, my mind is now more open, more willing to think outside the box, and I know, from that experience, that the most accurate or more accurate reporting of conflict comes not in real time but afterwards, whether in Northern Ireland, the north of Ireland or anywhere else.

As journalists, how we report and speak can influence how people think and react. Our words can conduct the orchestra; can create and contribute to a mood; can be blunt instruments that confirm worst fears, and, yet at other times, such as reporting a transition from war to peace, can be a kind of uplifting music to the many listening ears. How we report, the words we use and choose can change moods and minds – can both break and perpetuate cycles of violence.

12

LEADERSHIP

John, Lord Alderdice

In his classic text, *Leadership*, the great American historian, political scientist and biographer, James MacGregor Burns (1978), pointed out that the direction in which a community moved depended as much on followership as on what is usually called leadership. In this way, he helped to move the focus of leadership studies away from an almost total concentration on the personalities and behaviour of great men to the interaction and relationships between leaders and the communities on and through which they try to exercise influence.

In chapter 3, we looked at how understanding the causes and modalities for the appearance of terrorism is more informed by group psychology than that of the individual; however, we noted that individual psychology is still important in understanding the personality of those whom we would regard as leaders. There is much to be said about the psychology of political leaders in general (Paxman, 2002), and in politics the personality of the leader is a representation of some key elements of the psychology of the group he or she leads, as well as mirroring particular qualities and providing an inspiring role model (Benson, 2009). When the group and its requirements change, it will find another more representative leader. Some leaders in places of conflict stay in place for a very long time, because the conflict freezes development of the group and so the same leader is still an 'appropriate' person to lead decade after decade, at least in so far as representing the 'personality' of the group is concerned. Studies of the psychology of particular leaders can shed an interesting light on their cause and their followers (Falk, 2004; Robinson, 2001; Volkan & Itzkowitz, 1984) because in their very personality they tell us something about the group.

This is not only the case in the formal established leaders that would be widely recognised as such, but also in those who are chosen by young people as models to admire and emulate. Some of those with whom they identify are mates in their football teams and urban gangs. Some leaders are recognised local citizens in their community, and in many places religious figures play an important role. Sadly, known criminals who exude celebrity or power can become models for young people too. Other models are more recognisable national communal and political leaders; however, for most young people, celebrity leaders including footballers, pop stars and fashion icons exert a considerable influence, for good or bad. The person who most deserves the appellation 'leader' is the one who cannot only represent his community but also find a way of taking that community beyond their current position, improve their context and hand leadership over to the next generation with the community in better order.

One such transformational leader was Martin McGuiness, a leading figure in the Provisional Irish Republican Army (PIRA)[1] as well as in Sinn Fein, and at the time of writing he has been for some years the Deputy First Minister of the Northern Ireland Executive (government). Some time ago, I was working with him and a few other Northern Ireland and South African colleagues, trying to persuade political leaders in Iraq to grasp the opportunities for talks and a political negotiating process as an alternative to continued violence in their country. In the course of a passionate and very persuasive speech, Martin insisted that one of the key requirements for bringing violence to an end in a community is leadership. It was not, he said, something that just happened. Peace, progress and an end to violence only came through strong, persistent, persuasive and courageous leadership. He spoke with particular authority since he, Gerry Adams, and a small team of colleagues in the republican movement had done exactly that.

He spelt out to our Iraqi hosts how he and his friends in PIRA had come to the decision. After years of 'the 'Long War', they had concluded that while the British army, the British security services, and the Royal Ulster Constabulary[2] could not defeat them, neither could the PIRA defeat the British. Once they had come to the conclusion that they were at a stalemate, he said, they no longer felt that it was right to send young colleagues out to be injured, imprisoned and even killed, to no real purpose. It was a waste of their lives and therefore not something that he could morally sustain. The conclusion they drew was that they had to find another way to carry forward their vision of an independent, united Ireland, and so they sought out a political process that had the same vision but a different, non-violent political way of achieving it.

Of course, it was not quite so simple. There were other pressures. Loyalist paramilitaries[3] had been killing members of the republican and nationalist community – and there is now incontrovertible evidence that this happened with the collusion of some elements in the British security forces. It also subsequently became clear that there was a huge network of informers in the pay of the British security services; not only loyalists but some very senior republicans. In addition, the same leadership that had been in command of the republican movement for decades was getting older and may well have felt that a government car coming to their door to take them to work in a ministerial office might be preferable to a police Land Rover arriving to arrest them. There is still dispute about many elements of the decision and the process, including, for example, whether or not a message was sent by the republican leadership through a secret channel to the British government indicating that they wanted to cooperate to bring the violence to an end. But whatever the elements that contributed to their considerations and however they set out on the process, it is widely accepted that once the decision was made to move in the direction of a negotiated settlement, active leadership was of critical importance along the necessarily long, complex, circuitous and often dangerous road. I know from my own conversations that they had not thought that it would take so long – none of us did – and all of us made mistakes along the way, but the role of determined and sustained leadership was crucial.

We will return later to some of the key considerations for the republican leadership, but at this point I should make a declaration of interests or potential sources of bias in my own views. I was from October 1989 until June 1998 the leader of the Alliance Party of Northern Ireland.[4] On the completion of the 1998 Good Friday Agreement and its ratification in referendums in Ireland, North and South, elections were held to the new Northern Ireland Assembly, which was the centre-piece power-sharing institution in the new arrangements. After the election, I stood down as Alliance Leader and was appointed Speaker of the Assembly, a post I held until retiring in 2004. This was followed by a period of seven years as one of the four commissioners of the Independent Monitoring Commission (IMC) appointed by the British and Irish governments to oversee the running down of the terrorist organisations and the normalisation of security in Northern Ireland. I have served in various positions of leadership in a number of other national and inter-national political groups and organisations and as a negotiator, mediator or advisor in conflict situations around the world, and I have engaged with some leading figures who have been or are involved in 'terrorist' campaigns (Atran, 2010; Perry, 2010). My professional background was that of a consultant psychiatrist and uni-versity teacher in psychotherapy with a classical psychoanalytic perspective, and these experiences and theoretical ideas also inform my views of leadership. Psychological insight requires not only an intellectual model of human nature but also an acceptance that one may be mistaken and an appreciation of the perspec-tive of 'the Other'. Practical political leadership, on the other hand, often requires an undue confidence in one's own abilities, perspectives and principles and the singular importance of representing one's own people. If I am not unduly confi-dent, why should anyone else have sufficient confidence in me to suspend their own judgements in favour of mine? Yet this is a key component of leadership and its corollary, followership. Leaders often feel that a preparedness to question one-self in a crisis, and in particular to ask whether or not 'my people' are in the right, may be the beginning of the end of one's leadership. One may wish that people gave more thoughtful space to leaders to be human and have doubts and failings, but most leaders will feel that this is the kind of wishful thinking in which liberally minded intellectuals often engage, and is not something in which practical politi-cians can indulge. This may indeed be one of a number of reasons why genuinely liberal political parties rarely achieve an overall majority and are generally in gov-ernment as part of a coalition. There are additional complexities for leaders because the content of political belief and the process of politics may be conducted in parallel rather than in unison. A political leader may hold to the traditional political beliefs of his community but explore alternative ways of delivering them – a commitment to working-class interests may be interpreted as best served by being in the EU at one point, or being out of the EU at another. It may also be possible to maintain a commitment to a process, but change the fundamental narrative – while maintaining a commitment to the EU, the argument that its purpose is to prevent another war in Europe may be replaced with the argument that the purpose of membership of the EU is to maintain a position of power for Europeans at a global level. We will see later how changing the narrative is one of the ways that transformational leaders can help their community to move forward. However, at this point we should note that any consideration of the role of leadership in bringing terrorist campaigns to an end must appreciate these challenges and dilemmas, and leaders will often slip back and forth from one way of thinking to another – it will hardly be surprising that I would sometimes find my thinking more influenced by my psychotherapeutic 'self' and at other times by my political one.

It must also be appreciated that the process of transformation of a group's way of thinking is one of the most difficult challenges for the leader of a terrorist or insurgent organisation who believes that it is time to bring the politically motivated violence to an end. This brings us back to the question of what Martin McGuiness was referring to when he talked about leadership. What are the key elements?

In earlier chapters, we have explored how far the historical, political, social and economic background of a community can contribute to the creation of a context in which terrorism can break out. Indeed, without such a context, even the most determined terrorist will find it impossible to create a viable long-term campaign of violence, much less achieve any success. However, when a campaign of politically motivated violence is firmly entrenched and significant numbers of people are directly involved or implicitly supportive, even the removal of the primary 'causes' does not necessarily bring a terrorist campaign rapidly to a close. Using a medical analogy, one might observe that removing a patient from the toxic environment which has led to them falling ill does not necessarily cure them of the disorder that has taken hold. More importantly, when a group is formed, powerful attachments are created whose maintenance becomes an imperative for members beyond the achievement of any original purpose. Any threat to the survival of the group will meet with resistance for this reason alone. Martin McGuinness's message to the Iraqis was not just that leadership was a central and crucial requirement for getting to the table and negotiating a settlement, but the requirement for leadership continues right on through the implementation phase. Closing down a substantial community-based terrorist operation is not easy, if one is going to avoid damaging splits between those who want to change and those who want to continue, and splits in a terrorist organisation almost inevitably involve internecine violence and murder. Most notable in recent Irish history was the assassination in 1922 of Michael Collins, Chairman of the Provisional Irish Government and Commander-in-Chief of the National Army by some of his own erstwhile IRA colleagues when he returned to Ireland after negotiating the Anglo-Irish Treaty, which opened the door to independence, but accepted partition of the island. That murder of a key Irish leader who negotiated peace hangs heavy over all subsequent leaders. Some of Martin McGuinness's actions and statements have been essential to political progress, but profoundly unacceptable to some former friends and colleagues and potentially dangerous for him. In other words, the first criterion for leadership in such circumstances is courage; the physical courage to place one's life at risk, the intellectual courage to think the unthinkable, and the emotional courage to hold conflicting ideas in one's mind at the same time.

However, for leadership to be successful, the context must be conducive. I have referred to how leaders come to prominence because in themselves – in their very personality – they demonstrate something of the 'personality' of the community or group that they represent. An individual does not become the leader of a community just because he or she is the most intelligent, ambitious or talented candidate for the position of leadership, though these attributes are advantageous. More importantly, the angry community will chose a truculent leader; the smaller community which has an ambivalent attachment to the metropolis may elect a dependent personality; and the passive-aggressive individual may be identified by a group as their leader because his personality represents the resentful unhappy way that community feels. This tells us about the importance of the psychology of particular leaders because that can shed a very interesting light on their cause and their followers, as Volkan and Itzkowitz (1984), Falk (2004) and Robinson (2001) have shown in their studies.

I have also noticed that a key requirement of all successful leaders is an element of good fortune. Academics are hesitant to acknowledge such a thing, but some leaders do seem to be blessed with more regular breaks than others. However shrewd, strategic and tactically adept a leader may be, unless, as I have described above, he or she is working in a context that provides some opportunity for movement, it may be impossible to bring about a result. Most intractable conflicts have external stakeholders whose chronically damaged relationships play a key role. It is doubtful that the extraordinarily charismatic leadership of Nelson Mandela would have led to the end of apartheid in South Africa had not the end of the Cold War changed external attitudes. On the other hand, without an improvement in relations between Greece and Turkey, the Cyprus problem remains intractable, and Kashmir will hardly see a permanent peace until India and Pakistan find a way of addressing their historic disagreement. This is not to say that leaders must just wait for things to resolve. They can take active steps, but they do need the good fortune to be living and leading at a time when the key stakeholders within and without are prepared to build a new context. In the early 1970s there were some very able leaders in Northern Ireland – the unionist leader and prime minister, Brian Faulkner; nationalist leaders, Gerry Fitt and John Hume; and Oliver Napier of the cross-community Alliance Party were all politicians of considerable ability. However, at that time, key groups within Northern Ireland still harboured the view that they could have things their own way through the exercise of sufficient force. The British and Irish governments had also not yet fully appreciated that their interests were best served by a grand compromise and that the achievement of this outcome required them – the two governments – to be the joint drivers of the process that would achieve it. Tragically, in the early 1970s, good leaders came and went, and a very creative political initiative rose and fell, without any resolution because the key internal and external forces were not in positive alignment. It would take a quarter of a century before another real opportunity arose. So the second set of requirements for leadership is context and timing. A shrewd leader may, with persistence and perspicacity, contribute to good timing and a positive context, but having the good fortune to be born at the right time helps.

In chapters 4, 7 and 14, a good deal has been written about how the new context emerged in Northern Ireland. The terrorist organisations had tried a range of different strategies and tactics over the decades, some of which they had learnt from other groups and their own previous experience, and other tactics, such as the car bomb, they invented and were subsequently taken up by terrorist groups elsewhere. Despite this, they had seen little real progress in achieving their aims. The wider community had tired of the endless killing, and the two governments had a quarter of a century of working together within the European Union. Some local leaders had been replaced, but others had begun to modify their attitudes sufficiently to make possible an end of terrorism and a transition to a more peaceful democratic dispensation. In other words, in addition to courageous imaginative leadership within the terrorist community, it is necessary to have good leadership in the official and other non-terrorist elements of the equation, and most, if not all, must be operating in a context which makes progress possible.

While some of these remarks may seem very obvious – the need for a positive context and the presence of courageous leadership within and outside the terrorist community – it is only in relatively recent years, in the aftermath of the al-Qaeda attacks on the United States on 11 September, 2001, when the phenomenon of terrorism came to be regarded as a major strategic threat to the West, that the challenge of how terrorism can best be brought to a permanent end in a community has become the subject of more serious scientific study. Until then, it was regarded as obvious that these criminal acts simply had to be dealt with through robust security measures. It was only with the relative failure of simplistic responses that a scientific approach emerged that studied the evidence about what happens in terrorist and counter-terrorist campaigns and their outcomes. To date, perhaps the most thoughtful book on the subject is Audrey Kurth Cronin's review and analysis of how terrorist campaigns have actually come to a close, written while she was director of studies at the Changing Character of War programme at the University of Oxford between 2005 and 2007 and published in 2009. As we saw on p. 87 she reviewed 457 terrorist organisations that had been active in running campaigns since 1968. There were a series of different outcomes, but only very rarely were the terrorists successful in the cause they espoused. Mostly, they failed because of splits and in-fighting in the groups, a loss of momentum or relevance, massive state repression or decapitation of their organisation through the killing or imprisonment of their leadership. In regard to this last outcome, imprisonment was generally more effective in destroying the myth of the leadership's power, while assassination could produce martyrs to the cause. In the minority of cases where there was some degree of success, it could come about through negotiations; however, most negotiations with terrorist groups, while they could delay the ultimate end of their operations, generally reduced the death and damage they caused and usually led to them reorienting themselves in some way, for example, into democratic politics. She also pointed out that other forms of reorientation were more dangerous, for example, when they transitioned into organised crime (such as the narcoterrorism of FARC in Colombia and the Shining Path in Peru), or morphed into the insurgents holding territory, developing alternative state structures, and then sometimes sliding in into more traditional civil war or overt war scenarios.

In her analysis, Professor Cronin identifies six outcomes: *decapitation, negotiation, success, failure, repression and reorientation.* These outcomes are not all mutually exclusive. For example, decapitation may facilitate repression or contribute to failure, and negotiation may enable reorientation or even a degree of success. However, in all of them leadership plays a role, sometimes as a requirement for success, in other cases as a cause of failure; decapitation involves the removal of the leadership by assassination or imprisonment and failure must be seen as a failure of the strategy of the leaders. Negotiation is a role of the leadership, and reorientation requires the leader to reframe the group narrative and lead in a new direction.

While this analysis is both thoughtful and useful, there have been significant developments since the publication of her book. FARC has now engaged with the Colombian government, so the reorientation to organised crime may not be the end of the story. In Turkey, the death sentence on Abdullah Ocalan was commuted to life imprisonment because of the attempts by Turkey to conform to EU standards, and, as she observed, it looked initially as though this was working to reduce the level of violent activity by the PKK (Kurdistan Workers Party). However, the setbacks experienced by the peace initiative undertaken by Turkish prime minister, Recep Tayyip Erdogan, and instability in the region resulted in a resurgent PKK and then more recently new contacts with the imprisoned Ocalan. The story of Turkey and the PKK has also clearly a long way to go yet. Our models and theories are vital, indeed it is impossible to advance our understanding and communicate with other colleagues without them; however, our task as social scientists is not merely to hold to our current theories and analysis, but to follow the evidence where it takes us, being prepared where necessary to amend and sometimes even radically develop our ideas. As in religion, the progressive speculations of one generation can become the absolutes of conservatives in the next, so we must continually challenge our theories and submit them to new material as we go along.

Perhaps the most important potential outcome of the current wave of international terrorism, which has become clearer since the publication of Professor Cronin's book, is the widespread destabilisation of states from Afghanistan right across the wider Middle East and much of North Africa.

In the late 19th and early 20th centuries, anarchist terrorism was the tactic developed by weaker groups against a powerful state apparatus, and arguably this contributed to the end of empires that was the outcome of World War I.

After World War II, with the realisation of the two new superpowers that a nuclear conflict could be catastrophic, terrorist groups became a modality through which superpower rivalries could be channelled without endangering world peace. The end of the Cold War brought this phase to a close and with it some long-standing terrorist campaigns that were no longer sustainable. Some saw relatively peaceful, negotiated results, such as in South Africa, Northern Ireland and perhaps Nepal; some were 'decapitated' and left without much support as in Peru; and others were brutally put down, as in Sri Lanka. But now a whole new set of problems have emerged.

If in the past, the tactic of terrorism was the strategy of the weak against powerful states; terror, chaos and massive violence as seen in many parts of Africa and increasingly in the Middle East is the result of the failure of many weak states to be able to sustain themselves against powerful terrorist and other attacks. We do not yet understand the role of leadership in these groups, or how they function in a networked world of complex communications and fundamentalist beliefs, and it is not clear how far this failure of states is a crisis of certain regions, or may herald a major shift towards instability and a crisis of democracy itself. It was long assumed that if free and fair elections could be ensured, the people would generally elect fair, just and tolerant leaders and liberal democracy would be the result. When a very different outcome occurred in much of sub-Saharan Africa and tyrannical authoritarian chieftains were elected, it was excused as a developmental problem which would resolve over time. This turned out not to be the case and then, with the election of Hamas in Gaza and the subsequent developments of the Arab Awakening, it became increasingly clear that free and fair elections may result in intolerant, populist regimes that are a nightmare for minorities. Interestingly, it was an Islamist leader, Sheikh Ghannouchi, intellectual leader of the Muslim Brotherhood in Tunisia, who pointed out that a whole complex culture of democracy was necessary, not just elections and institutions (Tamimi, 2001). There is also a crisis of leadership in liberal democracy which ought to be preoccupying the public discourse more than some other matters. This takes us back to the requirements of leadership on the 'official' political side and in non-governmental 'civil society', for this element of leadership is at least as significant as that on the terrorist side.

Let us return to the experience of the Irish Peace Process. Albert Reynolds recounts how, when he was elected Taoiseach (Prime Minister of the Republic of Ireland) he called John Major, who had been elected British Prime Minister. They had known each other as Finance Ministers in ECOFIN – the Economic and Financial Affairs Council of the European Union – and so when he called and suggested an initiative on the Northern Ireland problem, although John Major was doubtful about the possibilities, he agreed to do what he could because of his friendship with Albert Reynolds. This was no small undertaking given the instability of John Major's own government, and it is a testament to the leadership of both men that they started what became the Irish Peace Process. It also speaks well for their successors that, even when they came from different political parties, they carried the process forward as a national rather than a merely governmental commitment. This is one of the requirements I have often urged on leaders in other places. Where a conflict resolution process is seen as a party initiative, it becomes prey to electoral politics. It must become a 'national' commitment that stands above partisan politics and is carried forward whether or not there is a change of government. This too is a question of leadership.

It should be acknowledged that the outcome in the Irish Peace Process owed an enormous debt not only to the containment provided by stable government-to-government relations at the political level but also to the role played by the patient and long-suffering British and Irish civil servants; a contribution that has not received as much attention as the leadership provided by the political leaders of the British and Irish governments and the high-profile interventions by President Clinton and the team led by Senator George Mitchell. These latter have rightly been given much credit for the Belfast Agreement, but the patient and sophisticated nourishing of the peace process through a quarter of a century is a demonstration of a remarkable degree of diplomatic professionalism by civil servants that one might well categorise as leadership from behind the scenes. It is an example of how long-term commitment is a key element of leadership. Some of the civil servants moved to new posts regularly, but others were identified to stay in post for much longer periods, and both the relationships they developed with politicians and the orderly way in which both civil services organised meetings, maintained records of meetings and contacts, and facilitated written agreements provided invaluable support and institutional memory for the process. The relationships they developed also created trust as they acted to liaise with government ministers, who were, in the nature of politics, birds of passage. They also sometimes addressed the needs of politicians for security concerns to be addressed.

Perhaps this is a useful point at which to refer to the security issues for politicians. In chapter 13, Professor Gerson describes how these challenges were addressed in the Netherlands. The situation in Northern Ireland was very different. Politicians were fully aware that their constituents were also in danger of being shot or blown up, and some citizens, especially those involved in the police, army, judicial system, prison service and many other public and private services, were daily in danger of their lives. Being 'security-aware' became a way of life for many people in Northern Ireland. As soon as I became Alliance Leader, the doors and windows of my home were replaced with bullet-resistant glass, alarms were fitted to my home and car and my family and I were given appropriate advice. The loyalist UVF had attempted to assassinate my predecessor as Alliance Leader, John Cushnahan, and he had to live under 24-hour police guard. No such attempts were made on my life, and so the same degree of security cover was unnecessary; however, my children grew up knowing that they needed to be wise about these things. Indeed, the security additions to my home were completed just as my wife was returning home after the birth of our youngest child, Joanna. This context, where a whole community lived in constant danger for more than a generation, is quite different from that experienced by the Dutch politicians described in the next chapter. Visitors noticed it much more than those of us who lived with it constantly (Little, 2009).

Understandably, in such a climate of threat, many people chose to keep their heads down and get on with living their lives and conducting their businesses as safely and unobtrusively as possible, but courageous leadership was also given by some elements within civil society. Business organisations such as the Institute of Directors, the Confederation of British Industry in Northern Ireland, the Chambers of Commerce and Federation of Small Businesses, the trade unions, and some other professional organisations made regular significant public statements about the help or damage to the public good of the stance of different political and terrorist actors. They also had useful private meetings and discussions which assisted political leaders to develop their thinking. There were also many useful smaller charities and NGOs established for the purpose of peace building or associated activities, such as the integrated schools movement, which worked to overcome the barriers of de facto segregated education. Even the press, which can sometimes be a significant part of the problem in their complex relationships with politicians and the communities which they serve, tried at times to play a positive role, most notably when the editors of the two morning newspapers in Northern Ireland got together and published a joint editorial. The significance of this development can only be appreciated when it is understood that *The Belfast Newsletter* (the oldest continuously published daily newspaper in the world) represented Protestant unionist interests and *The Irish News* was the Catholic nationalist morning paper. However, despite their historic differences of attitude and support, at a key point they came together to urge the whole community to unite in support of the peace process.

In a conflict which is often misrepresented as religious in nature (though religious identity clearly does play a key role), the four main church leaders[5] were generally seen as representing reasonably moderate and constructive attitudes. However, on one occasion during a meeting when I was Leader of the Alliance Party they asked what more they could do, and I pointed out that they were largely acting as chaplains to, and representatives of, their own people. If they were to be prophetic, I suggested, they would need to challenge their own people more. I suppose I was frustrated that they expected politicians who were dependent on votes to take risky positions while they, who did not depend on votes (at least not directly), seemed no more prepared to challenge their own people. In fairness, there was a major public appeal by Pope John Paul II during his visit to Ireland in 1979, when he called upon the PIRA:

> On my knees I beg of you to turn away from the paths of violence and to return to the ways of peace … Those who resort to violence always claim that only violence brings about change. You must know there is a political, peaceful way to justice.

Sadly, this had no impact, and the PIRA formally rejected his appeal a few days later; however, I suppose that I was also frustrated because I knew that while the grand public statements and appeals had little impact, there was a history of courageous behind-the-scenes work that had yielded results. The most dramatic of these were the secret talks held by a number of Protestant churchmen with the IRA in December 1974 at Feakle in County Clare, which led to a significant IRA ceasefire early the next year. More recently, it has become public knowledge that Father Alex Reid did much to assist the leadership of the republican movement find its way to the watershed ceasefire in 1994. A small minority of churchmen showed *courage* and *commitment* in trying to create a *context* for a peaceful outcome.

When a leader has decided that for the good of his people, things have to change, and is courageous enough to move forward, a key element in his role as a leader is in framing his people's understanding of their dilemmas. The term *narrative* is often used to connote the way individuals or groups construe their place in history. More than just a story, the narrative identifies key elements in the group culture. Vamik Volkan (2013) has identified the way in which chosen traumas and chosen victories play a remarkably powerful role in determining how a group acts and reacts. Many incidents in their history will barely be remembered, while others occupy a seminal role in shaping how a group of people not only identify with each other but respond to enemies and friends in any context. In developing the historic narrative to emphasise or underplay different elements, the language a leader uses and his models of understanding the nature of the problem are crucial. Let me give some examples.

For generations, and especially since the partition of the island by the 1920 Government of Ireland Act, the problem in Ireland had been perceived as a struggle over territory. For unionists, partition was a trauma turned into a victory – the Home Rule Bill that they so feared had been undermined by the creation of Northern Ireland as a province within the United Kingdom, and they had been given control of it. As far as nationalists were concerned, the victory of independence was marred, or at the very least left incomplete, by the traumatic loss of the six northern counties. For both communities, the struggle for control of territory was not merely a chosen trauma and a chosen victory but a constant celebration and grief. Organisations such as the Orange Order (a Protestant body) regularly dressed in distinctive regalia and marched along particular routes to show that they maintained territorial control. Flags were hung, and kerbstones painted in communal colours (the red, white and blue of the British Union flag in Protestant areas, and the green, white and orange of the Irish tricolour identifying Catholic streets and housing estates). Such a territorial 'zero sum game' was not amenable to resolution since even the notion of shared space connoted a loss of control. The Northern Nationalist leader, John Hume, realised this, and he more than anyone began to develop a new political language based on relationships. 'It was not the island that was divided', he frequently observed, for it was still one physical territory, 'It is the people who are divided about how they should share the island.' The implication of this reframing was that the political task was no longer to maintain control of territory or wrest it from the other side, but to rather resolve this division of view about how to share the territory – to address the problem of disturbed historic relationships between the different groups on the island. When he engaged with the leadership of the republican movement his question was whether the method (terrorism) was more sacred than the cause (Irish unity). The obvious answer was that the cause was more important, which gave him the opportunity to ask whether the violence could be abandoned if there was a better alternative. When republicans replied in the affirmative, Hume's challenge to the British and Irish governments was to develop an opportunity for Irish republicans to abandon the argument of physical force and espouse the force of democratic argument.

This development of a 'peace process language' was important for all the participants. Republicans did not speak of abandoning a failed violent struggle, but characterised their efforts as 'courageously taking risks for peace'. The unionist leader David Trimble did not describe his approach as defeating, or even accepting Sinn Fein (which would seem like a concession), but told his people that 'just because someone has a past it does not mean they cannot have a different future', putting the onus on Sinn Fein to prove itself and making it axiomatic that such a change should receive a positive response from unionists.

Communication through action is at least as important as that of words, and much of the process of peace or war involves political choreography and drama. Vamik Volkan (2004) describes how in 1989 Slobodan Milosevic literally raised up the ghosts of the past by having the remains of Prince Lazar exhumed, 600 years after defeat in the Battle of Kosovo in 1389, and parading the coffin around villages and towns, collapsing the sense of time and making the feelings of confrontation and struggle from the past intense, acute and powerful for his people in the present. In this way, he excited very dangerous feelings which overwhelmed current reality, including the humanity of their neighbours, and led to catastrophic violence.

In the Irish Peace Process, the opposite was achieved. The past was recognised as a tragic past, but a new agenda was created to make possible a shared, non-violent and respectful human future for all the people of the island. The fact that people could begin to share a programme in a broadcasting studio, or meet or shake hands was all carefully calibrated to move an exquisitely delicate process along. The language and the drama were also able to convey subtly different messages depending on which community was receiving them. This was brought home to me as I worked in the Speaker's chair in the new Northern Ireland Assembly. Those who had formerly advocated physical force as a solution to the historic problems of British-Irish relations worked, albeit with some difficulty, with those who wanted to maintain the British state. For Irish nationalists, the emphasis was on the changes that they had achieved. This could be symbolic, for example, when I made it possible for them to use the Irish language in the chamber and welcomed the Irish president on an official visit. They could feel confident that they were no longer second-class citizens because their culture and values were being given recognition at the highest level. For unionists, too, the symbolism of the union Flag still flying over Parliament Buildings, albeit on designated days rather than all the time, and the visits of Her Majesty The Queen to Stormont demonstrated that the link with the rest of the United Kingdom had been maintained, and was now accepted, in some measure, by those who had previously sought to break it.

The communication of new narratives through creative symbolism and new language are necessary but not sufficient achievements of leadership. Real change must be seen if it is to be believed. If the community has been torn apart and lives wrecked and destroyed by guns and bombs, it is vital that those weapons of war and the organisational structures that directed their use be transformed or decommissioned. In passing, I should point out that the term *decommissioning* is actually an example of linguistic leadership. In the early days of the process, one side was demanding the defeat of the other side and the surrender of weapons. I was trying to find a way to describe getting rid of weapons in more acceptable language and was exploring this with Proinsias de Rossa, a former IRA man who had left violence behind and led his group into democratic politics in a previous generation. He resolved my dilemma by suggesting to me the word *decommissioning* – 'Like you do with a ship when it has come to the end of her time', he said. The word removed the connotation of victory and defeat and became the accepted description of the process by which paramilitaries became convinced that the weapons were no longer necessary and were indeed a problem that they needed to dispose of, to the satisfaction of the whole community. Initially, it was thought that establishing an Independent International Commission for Decommissioning (IICD) with legal protections for those concerned was all that was necessary to make this happen within a couple of years of the Belfast Agreement. But by 2004, almost six years after the 1998 'Good Friday Agreement'[6] formally brought the Northern Ireland Troubles to an end, there had been no significant decommissioning of weapons or standing down of paramilitary organisations; republicans still did not support policing and the administration of justice in Northern Ireland (despite being in government), and the lack of trust this generated and demonstrated led to repeated collapse of the power-sharing government and suspension of the assembly, to the point where the whole peace settlement was in danger of unravelling. After a great deal of discussion between the British and Irish governments, they jointly established a four-man IMC, with one Commissioner each from Britain, Ireland, Northern Ireland and the United States of America.[7]

Despite the apparent commitment of the political leaders who had sat together at the table for years and eventually negotiated the 'peace deal', the Belfast Agreement did not have within it all the instruments necessary to ensure its full implementation. While the parties elected to the assembly were operating the democratic process, the paramilitary organisations on both sides[8] still had their arsenals and organisations intact. While most were said to be on 'ceasefire', all were still using some of their weaponry to exert control over people in their own areas through the threat and actual use of violence. In addition, each side had little confidence that they could trust the other not to restart the campaigns of terrorism and sectarian violence. In was well known that some of the political parties maintained more or less substantial links with paramilitaries on their side of the community. The IMC was put in place to find ways of exerting pressure on the paramilitaries to decommission their weapons and stand down their organisations.

At the same time, the British army and the Police Service of Northern Ireland were embarked on a programme of security normalisation[9] that was also monitored by the IMC under Article 5 of the International Agreement between the Government of the United Kingdom and the Government of Ireland under which the IMC was established. Over the period of more than seven years during which the IMC was in existence, we produced 26 reports, and all were published in full by the British and Irish Governments. Five of the IMC's reports were on this process of security normalisation, and 20 focused primarily on the paramilitaries. The most significant way in which the commission could exert pressure was through the legal requirement to produce these reports on the illegal activities of the paramilitaries and their relationships with the various political parties twice a year. The commission was also empowered to propose 'remedies' of various kinds, including sanctions, regulations and legislation, though it was for the governments to decide whether or not these would be implemented.

In Article 4(b) of the International Agreement, the IMC was required to assess in its reports whether the leaderships of paramilitary groups were directing violent and other criminal activities or seeking to prevent them. In the first report, when the commission was laying out how we would conduct the subsequent monitoring programme, two main questions of leadership were identified – the first about the relationship between the leadership of paramilitary groups and that of political parties, and the second about how to hold to account leaders of paramilitary groups engaged in continuing violence and other criminal activity.[10] In other words, it was recognised that leadership was a key element in finding ways of bringing this long and bloody campaign of terrorism and counter-terrorism to a close. One might argue that such a focus on leadership runs contrary to some of the theories espoused in other chapters about the importance of context and group responses in the emergence of terrorism and politically motivated violence. However, not only are these perspectives complementary, in addition we are not looking here at why terrorism might start but rather how it might be brought to an end, and the role and position of leaders of all kinds are of considerable importance in this phase.

In addition to all the qualities I have described above – various types of courage, context and timing, commitment, creativity in developing new narratives and communicating them persuasively and the value of external monitors that can hold leaders to account for the agreements they have made on behalf of the people – there is at least one other element which needs to be understood. In chapter 3, I outlined how people, when they get involved in terrorism, join groups which have a different way of thinking about morality and motivation than the rest of society. This is very difficult for people from stable societies to appreciate. They expect people, as individuals or as groups, to act rationally in their own best social and economic self-interest. It is clear, however, that this is not so. Those involved in terrorism – and the phenomenon is much more widely apparent in such societies – are not rational actors in that sense, but devoted actors who will defend sacred values even at the cost of their own lives and all else that they value (see also pp. 37 and 45). By sacred values I do not necessarily mean religious values. At an individual level, the life of my child is a sacred value – not something that can be traded. The flag of my country and the language of my people evoke feelings and attachments that seem bizarre to the person who says, 'but you can't eat a flag or stay warm wrapped in it'. The evidence considered in chapter 1 shows how powerful these values are when people are living in some sense of existential threat. It is also extremely difficult to engage in rational negotiation with groups and individuals operating on this basis. As a community moves from conflict to peace, and those who have been involved as combatants try to make the transition to civil society and take responsibility for the day-to-day decisions of government in the best social and economic interests of their people, this transformation from *devoted actors* operating on *sacred values* to *rational actors* functioning on *social and economic best interest* is a daily challenge for the political leader who tries to see his people through into the new dispensation. We are not yet clear about the ways in which this can best be achieved. In Northern Ireland, as I write, the sacred value challenge of flying the British Union flag over Belfast City Hall only on designated days rather than every day has sparked weeks of rioting and intimidation and death threats to some of my colleagues in the Alliance Party, even though this issue had been resolved at Parliament Buildings years before, when I was speaker.

Which takes us back to the start; however far along the process away from the use of physical force and violence we find ourselves, these remain elements of the human condition which will never truly go away. Those who choose to try to deal with them as leaders need not only an understanding of the challenges they face, and courage and commitment in doing so, but they are also well advised to remain humble about what we know and what we do not know and be constantly vigilant for the signals of what is actually going on among our people. David Owen, in his book on hubris in political leadership (2012), sets out clearly the disaster in store for anyone who fails to observe this last injunction to the experienced leaders about leadership. Leaders are no longer leaders if they lose their followers. If hubris takes over and they lose genuine understanding and empathy with the feelings of their people, they will not stay leaders for long.

Notes

1   The Provisional Irish Republican Army was the main Catholic nationalist republican paramilitary organisation, committed to achieving through the use of force an independent, united, socialist Irish republic. It was a breakaway in late 1969 from the Official IRA but quickly became the main organisation. There were various other

    smaller splinter groups over the years, including the Continuity IRA, the Real IRA and the INLA. PIRA was closely linked to Provisional Sinn Fein. In 2005, it formally ended its terrorist campaign.

2   The Royal Ulster Constabulary (RUC) was the Northern Ireland police force from the formation of Northern Ireland in 1921 to the completion of the Patten Reforms that emerged from the 1998 Belfast Agreement. They were transformed into the new Police Service of Northern Ireland (PSNI).

3   The term *loyalist* refers to Protestant, working-class unionists, who are often suspicious of middle-class groups of the same religious and political persuasion. They tended to be less successful politically, but many gathered into illegal paramilitary groups such as the Ulster Defence Association (UDA) and Ulster Volunteer Force (UVF). These engaged in public displays of strength, as well as intimidation, threats, extortion and organised crime to exert control over their own communities as well as bombings, shootings and murder of those they perceived to be Catholic nationalist republican and against union with Britain.

4   The Alliance Party of Northern Ireland (Alliance) was a cross-community political party, formed in April 1970, with a mission to find a peaceful, democratic shared settlement of the Northern Ireland problem. A broadly liberal pro-union party, it was made up of people from Protestant, Catholic and non-religious backgrounds with unionist, nationalist and non-aligned traditions. Its policy platform centred on power sharing within the United Kingdom and a strong Irish or North–South dimension.

5   The Roman Catholic Primate of Ireland (usually a Cardinal), the Church of Ireland (Anglican) Primate of Ireland, the Moderator of the Presbyterian Church in Ireland, and the President of the Methodist Church in Ireland regularly met, undertook initiatives and issued constructive joint statements. These four church leaders became something of an institution, representing as they did the overwhelming majority of church-going people in the island of Ireland, and all were organised on an all-Ireland basis. They met from time to time with most of the political leaders.

6   The 1998 agreement between the British and Irish governments and the various political parties, including those who represented the PIRA and the loyalist UVF and UDA, was initially known as the Good Friday Agreement because it was achieved on Good Friday 1998. However, Protestants who were opposed to it were angry with the attempt to give a positive 'religious' spin to the description, and so it is more properly known as the Belfast agreement after the capital city of Northern Ireland where most of the talks took place and where the agreement was reached – another demonstration of significance of language and description, and the need for flexibility.

7   The four commissioners were John Grieve (the former head of the Metropolitan Police Anti-Terrorist Branch), Joe Brosnan (former Secretary-General of the Department of Justice of the Irish Republic), John Alderdice (former Leader of the cross-community Alliance Party of Northern Ireland and at the time of appointment the Speaker of the Northern Ireland Assembly), and Dick Kerr (former Acting Director of the Central Intelligence Agency).

8   The Continuity Irish Republican Army (CIRA), the Irish National Liberation Army (INLA), the Provisional Irish Republican Army (PIRA), the Real Irish Republican Army (RIRA), the Loyalist Volunteer Force (LVF), the Ulster Defence Association (UDA), and the Ulster Volunteer Force (UVF).

9   This was a programme agreed between the British and Irish governments to return the British army presence over a period of two years (2004–2007) to normal peacetime presence – no troops or military vehicles on the streets, no shared army/police bases and no army lookout posts, guard posts (sangers) or military bases other than the 5,000 or so personnel who would make up the normal per-capita peacetime level of troops as in the rest of the United Kingdom and the Republic of Ireland. Police stations were also

to be transformed from military-style fortresses into community police facilities. While the army normalisation was fully completed within the time frame, the huge cost of the required changes to police stations and the threat from dissident republicans in some areas made this element of the normalisation process more drawn out.

10 Page 34 of the First Report of the Independent Monitoring Commission, published on 20 April, 2004.

13

SUPPORTING LEADERS UNDER THREAT AND THEIR PROTECTION

Berthold P.R. Gersons and Mirjam J. Nijdam

Introduction

Most politicians will die of natural causes, but some have died as a result of assassinations. E.J. Gumbel describes, in his book *Four Years of Political Murder*, that between 1918 and 1922, 376 political assassinations were carried out in Germany of which the assassination of the foreign minister Walter Rathenau is the most remembered. Four American presidents have been killed, and many more failed assassinations have been reported. In the Netherlands, such events are extremely rare. In 2002, the popular politician Pim Fortuyn was murdered by an animal activist. Two years later, the Dutch film maker Theo van Gogh was killed on his bicycle by an Islamic fundamentalist. Van Gogh had produced the movie *Submission* about the suppression of Islamic women together with the Dutch politician Ayaan Hirsi Ali.

To prevent new attacks and to enhance the safety of politicians, the Dutch government initiated the National Coordinator for Counterterrorism and Security (NCSC) in 2005. In this agency, threat intelligence was brought together with security and protection forces of the Dutch police with the aim of putting protective measures into place when the threat or risk reached such proportions that the politicians or other public figures were no longer able to take adequate protective measures themselves. Ayaan Hirsi Ali and Geert Wilders, both members of the Dutch Parliament at that time, already received death threats and needed protection. But other politicians also increasingly received threatening messages. Protection in this post-9/11 era has become an increasing activity with cameras, protected entrances and corridors, secure badge systems, armoured cars, surveillance teams, and constant intelligence sampling and analysis to prevent attacks on politicians.

In the same year, the psychological consequences of threat and protection became apparent to the NCSC, which then invited Professor Gersons to become their consultant (Gersons & Olff, 2005). Protection was not only a specialised skill of trained police officers, but involved the cooperation of those who needed protection. This cooperation, together with the support of the families of the protected politicians, could not be taken for granted. After the first experiences with providing advice and counselling politicians and their families under threat and protection, we began and published a systematic study on the psychological consequences of threat and protection (Nijdam, Olff, de Vries, Martens & Gersons. 2008; Nijdam, Olff & Gersons, 2010).

Death threats and protection

Death threats towards politicians are, apart from personal reasons, motivated to spread anxiety in the population and to influence the decision making of the politicians. Sometimes keeping the threat active is enough to draw attention towards the goals of the persons behind the threat. But killing the politician is showing power and audacity and making other politicians seriously frightened. Attacks on politicians can also help to silence a political opponent. Attacks from mentally disturbed persons on politicians, often without any warning, are the most dangerous

(James, Mullen, Meloy, Pathé, Farnham, Preston & Darnley, 2007).

The threats in the Netherlands from 2005 on were mainly related to some form of (Islamic) fundamentalism

(Stern, 2003).

To help politicians cope with threats, we first pay attention to the specifics of the threat. Often, the threat has become known through the Internet or an anonymous letter. Its aim is to intimidate the politician and to let him or her know that they are not safe any more. Sometimes the intelligence agency has discovered less explicit threats by listening to telephone calls or by tracking suspicious persons. The politician mostly does not know the potential attackers and their plans. The intelligence agency and the NCSC avoid sharing specific information with the politician for security reasons. The result is a very frightened politician, suddenly notified by the NCSC about a death threat. The lack of detailed information makes it extremely difficult for the politician to prevent the attack, to be well prepared, or even to imagine what could happen.

Some politicians are aware that their views are controversial towards, for instance, Islamic people. In such cases, a death threat is not completely unexpected. But even politicians who do not have such opinions can receive threats as representatives of the government. Threats have also come from individuals who hate certain politicians.

When the NCSC has identified a threat, they are legally obliged to provide protection. Depending on the risk analysis, the protective measures taken can be diverse. In extreme cases, the politician is not allowed to return to work or home and is sent directly to a safe house with protectors. Sometimes it is even necessary to send them elsewhere in the world. In such cases, the use of a phone or the Internet is prohibited because it can provide information to potential attackers. The decision to protect is often an immediate and urgent one which overwhelms the politician. Family, friends, colleagues and assistants gradually become aware of it. Less intense protection consists of being transported by protectors in armoured cars. The protectors wear bullet-proof jackets, and they have weapons on them. The protection is organised in different concentric circles around the politician. Some protectors (in shifts) in direct proximity of the politician will constantly accompany him or her. A wider circle of protection is composed of protectors who are on the lookout for signs of a planned attack. The home of the politician will be transformed with bullet-proof glass, cameras and other security measures and, constant police surveillance can be required.

All these safety measures are taken to protect the safety of the politician and of his or her family if needed. In 2005, however, the protectors were largely unaware that instead of providing reassurance, these measures actually increased fear in the politician and those around him or her.

Psychological reactions towards threats and protection

The threat of being murdered will immediately set off the stress response for survival (Olff, Langeland & Gersons, 2005). This response is mediated by the amygdala in the brain, which functions as an alarm centre. With sensory information such as seeing a sharp knife or a pistol directed at the person, the amygdala will inhibit the slower, reflective thinking in the frontal brain and start to prepare the body for immediate action by increasing the heart rate and oxygenation of muscles. This helps the individual to flee towards safety or to fight back. Freezing is also a possible reaction; the person then is not able to move or to control muscular movements appropriately. These are strong physical and psychological reactions. One feels tense, sometimes sweating or shivering, loses appetite, and is unable to relax.

From our experience, we have categorised the protection period into three different phases with their associated stress reactions. In these phases, the person's appraisal of the threat determines which stress reactions will occur (Olff et al., 2005). This sense of threat can vary over time and explains why protected persons, partners and family members differ in their stress reactions during the period of threat and protection.

The *beginning* phase starts when the politician is informed about a death threat and protection is introduced. Most politicians have no experience of protection and threat at such a level. The first reaction is to become bewildered, frightened and overwhelmed at the prospect of losing control of one's life and becoming dependent on others for safety. A common reaction is denial of the threat, resulting in noncompliance with the protection. Those who bring the unwelcome news are sometimes verbally attacked. Some politicians try to use their powerful position to overrule the actions of the protection agency. But some become so frightened that they cling to the protectors by constantly asking: 'Where are we going? Are they close? What do you know? How do you know we are safe now?', and other dependent behaviour. Others remain 'cool' and do not betray much emotion but later on become more emotional and may start to abuse alcohol. Protection may also be unwelcome because it is seen as a sudden intrusion not only into work but also into private life. Secrets and private relationships or habits may become known to the protectors. Reactions of family members, including the spouse and children, are often just as important in this phase. Sometimes the spouse is more worried than the politician, and each can start blaming the other for their reactions to the threat. The spouse may even ask the politician to leave this or her job. Especially when children have become a target of the terrorists, we have seen politicians who have stepped down.

In this phase, we normally see more intense emotions–fear, anger, sometimes crying, but also–feelings of guilt towards family and coworkers. They may suffer from sleeping problems, exhibit increased startle reactions as well as somewhat paranoid reactions, become easily irritated and lose concentration. These problems along with anger about the loss of control and the threat will influence the political opinions of the politician and influence decision making. The protectors and their supervisors may find these reactions difficult to understand and to handle.

Then follows the *consolidation* phase. After some weeks, protection becomes part of 'normal' life. Politicians 'enjoy' being freely transported and assisted in different ways by the protectors. It can even become politically profitable to show how much protection they need, for they now have good reason to blame the terrorists. This can also be stimulated by a less conscious process. Protection, in some ways, disconnects people from normal interactions, which would normally help the person to get certain points of view into perspective. Being threatened with death, however, increases the need to be more strongly convinced of one's existing convictions. People who do not share or accept certain viewpoints of one side or the other without criticism can be pressured to leave the group and may be blamed as a 'traitor' or as a disbeliever. Provocative behaviour on the part of the politician will provoke the 'enemy' and prevent termination of protection. It also can become difficult for the protectors not to become overly influenced by the ideas of the politician, since their lives are also under threat by virtue of being in the proximity of the protected person. 'Terror management theory' has shown that reminders of one's mortality in various contexts strengthen the person's cultural values and worldview (Greenberg, Pyszcynski & Solomon, 1986).

In addition, depending on their natural attachment style, some people will be inclined to form an attachment to their protectors and surrender control to them, whereas others tend to be antagonistic to the protectors and keep them at a distance (based on Hart, Shaver & Goldenberg, 2005).

However, a very different response can be exhibited by politicians under threat. They may start to evaluate their views and actions or even change how they perceive themselves and the world. This phenomenon – 'post-traumatic growth' (Tedeschi & Calhoun, 2004) – has first been found in cancer patients who expected to die soon. When life cannot be taken for granted, it becomes a vulnerable treasure. One starts to evaluate one's life and connections. Moreover, family and friends often become much more important than work, social position and money.

For those around the politician, the unexpected changes in interacting with the politician can be confusing. The topics of work and private life during protection often become an arguing point for partners who have nothing to do with the origin of the threat. They can become angry and complain about the 'stupid' choices made by the politician. Politicians often spend very little time at home with their family, which can cause family members to blame the politician's political ambitions for having led to this devastating situation. Protectors who are trained as specialised police officers or with a military background become unwilling observers of these quarrels. They try to distance themselves from these affairs. It becomes even more complicated if the politician or the partner becomes attached to their protectors and may even try to initiate romantic relationships with them. This also happens with hostages who are dependent on their hijackers (Symonds, 1980). Especially in a safe house, the protection situation bears some similarities to the experiences of hostages in terms of isolation, deprivation, psychological pressure and role inequality, and similar attachments can arise in the consolidation phase of protection.

The relationships of the protected person with family, friends and work will be influenced and compromised by the protection. Living under protection means loss of freedom in many respects. Going out for a stroll, to a bar or restaurant, to see movie, or friends and family will lose all its spontaneity.

The last phase is *withdrawal* from protection. One might expect someone to be happy about the renewed freedom when the message comes that there is no more danger, for instance, when a terrorist is killed or imprisoned. But more often the feeling of being safe sinks in much later than the message of new freedom. Protection agencies have recognised this phenomenon and have developed a routine to downgrade the protection step by step.

As human beings we perform many necessary behaviours automatically, such as driving a car, cooking, and going to bed. In a similar vein, when one is accustomed to protection, it takes time to adapt to its withdrawal and to return to normal circumstances. The habit of hyper-vigilance, learned under protection, will not be easily shaken off. The first reaction to withdrawal of protection is to start scanning your environment for danger again. The withdrawal of the protective shell will give rise to a feeling of renewed vulnerability. The politician wants proof of the new safety or does not believe the protection agency. Moreover, the secondary gain of free transportation and feeling important may motivate some to protest against the ending of protection.

Supporting by direct advice

As we have seen, politicians will react in various ways towards threat and protection. During *the beginning phase*, it helps if the politicians are reassured that their psychological reactions in the beginning are 'normal reactions when facing an abnormal situation'. This is an often-used choice of words in the direct aftermath of disasters and helps people to cope with their overwhelming experiences. When we start to advise politicians under protection, normalising their reactions is our first goal. This is sometimes called 'psycho-education'. In this setting, it means explaining the psychological reactions as a result of the unfamiliar death threat and protection. When a politician, and often also the partner, recognises that their psychological reactions are normal in the context of the abnormal circumstances, some feeling of control is regained.

We also explain that feeling fear is an important signal which is related to danger. When we feel fear, we immediately want to identify and assess the danger. Politicians under protection, however, cannot identify and assess the danger, and this uncertainty results in a state of anxiety. We explain that the feeling of fear initiates the stress response system; one becomes hyper-vigilant; the heart rate increases; emotions such as crying or irritability can appear, with aggressive outbursts; or emotions can be stifled. It becomes increasingly difficult to concentrate on matters not related to the threat and, most prominently, sleeping well often becomes impossible because one is on constant alert. Only when one is exhausted is sleep possible, and then only for a limited period.

The hyper-alertness makes keeping a normal work schedule difficult. Perhaps the terrorist wants to disrupt the politician's normal life and coerce him or her into accepting the terrorist's opinions. This is the case with instrumental threats, when the perpetrator wants to achieve a concrete result by force. Realising this often makes the politician extremely angry. Discussing and explaining these relations and reactions in an advisory session has been much appreciated by politicians and their family.

The psycho-education also includes warnings about the near future. It is worthwhile to warn protected persons against increasing their use of alcohol as a way of trying to feel less tense and to increase the chance of sleeping longer. Alcohol also impairs attention and concentration and can even increase the fear and emotions. Exhaustion can also lead to a depressed state.

We advise the politician to take note of his or her reactions and also those of family members and even assistants who become fearful because of the new situation. Then we start to discuss how he or she can best adapt to this new situation. Apart from keeping a daily routine with less work than usual, we explain and stimulate healthy distractions. Listening to or making music, exercising, sports and meeting with friends are examples of suggested activities. The protection results in a much smaller circle of movement than one is used to having. Because one cannot go out freely for a walk, physical activity at home or in a gym is a must.

Often it takes time and more sessions to help the politician and his family to adapt in steps to the protected state. In the beginning, they often have difficulty in trusting their protectors. The protected person lacks knowledge about the specifics of the threat and is therefore unable to distinguish between dangerous and less dangerous situations. One needs to learn to trust the protectors, and an optimal individual match is important. Some protectors are quite open, while others do not like to talk much. Their task is not primarily to socialise with the politician and his family, but to be on high alert and to maintain a professional distance. Politicians have repeatedly requested the agency to send only protectors who are already well known to them. However, the protectors work in shifts and, as a rule, routine is dangerous when one needs to be alert. Here, we see that the profession of protection may conflict with the needs of the protected person and the family.

The advisory meetings, as requested by the NCSC, are held by psychiatrists and psychologists who are specialised in interventions after traumatic events and in treating clients with post-traumatic stress disorder (PTSD). They can distinguish between normal and abnormal stress reactions. The role of an advisor, however, is different from that of a doctor or a therapist. When the NCSC asks the advisor to plan a meeting with a protected politician, it is seldom a request for medical treatment or psychotherapy. Therefore, we make it explicitly clear to the client that the aim of the meeting is to advise, not to diagnose mental problems. The involvement of the advisor is legitimate because of his knowledge and experience of normal and abnormal stress reactions, especially under threat and protection. The advisors are still governed by their duties as mental health professionals to abide by professional standards of confidentiality.

However, for a frightened politician, it is difficult to distinguish between these different roles, between a 'doctor', an advisor or a therapist. Regretfully, often the first reaction of a politician towards the offer of the NCSC to talk with a psychologist or psychiatrist about how to cope with the situation is a rejection. 'I am not crazy' or 'I do not need a shrink' are common reactions.

To overcome these negative reactions the NCSC has produced and distributed flyers with information about common reactions and about the advisory meetings. Also, politicians who have become familiar with threat and protection have offered to meet with the new protected persons and to tell them about the value of advisory meetings.

The advice will be different in the later phases. During *the consolidation phase*, there is usually less need for politicians and their families to meet with the advisors. Only new threats and disturbing new information, or complications in the interactions between the family and protectors, are reasons for new advisory sessions. Living in a safe house can become complicated when neighbours become fearful that they too may be caught up in an attack. When the threat persists for months, or even years, it can become a divisive issue for the politician and his or her partner and family. Both politicians and partners have to adapt to an abnormal life of protection and to cope with this unusual and often unacceptable situation.

It is sometimes difficult not to become suspicious towards unknown people, especially when the threat is coming from countries outside Europe. Here, confrontation with foreign-looking people can cause startle reactions. This phenomenon is called fear generalisation. When someone has been threatened, for instance by a coloured person, all coloured persons are then appraised as possible attackers. One loses the capacity to distinguish between real danger and triggers of past events.

During *the withdrawal phase*, the protection agency often likes to have an advisory meeting with the politician. Many psychological reactions about uncertainty and safety return and necessitate explanations and new ways of coping.

Complications

Advisors, as stated before, want to stick to their role and try to avoid making unnecessary diagnoses and offering treatment. However, as experienced mental health professionals, it is difficult not to see when suspicion – a normal response when one is protected – turns into a full-fledged paranoid state. Likewise, alcohol abuse and major depression are occasionally encountered in such situations. When an advisor is confronted with such symptoms, one has to discuss these observations explicitly with the politician if possible. In such cases, it is advisable to refer the protected person for treatment to someone outside the advisory team.

It has been helpful for us, as advisors, to understand the task of the protectors and the sometimes difficult interactions this can cause with the politician and his family. However, feeling dependent on the protector, or becoming friends with them, can become an unpleasant issue. Sometimes, politicians develop an intense attachment towards their protectors. Some politicians treat the protectors like servants; for instance, they may be expected to go shopping for the politician's family. This conflicts with their protective role and can cause anger among the protectors. We have also seen regressive reactions of politicians which complicated the protection.

In day-to-day life, people do not expect to be exposed to an accident, an attack or a life-threatening disease. However, when such incidents do happen, in the beginning it does not seem real. In the field of psycho-trauma, this is called the 'illusion of safety'. It is difficult to believe and to act as if a disaster could happen any day or that someone might die. Especially in the beginning phase, politicians sometimes do not want to comply with the protection. They sometimes, for instance, try to escape from the attention of the protectors. This behaviour can be understood as testing the reality of the threat.

Protection becomes a routine for politicians, such as ministers and presidents, who are in leading positions Here it is not a specific threat but constant unknown possible dangers that bring about the need for protection; for instance, it is always possible that mentally disturbed persons or 'lone wolves' will attack without warning. Without explicit threats, it is more difficult for the politician to comply with the protection and to accept the associated intrusion into their private life. Indeed, protection in itself sometimes stimulates fear in the protected person. Again, advisory meetings are advised in such situations.

Wider implications

To increase the general awareness of MPs, ministers and leaders of the political parties in the Netherlands about threats and protection and the need for psychological support, they have been informed at meetings with the NCSC together with an advisor. One can see this as an 'early warning system' to increase the feeling of responsibility and involvement of the leaders. This approach is also increasing their interest in other kinds of threat, which are much more frequent than might be expected. Hate mail is quite common, and politicians often receive threatening letters at home or are verbally attacked in public. This is often seen as insignificant, or 'part of the job'. The meetings help them to take threats more seriously and to inform the NCSC about those incidents.

The encounter with a personal death threat is a challenge for politicians. However, they are also confronted with the responsibility to respond to major tragedies and threats towards populations such as those that arise at times of war, or civil strife and natural or man-made disasters. As we saw on p. 91, politicians can be expected to experience the same or similar emotions to others faced with such problems. Both immediately and sometimes later on, they may become fearful, saddened, angry or depressed. They may attempt to cope by concealing or repressing some feelings while expressing others, they may make use of alcohol or other drugs for this purpose and this sometimes leads to abuse.

Their assistants or colleagues often turn a blind eye to these reactions and responses. They do not know how to handle them or how to help. Psychological advice as described earlier can be helpful in many such situations and can help politicians to feel less lonely at the top and better able to make wise decisions. At critical moments when the politician feels overwhelmed by emotions, it can be helpful to let the first wave of acute stress reactions die down before making high-impact decisions. For these reasons, it is important for an advisor to be an experienced mental health professional who is absolutely independent of the politician and who has nothing personal to gain.

Conclusion

Knowledge of stress reactions, trauma and PTSD has been applied outside the treatment room of the mental health professional. Expert knowledge of people's responses after disasters has been found to be useful.

In the Netherlands, in 2005, a special agency – the NCSC – was set up to protect politicians whose lives had been threatened. Soon after their first experiences of protecting politicians, this agency encountered psychological reactions in response to threat and protection which complicated their primary task of enhancing the safety of the protected persons. The help of specialised mental health professionals in the area of trauma and PTSD was requested to help the politicians cope with the situation in the best possible way. Further direct advice and consultation were found to be necessary but not easy to put into practice, mainly because of a certain stigma surrounding the issues. By using different approaches and tools, a more comprehensive programme has been developed. Advising politicians in the contexts of other stressful situations and encounters in their work has been found to be helpful and has important implications for future development.

14

OMAGH AND THE PEACE
PROCESS IN NORTHERN IRELAND

Nora Gribbin and Rodney Turtle

In chapter 4, we saw how two groups came into being in Northern Ireland, each seeing itself as a minority group whose security was threatened by the other. Protestants, fearing the larger Catholic south, and with an insecure attachment to Britain, bolster their memories of past victories in the annual marching rituals. Catholics have an equally insecure attachment to the Republic of Ireland while idealising a united Ireland.

We examined how the Northern Ireland Troubles emerged in the 1960s as a response to a civil rights campaign by the Catholic minority which was met by injustice, humiliation and disrespect by the Protestant majority, factors that, as we have seen (pp. 17 & 43), play a major part in the inception of terrorist acts. The Catholic minority were left feeling rejected and disempowered by the questionable form of democracy practised by Protestant leaders. Some turned to violence. In 1971, special powers were called on to reintroduce internment without trial of suspected terrorists. This only fuelled recruitment to the republican groups and escalated a cycle of violence which remained unbroken. In chapter 7, we saw how the killing of 13 innocent Catholic men and boys by the British army on Bloody Sunday undermined hopes of justice and was viewed by the Catholic population as an utterly unacceptable act by a hostile government. Different perspectives and responses polarised the two communities and further strengthened the extremes. IRA volunteers targeted the RUC and security forces, and in retaliation, Protestant paramilitaries targeted Catholics. A 'tit for tat' conflict continued for a third of a century at the cost of more than 3,500 lives and 36,000 serious injuries. It led to collateral loss and damage to a society across three generations; divisions deepened and the two communities became even more polarised. In short, the attempt by the British government/military to improve security in Northern Ireland (NI) by coercion undermined the fragile security of the Catholic minority which, in turn, retaliated in ways that only further undermined security in both populations.

Communal divisions extended beyond the traditional apartheid in schools and sports, and people increasingly sought comfort and solace with their co-religionists. Territories controlled by each group were symbolically marked by union colours or the tricolour. The tripartite relationships – between Catholics and Protestants, between Northern and Southern Ireland, and between Britain and Catholic Ireland – can be seen as dysfunctional and representing problematic patterns of attachment.

In this chapter, we examine the peace process which gradually restored hope of improved security on both sides of the conflict, and we consider why, when a devastating terrorist attack occurred – in Omagh – the event led to further reconciliation of the two communities while at another time, it would have had the opposite effect. As predicted by our model, changes in perceptions, and responses, in the media, the leadership and the populace, now diluted polarisation, opposed violent retaliation, and isolated the perpetrators.

The development of a peace process

Peace initiatives had been on the agenda of government and party leaders for 30 years. Eventual development of the peace process included recognition by the perpetrators of the futility of violence without prospect of victory, war weariness among the public and a growing acceptance that compromise was needed and that communication between the various sides, including the terrorists, would be needed.

> The provisionals (PIRA) had realised that their campaign to bomb Britain out of Northern Ireland and the unionist population into a United Ireland was a lost cause and they had better settle for power sharing.
>
> (Edwards 2009)

In chapter 1, Parkes showed how people become attached to nations, gods and the complex matrix of persons, ideas and assumptions with which they are associated. Such attachments cannot easily be changed by appeals to reason, particularly when the attachments are as extreme as they are insecure. It takes time and commitment to change patterns of allegiance and attachment, exactly what was necessary for the peace process to be fruitful. In chapter 2, Abrahamson explained why it is hard to change fixed prejudices, and in chapter 12, Alderdice discussed how a change of direction requires strong leadership, leaders taking risks, inevitable splits, and the context needs to be right. To make progress, an alignment of the internal and external stakeholders is necessary.

When the United Kingdom and the Republic of Ireland joined the European Economic Community (EEC) in 1973, the seeds were sown. Government ministers were now meeting regularly within the more impartial structures of the EEC. Practical working arrangements developed, mutual respect grew, and slowly Anglo-Irish relations began to change.

When the two governments, in the aftermath of the 1981 hunger strike in the Maze prison, found themselves facing profound threats to political instability both North and South of the Irish border, they had new and positive political relationships to build on. John Hume, one of the founders of the SDLP, had advocated broad-based negotiations between the three important relationships – between

Catholic and Protestants within NI, between the republic and NI, and between United Kingdom and the republic. In 1985, after intense secret talks between the two governments, the Anglo-Irish Agreement was signed by British Prime Minister, Margaret Thatcher, and Irish Taoiseach, Garret Fitzgerald. It set up bilateral institutions which laid the foundations of unprecedented cooperation between the two states to address the NI issue. It is unlikely that this could have happened without the institutional and new personal attachments between those in leadership positions which had developed within the structure of the EEC.

A turning point in the history of NI had arrived. Article One acknowledged there would be no change in the constitutional status of NI without the consent of the majority of the people of NI. On the other hand, new bilateral institutions were set up between Britain and Ireland, including a British-Irish Secretariat based near Belfast, a regular Anglo-Irish intergovernmental conference, and a British-Irish inter-parliamentary body. This all helped to improve relations between the United Kingdom and the Republic of Ireland. Even so, while democratic Catholic Nationalists of the SDLP now felt less isolated and more empowered, others feared compromise; the IRA continued its terrorist campaign; and Protestant loyalist paramilitaries felt betrayed by Britain's agreement to consult the republic over the future of NI and took revenge through further sectarian killings of Catholics. Indeed, the profoundly adverse reaction to the Anglo-Irish Agreement of almost all the Protestant unionist population of NI, and some conservative political figures in Britain, led to a serious political crisis. Their opposition could be interpreted as anxiety about the inherent threat to their previously strongly idealised (though insecure) attachment to the union with Great Britain. They were worried and suspicious of the agreement and terrified they were being 'sold out'.

Six years of diplomatic activity were needed to get political representatives of the two sides in NI to sit around a table to talk. Parties with terrorist involvement were absent – getting them there took a further five years. During the 'talks about talks' years, the parties edged slowly towards the table, certainly not by exploring substantive issues, but by discussing how they could best take the first few steps to engagement. Talks in 1991 consolidated some agreement: there would be three strands to the talks, each reflecting one of the three insecure attachment relationships.

At first the talks made little progress. Taoiseach Albert Reynolds and his British counterpart, John Major, had a good relationship and were pursuing what was to become the Downing Street Declaration. In April 1993, it became known that there had been unofficial dialogue between John Hume, the leader of the SDLP, and Gerry Adams of Sinn Fein. This prompted so much anger that John Hume threatened to pull out of the process. Major and Reynolds moved apart when it became clear that the British government had had its own 'back door channel' to republican paramilitaries for many years. Nevertheless, the Hume–Adams unofficial collaboration led to a draft statement encompassing self-determination and consent, and this was fed into the draft declaration.

McKittrick and McVea, writing about Hume, say

> In common with Garret Fitzgerald, he challenged the traditional nation-
> alist assertion that the root of the problem was the British presence. The
> historic mission of nationalism, he argued, was to convince unionism
> that its concerns could be accommodated in a new agreed settlement for
> Ireland. He built up an international reputation, accumulating consider-
> able influence especially in the republic and as a European MP, on the
> continent. In particular he wielded great influence in Washington, where
> powerful Irish-American figures such as Senator Edward Kennedy
> looked to him for advice. By the early 1990s he was, in sum, the most
> influential nationalist politician in Northern Ireland. His behind-the-
> scenes contacts with Adams interacted with events in the public domain.
> When Brookes made his 1990 statement that Britain had no selfish stra-
> tegic or economic interest in Northern Ireland he did so at the private
> prompting of Hume, who had been arguing this point in his talks with
> Adams. The thought that Britain was essentially neutral would play an
> important part in the embryonic peace process.
>
> (McKittrick & McVea 2001, p. 186)

With the talks stalling, an outbreak of terrorist killings in one week in October
1993 produced the worst death toll since the early 1970s with 23 civilians killed,
nine in the IRA Shankill bomb in Belfast and eight in a loyalist shooting on
Halloween night (after calling 'trick or treat') at a Greysteel pub in County Derry.

Against the backdrop of the continued terrorism, it was their intensive, often
secret and deniable conversations, which eventually included representatives of
the British and Irish governments and the paramilitary (terrorist) groups, which
led to a memorandum called the Downing Street Declaration in December 1993.
As we saw on p. 172 civil servants played an important role in preparing the
ground for change. The declaration included 'the DONE principle that the people
of the island of Ireland, North and South, had the exclusive right to solve the
issues between North and South by mutual consent'.

Alderdice (pp. 164-166) reminds us that leaders depend on followers in much
the same way that followers depend on leaders. Real change only takes place
when both are in tune. By 1993, support for the extremists had waned to the point
where acts of violence undermined, rather than rallied, their support. From now
on, widespread commitment to conflict resolution was to transcend the old political allegiances.

PM Major said in his memoirs:

> The process was on a knife-edge. I think it would have broken down had
> not the Shankill and Greysteel tragedies intervened.
>
> (McKittrick & McVea 2001, p. 194)

Another factor favouring public support for the peace process may have been the increase in the rising standard of living which came about in NI during the 1980s and 1990s influenced by international economic inward investment and around the millennium, the influence of 'the Celtic Tiger' in the republic. Subsidies of public services in NI resulted in the highest rate of public sector employment in the United Kingdom. Northern Ireland's unemployment rate was at its lowest at 6% at this time. Economic security seems to have made it possible for people to rethink their previously rigid adherence to old sources of supposed security and consider new solutions to their problems.

On 31 August, 1994, the IRA called a ceasefire. The scene was now set for serious negotiations involving all the key people. Framework Documents for a settlement were published by the two governments in February 1995, and a twin-track process developed later in the year to address the three-stranded political agenda, and the problems associated with getting rid of the terrorist weapons – 'decommissioning'– a term meaning voluntary surrender of their war materials. In many ways, the key to the process was not just that it was inclusive of all the key parties, but also recognition that no settlement could be achieved through force. 'Consent' was the principal foundation for any agreement.

As in South Africa, the wider international community played a role too, particularly the United States of America and President Clinton. His first visit to Ireland in 1995 as president symbolised his priorities. He provided economic assistance, expertise, encouragement and mediation. His envoy, Senator George Mitchell, involved Northern Ireland politicians in a 1995 USA Conference for Trade and Investment to help address the economy and employment and open up opportunities for an improved way of life. Visits were arranged for Northern Ireland politicians to other parts of the world to see conflict resolution at work.

> People in any conflict will only begin to turn away from violence as a means of solving their predicament if they feel that there is an alternative way to address their grievances, and that the prize of peace is worth the price of peace. The community needs to be weary of war and prepared to accept an outcome which is less than their ideal – a compromise – for the sake of peace. Central to this is the rebuilding of the rule of law.
>
> (Alderdice, Personal Communication)

Changes in codes, prejudices and assumptions

> If there is ever to be a durable peace and genuine reconciliation, what is really needed is the decommissioning of mindsets in Northern Ireland.
>
> (Mitchell 1999, p. 37)

We saw, in chapter 1, how attachments to nationalist and religious bodies can resemble love relationships in their resistance to change, even when change is a logical way of achieving goals.

Alderdice gives us an insight on one of these occasions.

> Coming into that meeting it was absolutely clear to me that everybody was going to be quite frightened, because there was a lot of hype and a lot of reactionary unionist talk about these guys selling the people out, and so on. And I had a sense that some of the nationalists were very frightened – because although they kept saying, 'We want you guys to meet us', you know, saying it over and over, in actual fact they never expected they would. They'd been asking the unionists for something they never thought they'd get. So, I thought, what can one usefully say in a situation like this? ... But I thought, well, if I was working with a patient and I sensed something was going to be very frightening, for him, I would speak about it, I would say there was anxiety and what it was. Now, politicians can't go into a meeting and say, 'I'm frightened!', but what I could say was, 'We're all very frightened here today. Everybody's terrified because we're afraid we may be selling out our people into the hands of their traditional enemies. This would be a terrible thing to do. It's a burden weighing on us, and there are people outside the meeting who wish us harm. But remember there are many people outside here who are wishing us well'.
>
> (Lord Alderdice quoted by Graham Little 2009, pp. 135, 136)

Senator George Mitchell's approach to his job as chairman of the multi-party talks was vital. He did not bring his own solutions but listened patiently and carefully to the different parties, excluding no one, and created a process where parties felt able to bring their proposals to him in the presence of each other. He built such trust that when the parties had exhausted the process, they asked him to bring forward his proposals. This work, building a process to create new attachments and revise myths rather than conjure up a solution, was at the heart of the conflict resolution. It required skill and stamina and, just as in the preparatory phase, it took some years. There were many aspects to the negotiations. Fundamental principles of democracy and non-violence became known as the Mitchell principles. (Mitchell 1999 p. 35). Careful use of deadlines, gradual building of respectful behaviour (even in the clear absence of feelings of respect), devices to break through when there was deadlock, and the imaginative use of different formats for the talks were just a few of the skills needed in this key phase of the peace process. Likewise, as we saw on p. 174–175, John Hume and David Trimble were bringing about gradual reframing with their 'peace process language'. The resemblance of these activities to well-conducted psychotherapy is irresistible.

The 1998 Belfast (Good Friday) Agreement and its implementation

In the new-style assembly in Northern Ireland, everything would be proportional. Neither of the two top elected officials could act separately; they could act only jointly and by agreement supported by a series of complex and overlapping legal and political protections and veto arrangements so that nothing could be done that was unacceptable to a significant minority of the community. There was a North–South Ministerial Council (bringing together ministers) and North–South Executive Bodies (staffed by civil servants) from Northern Ireland and the Republic of Ireland to deal with areas such as agriculture, economic development, environmental protection and transport (an arrangement which had been suggested at Partition but never implemented). The British–Irish Secretariat and the Anglo–Irish intergovernmental arrangements largely remained, but to them was added the variable geometry of a new British-Irish Council bringing together not only ministers from London and Dublin, but also the administrations in Scotland, Wales and Northern Ireland, as well as the Isle of Man and the Channel Islands.

In May 1998, there was overwhelming support in referendums in both Northern Ireland (71%) and the Republic of Ireland (85%) for the Belfast Agreement. An election in June to the new Northern Ireland Assembly had elected a majority of pro-Agreement candidates. In July, the election of David Trimble (Ulster Unionist Party – UUP) as First Minister and Seamus Mallon SDLP as Deputy First Minister was a symbolic power-sharing arrangement alongside ongoing preparations to devolve power from London.

While this political process was gradually addressing and changing the 'sacred' values (pp. 37 and 178) of most former IRA members, it would have been surprising if there were not a few extremists who remained strongly attached to what they saw as the 'pure' doctrines of the past. Republican dissident groups, the Irish National Liberation Army, Continuity IRA and the Real IRA (formed in November 1997), opposed the Provisional's and the Official IRA's (Gerry Adams and Martin McGuinness) compromise in the Belfast Agreement, regarding it as a 'sell-out' to the cause of Irish unity. Alderdice recognises the courage that it took for Martin McGuiness to change course (pp. 165–168).

The Reals '... are not regarded as a shady new group, but a continuance of a hard-line and purist tradition within old-style republicanism'. A former Quartermaster-General of the Provisionals had brought with him weapons and support, goodwill, much infrastructure and generous donations from major American groups. In consequence, the Reals were well able to carry out a terrorist campaign (Dingley 2001, p. 456).

The attack in Omagh

Against the backdrop of the peace process, the greatest single act of terrorism in the 30 years of the Troubles happened on 15 August, 1998. A bomb planted by the Real IRA killed 29 people and injured 370 others (60 of them seriously), from both communities in Omagh, County Tyrone. Of the 29 deaths, 11 were under the age of 18 (and included two babies) and 12 were women, one of whom was 34 weeks pregnant with twins. The predominantly Catholic town's victims included

Protestants, Catholics, a Mormon, two Spanish children, two from Donegal in the Irish Republic, and an English-born boy also living in Donegal.

Dingley's careful analysis of the bomber's likely intentions led him to conclude that Omagh was chosen because it was an economic, administrative, legal and military centre and an attack on the British presence and rule as a whole. 'Like many terrorist bombings it was aimed to send a message of an ability to strike at the heart of its opponents and register ubiquity, as well as simply causing economic, material, and disruptive damage' (Dingley 2001, p. 462). It was also only 30 minutes to escape by car across the border to the republic.

The attackers stole a maroon Vauxhall Cavalier car in County Monaghan the week before. They fitted it with false Northern Irish number plates, loaded the boot with over 200 kg of home-made explosives, and placed the detonating charge of Semtex in an Addis lunch box. Two Real IRA members drove from Dundalk, in the Irish Republic, to Omagh, where they parked on Market Street on a busy Saturday afternoon. An accompanying scout car with two members provided the getaway.

The car bomb was detonated about 3.10 pm following three conflicting warnings locating the bomb successively at the Court House, at an unspecified location in Omagh, and on a non-existent Main Street 200 yards from the Court House. In the event, the bomb was in Market Street, to where police, acting on the first message, had moved people away from the Court House but closer to the bomb. Finding no place to park by the Court House, the bombers panicked, chose another convenient location, and attempted to correct their mistake, but it was too late.

The bodies of several victims were never found, such was the power of the blast. Further from the epicentre, the blast tore limbs off many people. Heat from the explosion caused severe burns. The blast sent shards of glass and metal slicing through civilians. Besides those affected directly, injured or bereaved, it impacted the wider community significantly (Online Support & Self Help Group (OSSHG), January 2013).

An emergency response was mounted by the police, army, emergency fire and NHS services and civilians. The wounded were taken to the nearby Tyrone County Hospital, where a skeleton Saturday casualty staff were operating in battle-like conditions. Army jeeps and helicopters transported some of the wounded to other hospitals in a general atmosphere of shock and chaos. Confusion arose between the Tyrone hospital, the temporary mortuary and the meeting centre. Some casualties were taken to distant hospitals, with the result that relatives did not hear of the death or injury of their loved ones until Sunday or Monday morning.

The perception

Omagh and its inhabitants were never to be the same again. It was a deeply scarring event with a traumatic impact on the individual and the collective psyche. There was universal condemnation. An amateur video of the immediate aftermath and news reports as beamed around the world. World leaders responded:

President Clinton said it was a 'barbaric act intended to wreck Ireland's aspirations for peace and reconciliation'. Pope John Paul II stated that 'blind violence is attempting to impede the difficult path of peace and productive harmony which most discerning people are convinced is possible'. President Mandela urged political leaders 'not to allow this repulsive act to deter them from peace'. (Edwards 2009, p. 70)

The response

Leading political figures from Northern Ireland, the republic and Great Britain, together with leading religious figures from the North and South of Ireland, visited Omagh. Solidarity, grieving and cross-community sympathy were promoted and demonstrated by senior politicians and religious figures. With the local clergy, all were united to give support and solace, to say prayers at wakes and to officiate at funeral services over the week; 16 funerals took place on one day and eight on Thursday, 20 August, 1998. First Minister, David Trimble, was cheered for breaking an Orange Order convention not to attend a Catholic funeral. On 3 September, President Clinton visited, and the First Lady laid a wreath (Edwards 2009, p. 73).

Although the Real IRA realised that they had made a mistake that would seriously undermine their cause, they accepted responsibility for the bomb and expressed regret that civilians had been killed. Their regret must have deepened when they saw how their violent act and slaughter of civilians had strengthened a peace process which they had hoped to end. The leaders of their official wing (the 32 CSM based in Dundalk) and their associates were immediately ostracised and publicly denounced. Names of those alleged to be responsible for the bomb appeared in the newspapers. Sinn Fein leaders joined in the condemnation, though this new position brought a mixed response from the public.

Atrocious and enduring physical injuries had been inflicted. Psychological consequences of bereavement, acute stress reactions and adjustment disorders with depression and anxiety disorders were understandably prevalent. Physical pain and psychological pain such as post-traumatic stress disorder and symptoms linked to the catastrophic trauma were inevitable consequences.

Maxwell, in charge of the RUC emergency response to the Omagh bomb, says: 'The time-honoured RUC method for getting through terrible experiences was to get drunk on whisky with colleagues: psychological counselling was for sissies. But whisky offered little protection from the Omagh experience. Years later, I met one policeman who had been in the control room since 3 pm onwards who could not speak of what he had heard without dissolving into tears. Some of those who helped that day were never able to return to a normal life, and none fully recovered. A policeman who had wandered up and down the street carrying a head had to be invalided out of the RUC' ... Maxwell himself had two years of therapy. (Edwards 2009, p. 51)

Northern Ireland has high levels of practising Christians in a fairly stable network of a consistent population. Much exchange of information and support is through family, relatives and neighbours and within the framework of their respective churches. Father Kevin Mullan led prayers in Market Street a week after the bomb. 50,000 attended the Act of Prayerful Reflection. In Omagh, the close-knit community and infrastructure of the church would respond to support the injured, alongside the emergence of support groups and services. For many, the provision of a safe place and a trustworthy other with whom the afflicted could feel secure enough to tell their story reduces and addresses some of the symptoms of post-traumatic stress disorder (PTSD). The National Institute for Clinical Excellence (NICE) 2005 guidelines state that 'practical and social support can play an important part in facilitating a person's recovery from PTSD, particularly immediately after the trauma'.

The Omagh Community Trauma and Recovery Team (OCTRT) came into force three days after the bomb attack. It developed outside existing NHS services, and consisted of mental health staff and included GPs and other services as a multi-agency response to mental health issues. It existed for three and a half years as an obvious first contact, and during that time 700 people were seen. A large proportion of them had stress and mental health issues.

The Omagh Support and Self-Help Group (OSSHG) was founded in August 1998 to act as a resource for the adversely affected. It formed a multi-denominational support group representing the diversity of the victims. In October, Michael Gallagher, whose son had been killed, was elected chair.

An Omagh Fund was started and when donations reached a million, trustees were appointed to manage the fund. Internationally known Irish talent contributed to the album *Across the Bridge of Hope*.

Within the OCTRT, the delivery of a form of cognitive therapy was in line with existing evidence of the effectiveness of trauma-focused psychological treatment for PTSD (National Institute for Clinical Excellence 2005). Findings from an uncontrolled study of this therapy delivered three months to two years after the bombing were associated with improvements in post-traumatic stress disorder as large as those normally observed with cognitive therapy in randomised controlled trials of non-terrorism-related PTSD. This indicated an effective treatment for mental health problems triggered by violence (Gillespie, Duffy, Hackmann & Clark 2002; Behaviour Research and Therapy, 40, pp. 345–357).

It is not unrealistic to guess that involvement in the peace process was itself therapeutic and that containment of the powerful impulses to violence was responsible for producing what Alderdice calls '… the creation of a context in which the disturbed thoughts, feelings and behaviour of all the groups involved, as well as the causes of the disturbance, can be addressed' (p. 55).

Legitimising authorities

While the perpetrators wanted the opposite, the Omagh bomb on 15 August, 1998, inspired further resolve and determination to see the peace process through. Within days of the atrocity, the few dissident groups which had opposed the Good

Friday Agreement announced ceasefires. For the first time in 30 years, all the paramilitary organisations in Northern Ireland declared a ceasefire or suspended military operations (Mitchell 1999, p. 184).

Dingley suggests the Real IRA's activities and terrorist threat had the counter-effect of strengthening Sinn Fein's position in peace negotiations as long as they adhered to their ceasefire. He refers to an August report in *The Independent* news-paper of Gerry Adams and Martin McGuinness's new role in comforting relatives of terrorism after the Omagh bomb. 'This helped to foster a statesmanlike image of Sinn Fein, encouraging the view that its peace process policy was based on courage, wisdom and discipline'(Dingley 2001, p. 462).

Senator George Mitchell had wisely pointed out to the participants at the sign-ing of the Belfast Agreement in April 1998 that in many ways the hard part was just beginning. Early arguments over the semantics of the 'permanence' or 'com-pleteness' of the IRA's cessation of violence were just indications of the difficul-ties to be faced all along the way. Implementation would indeed prove every bit as challenging as he had suggested. Many hurdles remained.

The wording of the Belfast Agreement had not been clear on the decommis-sioning of weapons. Meanwhile, the unionist parties were angry about the British government fulfilling its commitments to prisoners in advance of the IRA decom-missioning of weapons when there was no clear commitment 'in terms' from the IRA that 'their long war was over'.

The new power-sharing executive

> ... challenged the unionist mindset and caused turmoil with that com-munity – Paisley still saying 'No' as loudly as ever and Trimble con-stantly preoccupied with fighting battles inside his own party, which amounted to his leadership being continually questioned, challenged and undermined. A still-functioning IRA added to his problems, especially questions that arose out of Columbia, Castlereagh and Stormontgate.
>
> (Rowan 2008, p. 63)

Reversing polarisation

It is ironic that the two enduring moderate political parties representing most of the Catholic and Protestant communities seemed to lose the support of their elec-torates later in the peace process. While the SDLP, led by John Hume and the Official Unionist Party (OUP), then led by David Trimble, were painfully engag-ing in the long peace process and their parties were elected to share power in 1998, their rivals for power were steadfast in their refusal to compromise. Hume and Trimble were recognised with a joint Nobel Laureate for peace in 1998. Without a hint of irony, Hume and Trimble celebrated the award with a visit to an arms factory to meet with workers and staff.

What happened next was an extraordinary shift in the positions of the previ-ously non-compromising parties. Both nationalist-leaning Sinn Fein and Ian

Paisley's (anti-Good Friday Agreement) Democratic Unionist Party (DUP) extended their support bases within their communities to become the largest parties after the elections in 2003. The DUP had always championed Ulster Protestant values and was still saying no to any power-sharing deal, while Sinn Fein was distancing itself from the provisionals and moving towards a place in mainstream politics. It took some years to achieve the necessary compromises to form a power-sharing executive in a devolved government in 2007.

In chapter 12, Alderdice discusses the formation of the Independent Monitoring Commission (IMC) in 2004 and his role in addressing the real obstacle of decommissioning, which had made no progress in six years. He also outlines the dynamic or interdependence between the leader and his or her followers. There seems to have been recognition that to gain power the new leaders needed to revise, if not abandon, their basic assumptions and offer their followers a new way out of the impasse.

While there is much speculation about this turn of events, Rowan (2008) describes the politics behind the inevitable toppling of Trimble and his OUP after the early power-sharing attempt in 1998 and the negotiations and events that led to the unlikely bed partners of the DUP and Sinn Fein:

> The DUP was a different party, however, and Paisley, like Adams, was a dominant leader. His people, or the majority of them at least, were going to follow him along whichever road he chose to walk; that was Paisley's huge advantage over Trimble'(Rowan, 2008 p. 65).

Rowan comments on this:

> ... We began to think the unthinkable: to consider the suddenly real possibility of a deal between Paisley and the Provos. The first time I said it aloud, it sounded so ridiculous – it had failed to work with Trimble, so how could it possibly work with Paisley? (Rowan, 2008, p.67).

For the Rev Ian Paisley, who had established himself at the intersection of religion and politics from the early 1970s, always in opposition to other leaders and shockingly anti-Catholic, this represented a dramatic shift (Mitchell 1999, p. 51).

Once the decommissioning process was confirmed, the republicans accepted policing by the new Police Service of Northern Ireland.

> The 'long war' was over ... The IRA was emerging from its war into the political process. Soon, one member of its (IRA) Army Council would be in government with the man who had vowed to smash Sinn Fein. There had been no sackcloth, no ashes, no surrender or photographs (of decommissioning), no victory or defeat, but peace and politics had finally been given shape through once unthinkable compromises. The Paisley-Provo deal was beginning to happen ...
>
> (Rowan 2008, p. 76)

In Rowan's role in providing a journalistic assessment, he was struck by

> how little the two sides knew about each other and just how far apart they
> were … That questioning from all sides told me something; I began to
> believe that this thing could work, that a deal could be done (Rowan,
> 2008, p. 68).

Theirs became the leading parties in the 2007 election for the Northern Ireland
Assembly and established the DUP's Ian Paisley and Sinn Fein's Martin Mc
Guinness, as, respectively, First Minister and Deputy First Minister in the assem-
bly. The chemistry (i.e., attachment) between the two men was so powerful that
some commentators called them 'the Chuckle Brothers' for their easy bonhomie.
For the year they demonstrated a good relationship – not only could they work
together, they seemed to like each other, though they never once shook hands.
Praise was heaped on their partnership and leadership skills.

Dudley Edwards is rather cynical about Paisley's virtues as a peacemaker and
points instead to how he split every organisation with which he was involved, first
by founding his Free Presbyterian Church of Ulster in 1951 and then his split with
unionism to found his own party, the DUP, in 1971. Ms Dudley Edwards suggests
that Paisley responded to the modernisers in his party and ultimately went into
government with Sinn Fein against the principles that he had espoused for years
to avoid splitting his party or being toppled. Ms Dudley Edwards suggests that his
wish to be the ultimate leader won out. She comments:

> What made it more piquant was that among the laudatory chorus were
> Gerry Adams and Martin McGuinness, two brutal former terrorists, who
> also saw the light rather late in the day.
>
> (Edwards 2007)

Paisley's sitting in government alongside Sinn Fein for the year would have required
a significant psychological cognitive shift on his part. Perhaps his growing knowledge
of the 'enemy' helped to inform and change his beliefs and shake a lifelong prejudice.
Perhaps the ultimate reward of leadership after 30 years of stalemate caused him to
put opportunity above principles to emerge as the consummate politician who changed
his direction for the greater good. Clarification may come in his forthcoming autobi-
ography at age 86. No doubt more frank accounts will eventually follow.

Prejudice, however, flows just below the surface and has its annual release in
the marching season when the historical victory in 1690 of Protestant King Billy
(King William III) over the Irish Catholic forces (assisted by the French) is celebrated. The parades are deeply polarising. They could also represent and demonstrate the insecure attachment and unease the participants (a small but persistent
section of the unionist and loyalist population) have with both the new Northern
Ireland and the old union. For sure, each year's marching season does little to
strengthen the new fragile reality.

University education and some other higher education facilities were in the past the first opportunity for many in Northern Ireland to experience mixed education and meet 'the other side' in a more informal way. Positive contact and education are known to reduce prejudice. The integrated schools movement has been desegregating education, exposing students to contemporaries they would not otherwise meet in an effort to reduce prejudice. While there are a few entering third-level education who have only had mixed religion and mixed gender education, it is disappointing that they often keep to their co-religionists at the secondary level.

Retaliation or restoration?

Counsellors and cognitive therapists are familiar with the value of goal setting and monitoring. We saw on pages 176–7 how the IMC provided a neutral body to monitor and contain acts of violence over a period of seven years. Their regular reports ensured that targets would be met. They also ensured that successes were recognised and failures rectified.

Over the years, since 1998, there has been a gradual decline in the number of deaths attributed to security problems in NI. Conflict-related deaths per annum dropped to single figures for the first time in 2004 and have remained below six in every year since (Police Service of Northern Ireland, 2012).

Despite the demands of the bereaved families and others for justice, no one was ever convicted for the deaths caused by the Omagh bomb. Charges brought in the Irish Republic failed to produce convictions. One man accused of murder was cleared by a court in 2007. It is reported that both the provisionals and Sinn Fein know who the bombers are. There was widespread criticism of the RUC's handling of the investigation. An impartial report by the police ombudsman made several recommendations to improve police performance.

Meanwhile, families of ten of the dead decided to pursue the suspects thorough the civil courts, where the burden of proof is lower, taking as their motto 'For evil to triumph, all that is necessary is for good men to do nothing'. They succeeded, and four men were held responsible for the bombing.

> HALLELUJAH FOR JUSTICE. For 11 years – backed by a Mail campaign – they refused to give up. Yesterday, these Omagh Families won an historic court case against the Real IRA bombers who slaughtered their loved ones … proving ordinary people CAN take on the terrorists.
>
> (*Daily Mail*, June 9, 2009)

Long-term psychological consequences of the Troubles

Kapur writes about his involvement with the support groups for the Trauma and Recovery Team (Kapur 2002 p. 317 from 1998. He describes the therapeutic response as a watershed in Northern Ireland's state of mind. For the first time, the psychological aftermath of trauma was being addressed, which, alongside dialogue and discourse, was becoming a new way of approaching problems in Northern Ireland. He argues that up until then Northern Ireland had remained in the distress and denial phase of the Troubles and was only now waking up to the level of destruction it had inflicted on itself (Kapur 2002, p. 316). Omagh Health & Social Services established a 'Reparative Group' to talk about the trauma of the past with international input bringing outside influence to an insular society (Kapur 2002, p. 327).

Bearing in mind the evidence that wars are commonly associated with overall declines in the use of psychiatric services, published studies in the late 1980s which showed the limited impact the Troubles had on the province's psychiatric services, with exceptions when the scale and numbers from outrages such as Enniskillen (1987) and Omagh (1998) overwhelmed services. Curran describes an audit in 2000 of his hospital's catchment area (some 10 square miles in North and West Belfast) containing half the city's population of Belfast and accounting for a third of all deaths, a third of all injuries and a third of all violent incidents in the province in 30 years where only 6% of psychiatric referrals to the services were precipitated by violence-related issues. But, as we shall see, this should not be assumed to indicate that the Troubles had no influence on the communal psyche. Curran speculates that possible mechanisms for this lack of presenting to services is denial, habituation styles of coping, social cohesion within sectarianism, and a finding that coping is more related to a person's perception and appraisal of violence than its actual level. Curran refers to Cairns and Wilson's suggestion that denial is a mechanism for coping with the stress of continuing political violence (Curran & Miller 2001).

The Trauma, Health and Conflict survey in Northern Ireland in 2008 grouped individual coping methods into the following categories:

'Get on with things'
  'Keeping busy and other methods'
  'Nothing was talked about'
  'Unhelpful ways of coping – substance use'
  A common pervasive outlook of Northern Irish people was that the Troubles were seen as 'normal'.
  (Ferry, Bolton, Bunting, Devine, McKann & Murphy, 2008, pp. 52–54)

In the geographical areas of actual street violence during that early phase of the campaign, the levels of suicide and depression went down, but in the penumbra – the areas around the scenes of violence, which heard the news, and feared what could happen – anxiety mounted, and the prescription of benzodiazepines is said to have risen.

In the early Troubles, there was an inverse relationship between homicide and suicide which later came into line with the trend in the United Kingdom in the 1990s where, while the overall suicide rate was reducing, there was an increase in suicide among younger men.

Later, evidence emerged that social and psychological difficulty from the Troubles years were emerging as a form of negative peace dividend. Curran detected that 'curiously in more recent years, when the violence has reduced somewhat, a rising trend in people seeking acknowledgement of victimhood'.

(Curran & Miller, 2001)

During the peace process, various reports were commissioned to research and make recommendations to address the legacy of 30 years of conflict. The Bloomfield Report, 'We Will Remember Them', published in April 1998, made several recommendations, among which were the establishment of a Commission for Victims and Survivors (NICVS) and a Forum (established in 2008 and 2009, respectively). A review carried out in 2011 made recommendations on fair assessment of need and funding and created a New Commission for Victims and Survivors in 2012 to ensure that resources were properly targeted. The Department of Health and Social Security report in 1998, 'Living with the Trauma of the Troubles', focused on the development of services to meet the social and psychological needs of individuals affected by civil unrest in Northern Ireland.

The research, reports and their recommendations were timely in thinking about and responding to the devastation after the Omagh bomb. The spontaneous creation of the OCTRT and the therapeutic effectiveness was consolidated and led to the establishment of the Northern Ireland Trauma and Transformation Centre (NI TTC 2002–2011). It had a province-wide remit to provide and deliver services to all victims of the Northern Ireland Troubles. Training and research in collaboration with the University of Ulster (UOU) resulted in a skilled workforce and a number of published papers on the impact of traumatic events on the mental and physical health of the adult population. Thus, there was a resource to help the further development and commissioning of services.

Primary data from the NI Study of Health and Stress (NISHS) clearly indicates that traumatic events associated with the conflict have been a prominent feature in the lives of the adult population and are associated with adverse mental health outcomes (Ferry et al., 2008; Ferry et al., under review). Among the striking findings from this body of research is that Northern Ireland has the highest rates of PTSD among comparable estimates produced from other countries. The adult population has an estimated 8.8% of individuals who have had PTSD at some point in their lifetime, while 5.1% had PTSD in the previous year. In addition, people are more likely to develop a range of other conditions such as depression, other anxiety disorders and alcohol problems, for example (Ferry et al., under review). There is a suggestion of a significant association between the experience of trauma and chronic physical health conditions (Ferry et al., 2008).

The economic impact of PTSD is reported. A third study focuses on the needs of the older adult population following earlier research which showed elevated exposure to traumatic events among individuals aged 45–64.

In a therapeutic controlled trial of cognitive therapy for PTSD related to the conflict, 58 consecutive patients attending the Northern Ireland Centre for Trauma and Transformation) between August 2003 and September 2004, often with co-morbidity and often having failed other treatments, were randomly allocated to receive immediate cognitive therapy or to a 12-week wait followed by cognitive therapy. Cognitive therapy was determined to be an effective treatment for PTSD related to terrorism and other civil conflict. Patients allocated to immediate therapy showed significant and substantial reductions in the symptoms of PTSD and depression and noticeable improvements in self-reported work-related disability, social disability, and family-related disability. In contrast, patients allocated to a no-treatment (waiting list) control condition showed no change. A previous finding that continuing physical problems had been noted to predict a less favourable outcome in those traumatised by the Omagh bomb was not replicated in the controlled study. Higher levels of depression than in other studies were particularly difficult to treat (Duffy, Gillespie & Clark 2007).

Conclusion

Bloody Sunday and the Omagh bomb were two 'terrorist' attacks which had the opposite results from those intended by the ones who perpetrated them. Bloody Sunday confirmed the injustice and hostility of the British forces and fed support for the old myths. In Omagh, the plan to undermine Protestant/British control by demonstrating its vulnerability confirmed the injustice and the hostility of the terrorist cause towards a peace process that had brought hope to many. In both cases, the actions that resulted at each point in the International Work Group's cycle in chapter 6 confirmed expectations based on this psychological model. Thirty years on, a war-weary society reacted differently to the Omagh bomb, providing an infrastructure over the following 15 years to heal and repair the wounds. The peace process seems to have succeeded because it was inclusive and gave time for respect to develop in leaders, the public and journalists on both sides. A turning point took place when those with large followings of attached supporters realised that changing some aspects of their assumptive worlds would lead to rewards rather than punishment, and so reflection allowed adjustment of core beliefs. It took many years for new ideas to spread from a few individual leaders to a large proportion of the population.

Elected politicians now share leadership and demonstrate a capacity for compromise at variance with their previous positions of 'No, Never' and the use of force. A new style of communication has been offered to the electorate which they can follow. Peace has been achieved through inclusion and compromise, though deep-seated beliefs and prejudices on both sides remain. A further task is to prevent myths of virtue and vice obstructing the necessary respect for oneself and others as trust has to be extended to 'the other side' to reduce the risk of cycles of hate, revenge and violence. Responsible leadership has to some extent modified mutual suspicion, though it may take some generations for this to filter down and its full effects to be felt.

Alderdice identifies the supporting and necessary infrastructure in reform of policing and the criminal justice system, the release of prisoners, the decommissioning of illegal weapons, and demilitarisation which were necessary. On the other hand, the wide-ranging reforms made by anti-discrimination measures, a whole range of commissions, ombudsmen, tribunals and equality bodies aimed to redress the former imbalance have been well received. Less contentious but equally central were the resources given to education, community relations and economic development, especially in targeting social need in underprivileged areas.

For 30 years, individuals and groups have adopted various coping styles to enable them to deal with the stress of conflict. As the province emerged from the Troubles around the millennium, research into the morbidity of the population, along with the commissioning of services, is helping to address the extent of physical pain and psychological consequences of the Troubles A change of attitudes, beliefs and assumptions is a challenge, though with the added benefit that a change of cognition may mitigate possible trans-generational transmission of 'tribal' myths and allow difference to be respected rather than be a cause of suspicion.

15

AFTER THE GENOCIDE

The peace process in Rwanda

Colin Murray Parkes and Peter Hall

We saw, in chapter 8, how, on 6 April, 1994, a terrorist act, the shooting down of an aircraft containing the presidents of Rwanda and Burundi, triggered genocide and led to the deaths of up to 800,000 persons in the course of 100 days. When Colin Murray Parkes visited Rwanda a year after the massacres, he wrote:

> In Rwanda the rule of law has broken down. People no longer sleep securely in their beds at night. Neither their own government nor the United Nations were able to protect them from the most appalling horror imaginable. They know that it could happen again and it probably will.
>
> (Parkes CM, 1998)

At that time, sporadic violence was still continuing, and a curfew was imposed during the hours of darkness. Gunshots and explosions could be heard from time to time, and UN observers reported numerous abuses of human rights about which they could do little more than write a report to the secretary-general. There were no police, and the observers feared that reporting attacks to the army would only lead to further abuses. Tens of thousands of people were awaiting trial in grossly overcrowded prisons, and there was no judicial system in operation.

A cruel irony of the genocide is how the extremism underlying its instigation was consolidated by the very international peace process that was intended to end the conflict. As we saw on p. 119, there is good reason to believe that it was planned and instigated by a powerful clique, many of whom stood to lose their power and their freedom if the Arusha Accords had been implemented. The assassination of the president, the moderate prime minister, and their supporters created the power vacuum that facilitated the coup d'etat, as well as triggering an appalling genocide, and the successful campaign by General Kagame's army (the Rwandese Patriotic Front–RPF) that ended the genocide. But peace processes are not always doomed to fail. Eighteen years after the RPF took control in Rwanda, not only has there been no recurrence of major massacres but, by all accounts, the country has become one of the most peaceful and rapidly developing states in Africa.

Javan: 'Just now I see a change, now its good, its very different. We have peace, we have security there is no problem. If I go to see my father after he was dead. I still remember that [meaning he is still haunted by the image of his father's dead body]. Now its OK, my health good ... We try to forget the genocide.'

Later in the day, apropos of nothing, he suddenly said:

They cut my sister's throat here [*pointing towards his right mastoid area and sliding his finger forward and down*]. It took her two days to die.

In this chapter, we examine how the apparent recovery came about and what psychological influences may have played a part in breaking the cycle of violence. Given the large number of possible factors, and the lack of solid evidence to validate various claims, our conclusions cannot be definitive. Nor can we be sure that the peace will hold. This said, the evidence is fascinating, and the reader will decide whether or not our guesses are justified,

Breaking the Cycle of Violence

It is useful to make use again of the model of the cycle of violence introduced in chapter 6. That chapter showed how the responses at each point in the cycle could aggravate and perpetuate the cycle. Here, we attempt to show how, in Rwanda, interventions in the cycle at each of the same points may have helped to break the cycle. At every point, we consider the viewpoint of three parties, the Tutsi victors (made up of survivors and returned exiles), the Hutu survivors (who still form the majority of the population), and the rest of the world. At each point, decisions were made. What were the consequences of those decisions?

1. The trauma

Our analysis starts at the point where, in July 1994, the RPF had driven the defenders into an enclave in the southwest of the country and General Kagame had accepted the Turquoise Zone and declared a ceasefire. Rwanda was in ruins, and huge numbers of indigenous Tutsi had been massacred. The RPF had indisputably carried out revenge killings on the Hutu population, most of whose own army had taken refuge in the Democratic Republic of Congo (DRC); fields had not been tilled, the police and judiciary had been wiped out, and the country was desperate for food and other resources.

Looking to the future, a correspondent for Kenya's *Daily Nation* wrote:

... the new guerrilla-controlled authority will require public acceptance to rule without wielding the big stick. Can they suppress a Hutu majority and conduct the business of government as if nothing is amiss? Could they possibly hold against Hutu military incursions if the population they ruled gave saccour [sic] to the enemy hiding rebels, feeding them and giving them vital information?

(Quoted by Alozie, 2007, p. 221)

Peace had been born out of the barrels of guns; it was, you might say, a 'victor's peace', but, as John Milton pointed out in 1645:

Who overcomes
  By force, hath overcome but half his foe.

What could be done to prevent the remorseless cycle from turning again?

2. How was this situation perceived?

Within Rwanda, both Tutsi and Hutu saw the situation as a disaster. Nearly every person met by Peter Hall (PH) and Colin Murray Parkes (CMP) during that first year had lost members of their families, often in the most horrific circumstances, and even the victorious troops had little cause to celebrate. To the Hutu majority, it was, no doubt, confirmation of their worst fears; the enemy had conquered, devils now ruled the land, and the rest of the world had let it happen.

The Special Representative of the Secretary of the United Nations, Sharyar Khan, visiting a hospital in Kigali for the first time, on 5 July, 1994, wrote:

I have never witnessed such horror, such vacant fear in the eyes of the patients, such putrid stench. I did not throw up, I did not even cry: I was too shocked. I was silent. My colleagues who had lived through the massacres were hardened: they had seen worse, much worse.

(Khan & Robinson, 2001)

General Dallaire, who quotes this passage, adds:

Khan was wrong when he wrote that the veterans of the genocide had become hardened to such things. We were simply putting off our feelings until later.

(Dallaire, 2003)

Albert Najambe was in Belgium:

My sister called on the phone and told me everybody has been killed, I thought of my parents and my young brothers and my cousin … I was feeling helpless and despair and guilty … The feeling of guilt for your loved ones, you know that you couldn't do anything. It was very hard.

As soon as possible, he returned to Rwanda.

> I found my sister, who survived. When she saw me she shook like this. She told me the details. I asked if there was hope that one of the children had survived ... [His baby had been left in the care of his mother, but both had been murdered] She was almost the last one to be killed, and she was a very good Christian. I told [my sister] I wanted to know the details, it was very important to me, my imagination would be worse. She told me mum was taken with the complicity of her own husband, a Hutu. My sister took almost 30 minutes, she was shaking, she gave me some details and told me mother's body had been put in a pit latrine ... Later I went again, they had begun reburying [the bodies] ... and we went to the pit latrine and it was only bones and clothes. I took her skull in my hands (*cradles an imagined skull*) ... And I tried to comfort my sister to be strong [but] I was the first to lose control and crying and shouted at people.

The few international journalists who stayed in Rwanda between the evacuation of expatriates in mid-April and the RPF's taking control of Kigali in early July did their best to describe accurately the terrible events taking place. The blame for any failure of interpretation of the significance of events lies more with their offices in Paris, London, Washington and Ottawa – and news agencies are careful about their use of words. The first time Agence France Presse (AFP) said 'genocide' was on 20 April after Human Rights Watch used the term, and then on 28 April, quoting Médecins Sans Frontières, and again on 3 May, quoting the Council of Europe. (Chaon, 2007). After news teams returned in large numbers, they focussed on the thousands of fleeing refugees who became cholera victims, thus lessening the impact of the enormity of the most recent massacres in eastern Rwanda.

3. What was the response?

The French and Belgian troops had been replaced by a small number of unarmed UN observers. By August, most of the Hutu army had fled, and the RPF were in control of the whole of Rwanda. The world had woken up to the horror of the situation, and aid was streaming into Rwanda from numerous government and non-governmental organisations (NGOs). Displaced persons (DP) camps had been set up to house over two million refugees in this and neighbouring countries, and medical care was provided. It was only after the Interahamwe began to dominate the camps and kill their opponents that the NGOs realised that they were supporting large numbers of genocidaires. And soon after frightened Hutus streamed out of the country, waves of Tutsi exiles were trickling in to take their places. Many had joined the RPF, and others were eager to be of help in supporting the survivors of the genocide.

The harm done by the massacres was not only physical; as we saw on pages 88–90, terrorist attacks can also lead to psychiatric disorders. PH, accompanied by a psychiatrist, Andrew Carney, visited Rwanda from 11 to 23 July, on behalf of Physicians for Human Rights [UK]. They carried out a survey (unpublished) of 248 adults and adolescents in the small towns of Rwamagana and Gahini, which lie south east of Kigali. This area was chosen as representing one of the more settled parts of the country. The massacres had persisted here for only two weeks, and it had been free from the conflict for nearly three months before they arrived.

Eleven of the respondents were RPF soldiers, the remainder being civilians, either internally displaced or inhabitants of the two towns. With only a handful of exceptions, the respondents were born within Rwanda: 64.5% of those questioned were women, 22.2% were widows or widowers, and 48.4% were single. They completed a well-established questionnaire used in the West (The General Health Questionnaire), and some parts of Africa, to measure levels of psychological disturbance in the community (Goldberg & Williams, 1988). This had been translated into Kinyarwandan.

The overall scores were high, with a mean of 9.66. Close to 90% exceeded the cut-off score of 7.00, which is established in the West as a measure of psychiatric 'caseness', that is, the critical score for diagnosing a psychiatric disorder. Many respondents reported symptoms, notably headache, appetite and digestive symptoms, and others reported difficulty in concentration, memory and judgement. While the questionnaire does not enquire about nightmares, many reported them either spontaneously, or on further questioning about their responses.

The investigators concluded that '… it is clear that unless resources are found to address the psychological needs of this profoundly traumatised society, there is a high risk of further bloodshed' (Carney & Hall, personal communication).

A similar study by Staub, Pearlman, Gubin and Hagengimana (2005) using the Harvard Trauma Questionnaire was carried out in 1999, five years later, at a time when Hutu had launched border attacks on Rwanda. It showed elevated scores of traumatic stress similar to those found in survivors of the Khmer Rouge Genocide. Despite being the victors, Tutsis still had significantly higher traumatic stress scores than Hutus (t (120) = 4.852, p < 0.01).

Throughout the war, each side had been preoccupied by the struggle to survive; now they had exhausted both their economic and psychological reserves. Faith in the lynchpins of security, their families, their communities, their state and their God were shattered, and they were now forced to rely on outsiders whom they had little reason to trust. But Rwanda had no alternative but to change.

The United Nations Children's Fund (UNICEF) performed a valuable role in organising camps for the 95,000 surviving orphans and displaced children who were separated from or bereaved of their families (United Nations Children's Fund, 1995) and, in October 1994, introduced a Trauma Recovery Program (TRP) led by a young American social worker, Leila Gupta. The Rwandese TRP staff recruited by Dr. Gupta had been living abroad at the time of the genocide; they included Eugenie Mukanohele (school teacher), Albert Najambe (child psychologist), and Charles Karakezi (psychology trainer). All had suffered multiple losses of family members; this meant that they were repeatedly reminded of their own losses.

> Eugenie: 'Working with children was difficult because of the stories that came out. At the end of the day I had a headache – it felt about to explode. But I had to help them … you know, at first I cried because of all the stories – "Why, Why this?" Other times I was helped by the fact it was common [shared].'
>
> Albert: 'It became bad a year later for me. Late 1995, I'd just divorced, it was too much for me. Nothing appeared on my face, I was still smiling and doing my job, to feel more alive, but years later I had blood pressure problems and diabetes, it was just too much. It (my marriage) was the only thing left. It felt like the Titanic – now what for? I didn't ask for help. I thought this is the kind of thing you just manage. [Didn't UNICEF help?] No. I did not ask for help. I knew what it is, and I thought I would get over it. The more you feel it, the more you work out, help others. It had worked well before. I became a workaholic. But still I love it.'

Even so, their participation in the project gave meaning to their lives and helped them gain trust when helping others in the schools and orphanages.

The TRP contained three main elements: (1) they trained a network of trauma advisers who then selected and trained social agents, including teachers, social workers, health providers, orphanage 'centre' staff, from across Rwanda, who would support children and their families or carers; (2) they helped set up a National Trauma Recovery Centre in Kigali to provide more expert help to those requiring it; and (3) a public education and support programme in the form of radio broadcasts in the Kinyarwandan language. By 1996, the TRP had employed 6,193 social agents, who came from many professions and included a number of clergy and religious Christians. In the end, they had taken part in integrated community programmes involving 145,000 children and families in all parts of Rwanda (United Nations Childrens Fund, 1997).

> Eugenie: 'It was a good programme, we did a lot and we helped people understand what was happening to them, that they were not going crazy.'

In 1997, an independent evaluation of the impact of the programme on children concluded that 'the training of social agents was in many ways an appropriate intervention. The outreach was significant and there is little doubt that this training had an effect to the benefit of many children' (Jensen, Neugebouer et al., 1997). The main problem was the paucity of professional trauma specialists needed by the many children and adults with lasting evidence of traumatic stress disorders. To this day (July 2012), there are only four Rwandese psychiatrists working in Rwanda, although they make good use of a wide range of other mental health professionals.

Even so, the trauma advisers reported how good it was to see the children 'come alive' when they were permitted to draw pictures and to express their thoughts and feelings about the horrific events that they had witnessed. Gupta prepared, and UNICEF published, an educational booklet in Kinyarwandan using these pictures as illustrations.

The interaction between the Rwandese who made up the bulk of the 'carers' and the professional psychologists, psychiatrists, counsellors, priests and others who arrived in Rwanda from the West in the hope of helping was crucial to the success or failure of the enterprise. But they were not all welcome.

> Albert: 'We had colleagues from other countries, and we would say "They are just mercenaries. They cannot understand ... Short-term finance and leaving to play golf. They do it for the money".'

No doubt we were better paid than the Rwandans, and most of us were aware of our ignorance of Rwanda, but most of us welcomed the cultural awareness of the Rwandese psychologists, social workers, and others with whom we worked at UNICEF, and we respected their special knowledge and skills. They, in turn, appreciated learning about traumatic stress, complications of bereavement, and intervention strategies that had been successfully implemented in other war zones.

Their capacity to repress emotions may have helped the Rwandese to survive the extremes of trauma without 'breaking down', and some found that they could redirect their repressed discontent into worthwhile activities, but there were others in whom it was causing problems. Only by avoiding painful topics could powerful feelings be avoided, but, as a result, issues remained unresolved. Anger, which is a natural reaction to bereavement, is particularly problematic following man-made deaths. In Rwanda, there was good cause for rage; it was dangerous to repress it and dangerous to express it.

The main cultural difference was that, whereas in the West it is severe and pro-longed grief that is the most common complication of bereavement, in Rwanda it was repression and avoidance of grief that was causing difficulties. This confirmed one of Parkes' observations that repression and avoidance of grief are most common in countries at war and in warlike races (Parkes CM, 1998).

It is important to make a distinction between traumatic stress and grief. The experience of traumatic stress was producing emotional numbness, haunting memories, dreams and 'flashbacks' which were so painful that they led to avoidance of reminders of the deaths and other horrific events. As we shall see, pp. 217, many people were suffering from post-traumatic stress disorder (PTSD), for which psychological treatments were only beginning to becoming available.

> Claudine: 'Often, at night, images crowd in as dreams. I see faces again that look at me without saying a word; and when I wake up, I feel disquiet

214

between me and those who were cut [up] … I am very shaken by this curse, but I bottle it up within, I stop it from spilling out – I remain calm for the children.'

(Hatzfeld, 2000, pp. 148, 150)

Recovery has been aided by universal health insurance and a national policy for mental health.

Dr Naasson Munyandamutsa, a Rwandese psychiatrist and vice-director of the Institute for Research and Dialogue for Peace (IRDP), has been in medical practice in Rwanda since 1989 and has been studying issues of security and insecurity during much of that time. He was working at the University of Geneva when the genocide took place. In 1994, he returned to find his family dead and decided to remain in Rwanda in order to help traumatised people. He agrees with CMP that a big problem after the genocide was caused by the repression of feelings.

Naasson: 'Many people never had the freedom to express themselves, to think about their relationships. They keep quiet … They need time and space to think together.'

Rwandese social agents all agreed that helping people to tell their story in their own words, to cry, to grieve, and, in a safe place, to express their anger and bitterness enabled them to heal their trauma. Other techniques included journal writing, drawing (particularly with children), role play, and small group discussions, all of which have been found useful in subsequent research into the treatment of traumatic and complicated bereavements (Boelen et al., 2003; Shear et al., 2005). It was hard for people to recover purpose and meaning in a world whose structures of meaning had collapsed. Naasson calls this 'Participatory Research', by which he means an interactive process by which people work together to solve problems. He has tried to create safe places '… where they can change progressively and where it is safe to disagree'.

At the time of the first anniversary of the genocide, Dr Gupta invited one of us (CMP) to speak on the radio, and at a National Training Seminar which was attended by members of the government, local community and international implementing organisations. CMP spent several days before the conference talking to Rwandese people and preparing his teaching materials. Although his lecture at the conference was marred by poor translation, it was well supported by another speaker, a Rwandan psychiatrist, Athenase Hagengimana, who had already found that some of the techniques of bereavement and trauma counselling used in the West were valuable in helping Rwandese people.

Before Parkes left Rwanda, he had prepared a revised version of his lecture that was subsequently translated into Kinyarwandan and circulated to the counsellors/para-professionals of the TRP. His last duty in Kigali was to speak on the radio for half an hour about the psychological consequences of traumatic bereavements and the ways in which they could aggravate cycles of violence. This was part of the TRP's regular broadcasts on topics that included the identifying of trauma symptoms, reassuring people about the normality of their reactions, and offering simple, cul-turally appropriate, expressive techniques that included story-telling, praying, drawing and singing songs to facilitate coping with traumatic memories and grief.

Since then Rwanda has put much effort in getting trained trauma counsellors, psychologists, nurses, and other mental health professionals to help in the process. It is not yet possible to disentangle the effects of the various psychological, social and spiritual interventions that were undertaken. These included elements of trauma counselling, bereavement counselling, anger management, cognitive restructuring, and care at both individual and group levels.

A good example of a programme that attempted to combine these elements is that developed and evaluated by Staub et al. (2005). It contained elements that were widely adopted in the TRP and provides evidence suggesting that psychoso-cial interventions not only reduce the high levels of traumatic stress that were still prevalent five years after the massacres, but that it may well have contributed to reconciliation between the tribes. By 2007, 14 years after the genocide, another study of 400 widows and orphans of the genocide found only 8% with continuing prolonged grief disorder and similar levels of clinical depression, PTSD and clin-ical anxiety, most of them in the same individuals who had several diagnoses (i.e., high levels of co-morbidity) (Schaal, Dusengizemungu et al., 2012).

> Eugenie: 'I think many people are recovering. Many, like me, realise that
> it is no good dwelling on the past.'

Once a measure of security, or stability, had been achieved, the need for counsel-ling diminished, but UNICEF and other organisations continued more focused support for orphans, numerous sufferers from AIDS (including many of the women who had been raped) and the problems that faced the many families who were now returning from displaced persons camps and the neighbouring countries and needed to be reintegrated in their communities.

Along with all the interventions by outsiders came what can best be described as an Anglo-American zeitgeist, an optimism that stemmed from many years of peace, opulence and security, in a world where violence and violent death is newsworthy because it is exceptional and most people can expect to survive into old age. By the very act of visiting Rwanda and sharing our limited knowledge, we offered hope to this benighted nation that they too could escape from the traps of their own history. In accepting our material aid and personal care, they must have hoped that some of our good fortune would also rub off on them. But it was people directly affected by the genocide who recognised and found a solution to one of the most important prob-lems, the loss of personal care and attachment among people bereft by the genocide.

Ngoga, who was an orphan, found himself one of 24 children in the care of an uncle.

> Ngoga: 'Someone can give you whatever you want, but no one can
> replace your mother and father and brothers and sisters.'

He joined an organisation Association des Etudiants Et Éleves Rescapés Du Genocide, (AEERG) for orphans of the genocide. These children supported each other and

> ... we started to create 'Artificial Families' – We had a mother and father and children, ten to twenty members would choose our own Mum. I started to have someone the same age as me as my Dad and my Mum [Could you touch and cuddle each other like Mum?] Yes, Yes, and when we got our school reports we had to discuss them with our 'Mum' or 'Dad' ... We say it was artificial and we could not imagine that working, but we began to feel that we had a real family, not an artificial family. The family even had a name that was our belief. For instance, if the name of the family is 'Chesare' that means 'Hope'. We had to strive for hope. It kept the belief alive.

As the years passed, these surrogate families stay together and even attend graduations, marriages and other family events.

The idea that others can substitute for the missing members of families has also been taken up by AVEGA, the Association for Widows of the Rwandan Genocide, whose chief executive, Odette Kayirere, says that the genocide

> Odette: '... left most of them without children, without direction, and AVEGA gives new hope. To create this, every member of AVEGA is a member of the family, one is my mother-in-law, another can be a cousin ... We created that kind of family relationship in the organisation'.

Both of these organisations also provide information, chat groups, psychotherapy and a variety of other services too numerous to list here. Ngoga, who now runs the Gradués et Rescapés Du Genocide (GERG), the graduate branch of AEERG, says that, of the 40,000 children orphaned by the genocide, 90% are now members of one or other organisation, and Odette reports that all of the 193,434 genocide widows are automatically members of AVEGA. Of these, about 9,000 have sought help for the treatment of traumatic stress, of which PTSD is the most frequent. She takes it as a sign of recovery that this number has dropped to only 2,675 today. AVEGA now makes use of 800–1,000 volunteers.

Despite evidence for improvement in many symptoms and mental health problems, claims that the incidence of post-traumatic symptoms is decreasing have not gone unchallenged, and both Betty Gahima, who runs Benishyaka (an NGO for widows and orphans, single mothers and unaccompanied children), and Dr. Naason report increases in the numbers seeking help for these problems in recent years. Naasson's study in 2008/2009 showed that around 28% of Rwandans aged over 15 had trauma-related problems, the highest rate worldwide.

4. Legitimising authorities

From the point of view of the world and of Rwanda, the war was over, and General Paul Kagame had achieved his primary objective. The world's sympathy had been aroused, and Kagame's troops were the saviours of Rwanda, having put a stop to the genocide.

From Kagame's perspective, the conquest of Rwanda could easily have become a pyrrhic victory. The battle had been won at enormous cost, and the country was bankrupt. He was also aware that he was now the ruler of a nation of Hutu, most of whom would welcome his death or overthrow. His position was anything but secure. He recalls the faces of the survivors:

> You would look in their eyes and see a blankness. They were just wondering how it was possible to cope with everything they had seen.
>
> (Grant, 2010)

Like many of those who seek help from psychiatrists, Rwandese people were suffering from the traumatic consequences of their personal and national history. Looking back on the situation, 16 years later, he reflected:

> For me, this fragility is to be expected. Sixteen years is a very short time, and the trauma runs much deeper than people from outside, however well meaning, will ever understand. Sometimes our partners from other countries ask us why we have not got further with our reconciliation, as if we possess a magic to just get rid of this tragic history of ours. No, we have to find a way to live with it and also to build a new nation. The first phase was to achieve peace and stability, and now we are moving forward with development. And if Kagame, for one reason or other, is no longer there, people can look back at everything that has been done in sixteen years, and they can feel a part of it, and be reassured that this stability will continue.
>
> (Grant 2010)

Brought up in the English-speaking former British colony of Uganda, he had visited the United States and had already met many Western leaders. Capitalising on the sympathy and guilt that the genocide had engendered, he gladly accepted, and continues to accept, offers of financial and other support from many directions. He came to rely upon the World Bank, the IMF, the United Nations High Commissioner for Refugees (UNHCR), and on influential leaders in the United States and Britain, notably President Clinton and Prime Minister Blair, whom he persuaded to back him. This, in itself, is remarkable, for they had little to gain from investing in an African nation destroyed by internal conflicts, and with few marketable assets.

At the same time, Kagame has learned the hard way not to trust his benefactors and is careful not to pass control of his assets into their hands. He is scornful of the motives and ignorance of the 200+ NGOs who have descended upon his country:

They come here knowing almost nothing, understanding almost nothing, and they judge and criticise and tell you what you should do. A big part of the misunderstanding is that they expect us to be a normal country, like the ones where they are from. They do not understand that we are operating in a very different context.

(Grant, 2010)

This idea of countries being 'normal' or 'abnormal' raises important questions. Most people see their own country as normal, and others are judged by comparison with our norms. Not so Kagame; he had travelled enough and read enough to know that Rwanda is very 'abnormal' by comparison with most other countries, but that did not mean that he had fallen into the trap of mistaking abnormality for madness, or badness.

Kagame's childhood dream may have started as an attempt to restore the privilege and power of the Tutsi aristocracy into which he was born, but it changed along the way to an attempt to escape from that self-same trap. He is no pacifist and admits that 'even with all the hardships and hunger, war is straightforward and clear-cut' (Grant 2010), but he is wise enough to recognise that military solutions are not always the best. He is a pragmatist:

I try to look at problems very clearly and think, 'How do we get out of this? What will work? What will be the consequences for the people involved?'

He constantly searches for practical solutions. It helps that he is an avid reader.

Mainly it is books about economics, business management, development issues, politics, international affairs … I get newspapers from Britain and other countries twice a week, and read them almost page to page. Sometimes I find I'm reading things I don't even need to read, because my mind is still hungry. I don't need much sleep. Four hours is enough.

(Grant, 2010)

Kagame had fought in a succession of tough wars, and he had learned to be tough. African history records many such conquerors, rebel leaders whose power has been won by force and who see no alternative but to maintain it by force. They see their armies as their main source of security, and several have gone on to plunder their own countries in order to pay and arm their troops. However, once they have achieved power by rebellion, they know that it is dangerous to place too much power in the hands of their military colleagues, they share it only with those they can trust, most often members of their own families. Too often, they exploit the assets of their nation by trading with others and keep the profits for themselves and their families. There is a crazy logic to this model, for it becomes dangerous to share these assets with anyone who might then use them against you; the usual policy is to keep the poor poor, to develop a large secret service to watch for signs of dissent and to punish dissent with ruthless cruelty.

Kagame understood that world all too well. He now found himself the head of state in a country in which his own tribe were a distrusted minority. He set about a process of detribalisation, acculturation into a new context in which ethnic distinctiveness was eradicated, in which it was to be replaced by a meritocracy in which problems would be solved by those best qualified to solve them, regardless of ethnicity, or so he claimed.

We saw, in chapter 1, that negative codes, prejudices and assumptions are an inevitable consequence of our humanity and that they give rise to myths of both virtue and of vice that can increase the risk of cycles of violence. In Rwanda, the most influential of these was undoubtedly the negative perceptions of Tutsis held by Hutus and of Hutus by Tutsis. Kagame recognised, from the outset, that he must do everything in his power to reduce that prejudice and to undermine the myths by which it was supported.

He knew that this would not be easy as such myths exist to keep us safe, and a direct attack on the mythology would increase anxiety and might well aggravate the situation. On the one hand, his fellow Tutsis would find it hard to give up their assumptions of militant, masculine superiority, an attitude that had been fed by their success as warriors. On the other hand, the Hutu population had long blamed their problems on the Tutsis, who had become a scapegoat for the failures of their governments and for the poverty into which most of them had been born. They saw no reason to trust their conquerors.

Yet, within Rwanda, both sides must have realised that continuing the inter-ethnic animosity would be fruitless, and that renewed hostility would make a bad situation much worse. Kagame set about creating two new myths, national narratives that would replace the traditional myths with positive alternatives that might prove viable, those of feminism and nationalism. The myth of the Tutsi held that they are great warriors and cattle owners; brave and heroic in battle; ruthless with themselves and others; and ambitious for power. Their men tend to seek power and sometimes achieve it; their women are weaker but tend to be more trustworthy, tender, self-sacrificing and loyal to those they love. Men may be cruel, when necessary, to maintain their power.

Kagame's genius has been to recognise that the victorious Tutsi minority would feel less threatened by sharing power with women than with men, and the conquered Hutus would feel less threatened when ruled by women than by male Tutsi warriors. He introduced women into government posts and built support for an educated middle class who were prepared to set aside their tribal differences. To this day, Rwanda has a larger proportion of women in government than any other country.

Another source of tension was that between the Hutu agriculturalists and the Tutsi cowboys, whose long-horned cows had become a symbol of their superiority, despite the fact that, in modern times, this strain of cow was a poor producer of both milk and meat. The Rwandan government introduced better breeds, and Kagame pronounced the principle of 'one family, one cow'. This ideal may be impractical, but it establishes the idea that every Rwandan is entitled to the status of the cowboy.

At the same time, Kagame was to create a more realistic national narrative of a united, egalitarian people that work hard together to bring about a new Rwanda, rising like a phoenix from the ashes of the genocide. He introduced an educational programme to replace ethnicity with nationalism and reinforced it with a new constitution, enacted in June 2003, in which Article 33 states:

> Freedom of thought, opinion, conscience, religion, worship and the public manifestation thereof is guaranteed by the State in accordance with conditions determined by law.

At the same time, he limited some freedom, becoming intolerant of intolerance:

> Propagation of ethnic, regional, racial or discrimination or any other form of division is punishable by law.

Of course, it was easy to write ethnicity out of existence, but less easy to deny its continued cultural existence. Trust of other people is something that has to be earned, not legislated.

> Eugenie: 'I agree that legislation doesn't stop feelings, but at least it can help manage them. And I think what is helpful is sensitization, education about respect for other people's lives and human rights (which is done on an ongoing basis). I don't think it's correct to speak about former Hutus and Tutsis. The policy is to get people to see themselves as Rwandans first.'

One consequence of Kagame's detribalisation programme is the difficulty that now arises in distinguishing former Tutsis from Hutus for the purposes of research. I suspect that most of our interviewees were former Tutsis, if only because they were less likely to conceal that fact. But CMP met at least one self-declared 'Tutsi' whom friends later identified as a Hutu. Knowing that nobody is now either Hutu or Tutsi, CMP asked a taxi driver to which tribe his parents had belonged. He replied 'I don't remember'. The law against tribalism may have driven it underground.

In 2010, Kagame was re-elected as President, receiving 93% of the votes. Allowing for the fact that there were irregularities in the voting process and intimidation of journalists (Bureau of Democracy, Human Rights, and Labor, 2010) the turnout was very high, and this is a remarkable indication of his popularity in the country that he conquered.

5. Reversing polarisation

'The whole nation has peace as a goal', says Dr. Naasson,

Perhaps it is fortunate that Rwanda has little mineral wealth, because this has kept it out of the hands of the most ruthless capitalist economies. Rwanda's main cash crop is coffee, but as we have seen, that made it vulnerable to the forces of nature. Rather, Kagame insists that Rwanda's biggest asset is his people. Building on a good educational system based on the French model, Rwanda already had the infrastructure for an educational programme which, in the course of a few years, is training a young generation of entrepreneurs and computer whiz-kids who aim '... to turn Rwanda into the high-tech commercial, banking and communications hub of east and central Africa by 2020' (Grant, 2010). It would, however, be wrong to paint Rwanda as computerised since, as of 2008, only 3% were able to use the Internet (Bureau of Democracy, Human Rights, and Labor, 2010). Even so, 'Nothing succeeds like success'; within 15 years this programme has achieved sufficient stability to attract investment and enabled Rwanda to move from being one of the poorest countries in the world to one with the highest growth rate in Central Africa. At the same time, the government have reduced the country's dependence on international aid from 100% to 42%. The World Bank and the International Monetary Fund have helped it to adopt reliable methods of financial record-keeping, management and control to ensure that the money is used to promote growth and long-term independence.

We saw on pages 96–7 that polarisation is often supported by rewards for conformity with hostile plans, prejudices and behaviour, and punishments for nonconformity. By the same token, depolarisation in Rwanda has been supported by conformity with the new model.

The greatest obstacle to depolarisation was to be found among the large numbers of Hutus who supported or carried out the genocide. Some of these remained within Rwanda, either awaiting trial in the prisons, or silent in the community; others had fled the country and were now in similarly overcrowded DP camps. By 2001, it was apparent that it would take many years to reinstate the legal system that had been destroyed by the genocide and its aftermath. As many as 120,000 prisoners were awaiting trial in dreadful prisons in which many thousands were to die of infectious diseases caused by overcrowding.

To solve this problem, Kagame set up over 8,000 local courts, or 'gacaca' (pronounced ga-CHA-cha), resembling those formerly run by village elders for the settlement of local disputes. Nine judges for each court (most of them former Hutus) were selected by their local community and received some basic training. No lawyers were involved, but trials took place in public, and both accusers and accused were free to call witnesses. Punishments of up to 25 years could be handed down but half of the sentence would be spent in 'community service' and the duration of the sentence would be halved if the court was satisfied that the prisoner had confessed and offered an apology and/or compensation. About 25% of cases led to an acquittal (Clark, 2012, p. 7).

By 18 June, 2012, when gacaca was finally ended, over a million accused persons had been tried. No doubt, witnesses were intimidated, and threats seem to have increased in the later stages; as a result, while some guilty prisoners walked free, others became the victims of false accusations. Yet the whole enterprise cost only 40 million US$, while the International Criminal Tribunal for Rwanda cost

1 billion US$ and tried only 69 cases over 15 years (Clark, 2012, p. 7). The most severe criticism of the gacaca system is that it excluded crimes committed after the successful invasion (Longman, 2010). But the involvement of the community in all aspects of the system probably made the overall result acceptable at the grassroots level and reduced the level of fear.

Dr. Naasson attaches much importance to the psychological consequences of this system of justice:

> Naason: 'The gacaca system established a binding legal framework in which community members were able to ask questions about the past, no matter how terrifying they might be. That takes a lot of political courage which is absolutely essential if a society is to recover ... By setting up the gacaca process, our society has chosen to go with the belief that truth heals. But things are not that simple. The truth can also hurt. Some of the truths that were revealed during the gacaca process were quite trauma- tising for our society. And then the truth often differs in the eyes of the beholder – perspectives differ depending on whether you are a victim or a perpetrator.'
>
> Ngoga: 'Before gacaca I could not go to my homeland. I was again afraid they would kill me. There were too many people who killed my parents, my uncles and aunts, how could I go back? Gacaca helped survivors to return to our homelands ... we had the courage to return to our homeland. [*To hear people saying 'I'm sorry'? CMP*] Yes. People even sometimes told the truth.'

As Paul Kagame put it at the closing of the Gacaca Courts in 2012: 'It challenged every Rwandan into introspection and soul-searching that resulted in truth-telling, national healing, reconciliation and justice. And it worked because Rwandans largely believed in it ...' To the outside world the courts seemed to resemble the 'Peace and Reconciliation' process that had been established in South Africa and, although that is only partly true, it has helped to cement acceptance of Rwanda's recovery.

One other problem that has created new difficulties is the return of refugees from other countries. Unlike General Hagyarimana, who had blocked the return of refugees on the grounds that Rwanda was already 'full up', Kagame attempted to solve the problem by encouraging them to return. By 1979, the massive influx which resulted, together with the natural population growth rate, increased the country's population by 1.6 million (25%) (Food & Agricultural Organisation of the United Nations 1997). This remains a potential source of future unrest.

One other attempt at depolarisation has been the establishment of reminders, memorials of various kinds, and an annual ritual commemorating the genocide. This provides an opportunity to mourn for the dead but is also a reminder of the horrors.

Eugenie describes the event that took place on the 10th anniversary, on April 7, 2004:

A big crowd had gathered at the National Stadium in Kigali. As it can easily be understood, the speeches on that day were rather sad. In the stadium, there was deafening silence and the atmosphere was tense. Suddenly, a scream was heard of somebody who was shouting in the local language, 'They are here ... they are going to kill me!'

Shortly afterwards, another scream, and another and another ... Screams were coming from all the corners of the stadium. It was only at that moment that I realised there was still a lot of trauma among the Rwandan population and that indeed, time alone doesn't heal trauma.

(Personal communication with CMP 2004)

This kind of abreaction is clear evidence that a minority of Rwandans are still vulnerable to reminders of their trauma. They were mentioned by several of our interviewees and have become a worrying feature of these annual rituals. As a result, attempts have been made to minimise the trauma during Remembrance Week. 'They used to show the films, but now they don't. Visual images they no longer show that on TV. This year the focus was on the future.'

6. Retaliation or rebuilding?

In Rwanda, the peace has lasted for nearly 20 years. Dr. Jean Ruzindaza, psychiatrist and director of the Genocide Survivor's Advocacy Unit, sums up the present situation.

> Jean: 'On the surface, Rwanda is now safe and people physically secure. Work is available and there is hope for the future. But those who lived through the genocide know that all of this could be lost. It happened once and could happen again. The past is still present.
>
> Fear is not tangible. We are safe but we don't know it ... It takes time for those who have lost it, to regain their confidence in themselves and to trust authorities. They will trust individuals but not the bodies that they represent. Everyone had trauma – it continues but is rarely explosive ... Communities are now more caring. There was a time when someone who cried was ignored, now they will receive support.'
>
> Albert: 'Sometimes I feel strengthened – if I've come through this I can face anything. And my religion is more strong. I have remarried and I have one boy ... We've been waiting for him for seven years ... You can burn a forest and the trees grow and become stronger. I feel there is something stronger than me that is pushing out ... I feel like a hen hatching eggs. The young is pushing out.'

It would be naive to suppose that Rwandese society has been completely changed. Kagame's critics, including some from African Rights, have complained that his English-speaking Tutsi friends now occupy many important government positions, that the army remains both male and Tutsi and that his attempts to outlaw 'divisionism' have only forced it underground. They claim that the law against 'divisionism' has been misused to stifle political opponents, some of whom have been assassinated, and that it is time to hold democratic elections.

In addition, a number of new 'divisions' have become apparent. These include distrust of English speakers by the older residents and distrust of French speakers by the new immigrants, who learned English in former British colonies and have educational opportunities and better jobs then the francophones. Likewise, people from rural communities are envious of the urban population, who are seen as benefiting more than they from the economic recovery.

Amnesty International reports that, in March 2010, following grenade attacks in the run-up to the presidential elections, a pattern of unlawful detention of suspects was detected. 'Amnesty documented 45 cases of unlawful detention and 18 allegations of torture or ill-treatment at Camp Kami, Mukamira military camp, and in safe houses in Kigali.'

It is no more our role to idealise or to judge Kagame but to understand how a man who has achieved so much can have permitted crimes of this nature and to observe that, in many countries, such behaviour is the 'normal' way of treating suspects and political opponents. Indeed, we saw on page 69 how Kagame's experience of guerrilla warfare in Museveni's army and his subsequent appointment as chief of intelligence may have blunted his empathy towards opponents.

Since 2010, the number of reported abuses has diminished, and Rwandan authorities have taken some positive steps to combat torture, including agreeing to ratify the Optional Protocol to the Convention against Torture and inviting the UN's Special Rapporteur on Torture to visit Rwanda (Amnesty International, 2012).

Nevertheless, CMP was struck by the pervading presence of army and security services still in evidence when he visited Rwanda in July 2012. The violations of human rights seem to reflect continuing distrust, conflict between retributive and more tolerant elements within the army, and a natural tendency to overreact to terrorist threats.

Eugenie: 'Regarding obstacles to freedom of speech, I think there is enough freedom for all that brings constructive input, but zero tolerance to anything that is likely to destroy what has already been achieved. So far, the lay population appreciates the security they feel now, [but] … there are some politicians who still believe in democracy based on the ethnic majority. In my opinion, democracy should be based on ideological majority.'

According to the Belgian Development Agency, Rwanda, 2007:

Regardless of the efforts made since 1994 for the socioeconomic development of the country, Rwanda remains one of the poorest countries in the world, with almost 57% of population living below the poverty threshold. Less than three quarters of the population have access to drinking water, whereas less than half the population have no hygiene or sanitation facilities. There is one doctor per 18,000 inhabitants and one nurse per 1,690 inhabitants; healthcare service usage is 70%.

All change is assessed by comparing it with the situation that preceded it, and as one of Mandela's fellow prisoners, who now guides visitors to Robben Island, put it to CMP: 'Half a loaf is better than no bread.' Most people are prepared to tolerate injustices and violations of human rights provided that they have food in their stomachs and a good chance of surviving. Small wonder that, in successive elections, over 90% of the population has voted to keep President Kagame in power.

International developments

During the 60 days before Operation Turquoise had come to an end, a substantial Hutu army had escaped across the border along with their weapons. The continuing battle between Hutu and Tutsi forces was to play a major part in the Second Congo War, which lasted from 1998 to 2002, and is sometimes referred to as The Great War of Africa. In it, several million people were to die, most of them from starvation (Peterson, 2001). The cycle of violence continues, and Rwanda is one of several neighbouring states that have been accused of aiding rebel forces in the DRC in defiance of UN-monitored peace agreements, and in pursuit of mineral and other wealth (Guardian, 2012).

In many ways, Burundi resembles Rwanda. It too has suffered from long-continuing hostility between Tutsis and Hutus, the main difference being the continued domination of the Hutu majority by a Tutsi minority. This resulted in a long series of massacres and terrorist attacks between the two sides. However, in 2004, things took a turn for the better; both sides agreed to share power, and a UN peacekeeping force was sent in to monitor the agreement. Two years later, it was possible to withdraw that force, and since then peace has been maintained. It seems that some of the success of the recovery of Rwanda has rubbed off on its near neighbour.

While these developments were taking place in Rwanda and Burundi, the international community was also responding to the Rwandan genocide. One of us, Peter Hall, had visited Rwanda in July 1994, on behalf of Physicians for Human Rights-UK (PHR-UK), and his testimony was used to stop medical genocidaires practising medicine in countries to which they had fled and, later, to provide evidence to the International Criminal Tribunal for Rwanda. In May 1999, PHR-UK joined forces with like-minded NGOs to develop a coalition, the International Campaign to End Genocide. They sought to improve structures available to the international community to prevent, suppress or punish genocide by methods including the training of a rapid response force and the establishment of an independent international criminal court.

The campaign did not have long to wait before its capacity to meet its ambitious objectives was tested. In August 1999, it responded to the attempted genocide in East Timor by forming an East Timor Crisis Group. The immediate goals were to get an international peacekeeping force into East Timor and to provide aid for displaced persons. PHR-UK took the lead in appraising the UK foreign secretary of the need to create an International Criminal Tribunal for East Timor. The following day, Robin Cook, the foreign secretary, publicly announced his support for the creation of this tribunal. Pressure from the West forced Habibie's Indonesian government to cede control to an international force. The UN Commission on Human Rights instigated a commission of enquiry, and East Timorese refugees forced into West Timor were allowed to return home.

In March 2003, the proposal to create a Special Adviser on the Prevention of Genocide in the United Nations was first put to Kofi Annan, secretary-general of the UN, by PHR-UK's senior adviser, Bernie Hamilton and reinforced some months later by PHR-UK member, CMP. Parkes wrote a letter to Kofi Annan, whom he had told about the work in Rwanda after a church service in New York for British nationals bereaved in the 9/11 attack on the World Trade Center.

I am a member of Physicians for Human Rights and would like to endorse the proposals which they have made, in conjunction with the International Campaign to end Genocide and Genocide Watch, to mark the tenth anniversary of the genocide in Rwanda by the creation of a United Nations Genocide Prevention Focal Point. This would act as a watchdog, alerting you and the member nations of the build up of tensions likely to lead to future genocidal conditions and drawing on the experience of genocide scholars, lawyers, politicians and others to reduce that risk ...

(Parkes CM, 21 November, 2003)

On 7 April, 2004, the tenth anniversary of the start of the genocide in Rwanda, Bernie Hamilton was in Geneva to hear Kofi Annan announce to the UN Commission on Human Rights that he was creating the post of Special Adviser on the Prevention of Genocide. A former political prisoner, Argentinian Juan Mendez, was appointed, and his role was 'to ensure that the Security Council is informed fully and in a timely manner about situations of threats of genocide which also represent threats to international peace and security' (Dingley, 2001).

Another lesson which has international implications is the recognition of the value of women in peacekeeping. On 13 September, 2012, Ban Ki-Moon, secretary-general of the UN, addressed the United Nations General Assembly:

We must also continue to enhance the participation of women in peace processes.

We are now providing gender expertise and appointing women in most UN mediation teams, though there is still clearly room for improvement.

More and more of our teams are making genuine efforts to consult with women's organizations systematically throughout the mediation process.

There are a growing number of female senior officials who undertake mediation as part of their duties in field missions – and, as I state in my report, I remain committed to appointing a female United Nations envoy to lead a UN mediation effort.

Kofi Annan, the first secretary-general of the United Nations to be chosen from within the ranks of the UN, has recognised that whereas the UN initially brought together the interests of the nation-states, it was originally set up to represent the people who make up those states. In recent years, it has been realised that governments sometimes act in their own interests rather than in the interests of the people whom they govern. The International Criminal Court has indicted political leaders who commit crimes against their subjects; the Security Council has authorised UN troops to take control in situations where 'terrorists' have seized the reins of power by coups d'état and conducted acts of genocide or other abuse of substantial populations; the World Bank has used its own resources to influence leaders whose actions are seen as contrary to their nation's interests, and the UN secretariat has developed close working links with non-governmental organizations whose aims are truly international (Annan, 2012).

Conclusions

Eugenie: 'Today, the fear has decreased as people now live together in their villages. The government efforts to sensitise the population about the necessity of reconciliation has been instrumental in this. Also, the Gacaca courts which have made it possible to render some justice to both the survivors and those suspected of participating in the killings have played a role in reassuring people. The majority of Rwandans have learned that it's no use dwelling on the past but rather building and improving their lives. This is also true for me, indeed I have learned to live with the loss of my loved ones for life to be possible!'

Rwanda is winning. The world has taken pity on one of its smallest, weakest and most desperate countries and is attempting to love it to life; the Rwandans are finding new, more positive myths to replace the old negative ones; and a tough, suspicious warrior leader has discovered how to charm and work with women, politicians, industrialists and bankers. Psychologists may have played a small part, by providing psychological first aid when it was most needed, setting up secure bases from which people could begin to explore ways out of the monstrous pit into which they had fallen, by encouraging people to take stock and talk about their distress, and helping them to regain sufficient confidence and self-respect to look forward rather than over their shoulders. The world, as embodied in its many-headed institutions and leaders, has opened the door to its own success, finance and know-how, bringing hope to a hopeless case. While his human rights record is not good, pragmatic Paul Kagame has proved that he can be a brilliant strategist at home as well as in battle. In the great continent of Africa, the success of Rwanda is viewed with interest, and others are beginning to follow its example.

16

SYNTHESIS AND CONCLUSIONS

Colin Murray Parkes

You never change things by fighting the existing reality.
To change something, build a new model that makes the existing model obsolete.

— Richard Buckminster Fuller

The reader will by now be aware that the contributors to this volume each bring their own frame of reference to the task we face, and my role as editor is not to force them all into the same bed. Indeed, any attempt to do that would soon bring home the impossibility of one person speaking for us all at this point in our discourse.

Anthony Glees reminded me that 'the purpose of this study was to take two public policy issues, terrorism and counter-terrorism, and see how a group of experts, predominantly drawn from psychiatry and psychology, would approach them in a critical format and advance novel but hard-nosed solutions. As such, the book is a contribution to public policy, and to its being debated, rather than to the further study of psychiatry, or thanatology. This book is about experts reaching out, moving beyond their comfort zone and arguing normatively, not just positively, about a major issue of our time'. He is right, but we need to be careful about what we mean by 'counter-terrorism'. Most of our contributors have seen our responses to terrorism as extending beyond the obvious steps to obstruct and eliminate terrorists, important though that may be, to examining the roots of terrorism and of the 'natural' responses in the hope of finding more radical solutions to the problems to which they give rise.

With these words in mind, I shall test the tolerance of both my fellow contributors and my readers by taking advantage of this opportunity to summarise what I see as some of the lessons I have learned and highlight some of the challenges that remain.

It seems to me that much of it comes down to security. Our attachments to all that we love and hold sacred – our families, our gods, our homes and homelands – all function to keep us and our genes safe in the world, and as such they are our most precious possessions, our most priceless treasures. So are those attachments of the attackers and their supporters. Both terrorist attacks and the insecurity which causes them upset the balance between our security and that of the people whom the terrorists hope to, and may indeed, represent.

It is natural and indeed quite proper for the attacked to defend themselves, and in some circumstances it would be suicidal not to. That is what the security forces are for. They have to find the right balance between meeting violence with the violence necessary to maintain our security without shattering the security of peaceful others, and that can only be achieved by understanding and respecting *their* sources of security. It is sad that the term *security staff* has come to mean officials with guns who protect our gates, rather than friendly people who make us feel welcome and, like good parents, combine the roles of protector, supporter and informant.

Relevant to the response to terrorism is the model of the police's family liaison officers (FLOs), who, in Britain, have now replaced the macho detectives who investigated violent crimes and controlled disaster situations. They recognise that it is quite possible to combine the roles of investigating officer and family supporter to people in crisis. They enter homes and meet families who are facing great trauma and loss with empathy and kindness even when they expect their overtures to be rejected. This does not mean that they deny the need to take control, like good parents, when it is important to set limits; and that sometimes means meeting violence with firmness and strength.

In this book we have seen how, faced by the loss of those they love and trust, human animals are programmed by evolution to experience powerful impulses to actions which may themselves increase the danger. But these impulses can also save us, and without them none of us would be alive today.

There is a measure of truth in the saying that love is blind, and it is no surprise to find that we, like the terrorists, overvalue the people, communities and gods to whom we are attached. Myths of the superiority, wisdom and strength of our own family and tribe are inevitable, and we enjoy the pride, the enhanced self-esteem and sense of security that comes from such relationships. Sadly, these myths are also likely to be associated with negative myths about outsiders, their inferiority, impurity and enmity. These enable us to exploit and even kill them without undue self-reproach. It seems that love cannot make the world go round, but it can make it grow pear-shaped.

We saw how Catholics and Protestants in Northern Ireland, and Hutu and Tutsi youngsters in Rwanda, joined with others in riots with enthusiasm, and some of those who subsequently joined the terrorist sides took pleasure in hunting and killing their supposed enemies. We also saw how each side tends to overestimate its own strength, courage and resources while underestimating the strength, courage and resources of its opponents.

We have seen how important it is to distinguish a deadly event from our perception of the event and from the way we respond to it. What actually happens in a terrorist attack, and what we see happening, are two different things – the news has usually been chosen by informants (notably the media), and what we make of it is determined by our choice of informant, by the emotions evoked and by the sum total of memories and assumptions out of which we recognise and make sense of our world. The chances of distortion are great, and we all experience something different. Yet we must act together if we are to respond.

Between the moment of perception and the moment of response, there comes a pause. Our brains are alerted, we are never more 'switched on'. During that pause, we digest the information we receive, followers look to leaders and leaders to followers, and out of that interaction comes a group reaction which may be quite different to the reaction of any one of us alone. We find ourselves drawn towards others who share our myths and united against the supposed attackers and their supporters. Polarisation often escalates the conflict and leads to retaliation and another turn of the wheel of deadly violence, but awareness of that danger can change our responses.

Group interaction can also lead to de-escalation. We do not have to be pawns in the hands of our emotions, and the cycle of violence is not inevitable. Our studies have shown how children can be helped to stand aside from the traps in which they are entangled and to resist the magnet of violence. Is it possible that adult education can meet the same challenge? We saw how, in both Rwanda and Northern Ireland, substantial numbers of people have become disillusioned with the use of deadly violence and have accepted leaders who offer alternative ways to find security and, with it, peace. Are there ways to speed up disillusionment with violent solutions?

All change is painful, even change for the better, and changing patterns of attachment are the most painful of all. We have seen that such change is a process of grieving akin to the grief we experience whenever we lose something or someone we love. In both Northern Ireland and Rwanda, the peace process has been slow because it takes time, patience and group process to change the attachment patterns and the obsolete assumptions on which we have learned to depend.

In Rwanda, new leaders achieved power by force of arms, and social change was enforced by law. Many of those who were held responsible for abuses of genocide and other crimes by their neighbours were punished, but the punishment was not excessive, and retribution is now virtually at an end. Security was largely brought about by non-coercive means, many of the new leaders are women, few are warriors, and security is enhanced by education, by community involvement and by economic support and advice from other countries. Little by little, new myths have taken the place of the old destructive ones. Now support from outside is dwindling, and the Rwandese are becoming autonomous. Even so, although 20 years have passed, the cycle of deadly violence continues to rage in nearby countries, and in Rwanda fear of a return to the old patterns of attachment is undermining the trust that would make possible a true democracy.

In Northern Ireland, it was leaders in Great Britain and the Irish Republic who met and worked together in the European Union and started to understand each other; this camaraderie eventually extended to the warring parties. Moderates initiated the process, but it was not until extremist leaders to whom the two communities were attached, in Sinn Fein/IRA in particular, took significant initiatives to end

SYNTHESIS AND CONCLUSIONS

the war, that substantial de-escalation took place. They met with neutral commissioners and led the way, persuading their followers to decommission their weapons
and their minds. The long-standing attachment to these leaders enabled new myths
to grow out of the old. The Omagh bombing proved the acid test of community
commitment to the new assumptive world and left the remaining terrorists isolated
and discredited. Here too, economic security and the support of allies trusted by
both sides, notably the United States, helped to foster the security that is the sine
qua non of the psychosocial transition to new patterns of attachment.

These issues were well summarised on 13 September, 2012, when one of our
contributors, Lord Alderdice, addressed the General Assembly of the UN in a
debate on 'Strengthening the Role of Mediation in the Peaceful Settlement of
Disputes, Conflict, Prevention and Resolution'.

He said:

> ... Powerful feelings affect the way that we think. Even when it is to our
> disadvantage, we cannot just dismiss our feelings. Powerful emotions
> actually affect not just what we think but the way that we think; they dis-
> turb our capacity for rationality and acting in our own best self-interest.
> This is true also of groups, communities and whole nations of people ...
>
> In every part of the world where I have studied the outbreak of terror-
> ism and profound violence, I have found at least one group of people
> who feel that their culture, their values and their people have been
> treated unfairly and profoundly disrespected. When they have been
> unable to right what they perceive to be this terrible wrong, they have
> turned to violence, not out of rational self-interest, for their people rarely
> benefit from the violence; they usually suffer terribly.
>
> This is one of the mistakes that people from stable societies often
> make in addressing violence in other places. They try to interpret the
> events using a rational actor model, when what they are observing are
> 'devoted actors' motivated not by social and economic drivers but by
> 'sacred values' – by which I do not mean religious values but values that
> transcend economic benefit – the value of the life of my child is a sacred
> value. I cannot trade that without losing part of my very humanity ...
>
> Forgiveness, like trust and reconciliation, is not a prerequisite for
> starting the process of addressing such conflicts, but is a result of a
> successful process of doing so. However, while trust tends to grow out
> of the experience of working together in a human relationship with the
> other side, forgiveness is much less common, much more difficult and
> very painful.
>
> The key element in building trust, achieving agreement, ending
> violence and eventually contributing to reconciliation is the construction
> of a process through which by direct engagement with each other, the
> two or more, sides begin to see 'the Others' as human beings who have
> their positive as well as negative elements. If you treat others as less

human than you and your people, they will feel able to treat you and your people as less than human too.

These then are some of the key issues in mediation work with groups in violent conflict:

The power of the past – with repetitions and reactions to hurts, over centuries not just years.

The impact of the emotions – I react not out of rational self-interest but emotionally, and often to my cost. The toxic effects of injustice and humiliation – resulting in devoted actors, who, if they find no other way may react with self-destructive violence in what they perceive to be a higher cause. If you humiliate me, I will remember it forever and find it hard ever to forgive. The need to construct a robust process through which I begin to relate directly to 'the other side' as human beings with good in them as well as bad, and recognizing the faults on my own side in the past and the present.

The recognition that social scientists can throw new light on old problems does not mean that we have all the answers. Psychology and psychiatry have lagged behind other sciences, but that does not mean that our contribution is valueless. Much of our theorising has been speculative, and it will require more research and interaction between the various schools of psychology, sociology and psychiatry before we can truly call our work in this field 'hard-nosed'.

In the introduction to this volume, I asked if palliative care, the body of knowledge that has revolutionised the care of patients and families faced by deadly illness, has something to teach people in communities faced by deadly terrorism. In both situations, people are faced with threats to their own survival and the loss of loved ones. A recent IWG workshop concluded that, in both situations, people need (1) to obtain reliable information, (2) to face the painful reality of death, (3) to find a safe place, (4) to make secure relationships, (5) to relinquish long-standing assumptions about the world (decommission mindsets), (6) to grieve, and to commemorate and value the lasting bonds that remain to those people and other objects of attachment that are now lost, (7) to apologise and make restitution for any failures, (8) to forgive or accept the failures of others, (9) to let go of what they cannot have, on the way to accepting and enjoying what they can have (reconciliation), and (10) to prepare for future threats, losses and change (IWG, 2011). In palliative care, it is the support with all of these problems that can often bring relief of distress, calm reflection, peace of mind, security in the face of death, and maturity in its aftermath. Could similar kinds of support be developed for people faced with deadly terrorism?

Given that resistance to changing mindsets results from fear, the first step may be in finding ways to support the front-line of responders. Brian Rowan acknowledges the dangerous and stressful time in his life as a journalist reporting the Troubles when '... the BBC offered me some counselling, and I can remember feeling insulted, thinking that this offer in some way suggested weakness on my part. Many years later, I realise that the penny was beginning to drop in terms of what was being asked of those involved in the reporting of our conflict/war'. For the journalists' sake and for ours, they may be wise to think again.

Of course, psychiatrists and psychologists are also caught up in their own assumptive worlds, blinkered by the limitations of the human brain. We have our own attachments and agendas, and others may be right not to trust us. One object of this volume is to put our cards on the table, to let others judge and share in the insights and assumptions that we make, to disagree, to take what is useful and junk the rest. We are all in this together.

Lord Alderdice has acknowledged the very different roles required of the politician and the psychotherapist. Yet he remains a good example of a psychiatrist who has, patiently and unobtrusively, made use of his skills in both fields, to play a significant part in a peace process. Professor Gersons and Mirjam Nijdam have shown that psychologists can support politicians and help to minimise the psychological impact of threats that could easily impair their judgement and decision making at a time when these skills are most needed.

In the past 50 years, hospices and other palliative care services have sprung up all over the world. Is it possible that, 50 years from now, leaders, communicators and communities faced with life-threatening violence will obtain similar support, not from psychiatrists or specialists in palliative care, but from a new kind of psychological, social and spiritual care that is now, as Albert Najambe would put it, 'pushing out'?

REFERENCES

Abrahams, M. (2006) Why terrorism does not work. *International Security* 31(2): 42–78.

African Rights (1994) *Rwanda, Death, Despair and Defiance*. 'African Rights', 11, Marshallsea Rd, London SE1 1EP.

Ainsworth, M. D. S., Blehar, M. C., Waters, E., and Wall, S. (1978) *Patterns of Attachment: A Psychological Study of the Strange Situation*. Erlbaum, Hillsdale, NJ.

Alderdice, J. (1991) Liberalism and fundamentalism, '*80 Club Lecture*', published in *Liberal Aerogramme* (2003), 46: 13–17.

Alderdice, J. J. (2003) Terrorism and the psychoanalytic space and terrorism at close quarters. In *Terrorism and the Psychoanalytic Space: International Perspectives from Ground Zero*, Cancelmo, J. A., Tylim, I., Hoffenberg, J. and Myers, H. (eds.) Pace University Press, New York.

Alderdice, J. (2005) Understanding terrorism—the inner world and the wider world. *British Journal of Psychotherapy* 21(4): June 2005.

Alderdice, J. (2007) The individual, the group and the psychology of terrorism. *International Review of Psychiatry*. 1, (3), 201–209.

Alozie, E. C. (2007) What did they say? African Media Coverage of the first 100 days of the Rwanda crisis. Ch.17 in *The Media and the Rwandan Genocide*, Allan Thompson (ed.). Fountain Pub., Kampala.

American Psychiatric Association (2013) *Diagnostic Statistical Manual of Mental Disorders. 5*th *edition (DSM5)* American Psychiatric Association, Washington DC.

Amnesty International, Human Rights Watch, Inter-African Union of Human Rights, International Center for Human Rights and Democratic Development, International Federation of Human Rights Leagues (1994) Declaration of Five International Human Rights Organizations Concerning the Delays in the Implementation of the Peace Agreements in Rwanda, March 15.

Amnesty International (2012) Rwanda Shrouded in Secrecy: Illegal Detention and Torture by Military Intelligence. Amnesty International http://www.amnesty.org/en/library/asset/AFR47/004/2012/en/ca2e51a2-1c3f-4bb4-b7b9-e44ccbb2b8de/afr470042012en.pdf (Accessed 9th October 2012).

Annan, K. (2012) *Interventions: A Life in War and Peace*. Allen Lane, Penguin Books, London, New York, etc.

Anyidoho, H. K. (1997) *Guns over Kigali: The Rwandese Civil War, 1994: A Personal Account*. Fountain, Kampala, Uganda.

Aron, R. (1966) *Press and War*. Weidenfeld & Nicholson, London.

236

Atran, S. (2010) *Talking to the Enemy: Violent Extremism, Sacred Values and What it Means to be Human*. Allen Lane, London.

Baddeley, A. (2007) *Working Memory, Thought and Action*. Oxford University Press, Oxford.

Bardon, J (1992) *A History of Ulster*. Blackstaff Press, Belfast.

Baumeister, R. F., Mascampo, E. J. and Vohs, K. D. (2011) Do conscious thoughts cause behavior? *Annual Review of Psychology* 62: 331–361.

Beck, A. T. (1976) *Cognitive Therapy and the Emotional Disorders*. International Universities Press, New York.

Beckerman, Z. (2009) The complexities of teaching historical conflictual narratives in integrated Palestinian Jewish schools in Israel. *International Review of Education* 55: 235–250.

Belgian Development Agency (2007) Report Rwanda. http://www.btcctb.org/en/node/29 (Accessed 14th February 2013).

Benson, J. (2009) The Northern Ireland conflict and peace process: The role of mutual regulatory symbiosis between leaders and groups. Ch. 9 in *Leadership in a Changing World*, Klein, R. H., Rice, C. A. and Schermer, V. L. (eds.) Lexington Books, Lanham Maryland.

Berkowitz, L. and LePage, A. (1967) Weapons as aggression-eliciting stimuli. *Journal of Personality and Social Psychology* 7: 202–207.

Blaug, R. (2012) How power corrupts: Video of lecture recorded at conference on 'The Intoxication of Power: From Neurosciences to Hubris in Healthcare and Public Life'. Royal Society of Medicine. http://www.rsmvideos.com

Boelen, P. A., Van den Bout, J., De Kejser, J., and Hoijtink, H. (2003) Reliability and validity of the Dutch version of the Inventory of Traumatic Grief (ITG). *Death Studies* 27(3): 227–248.

Bowlby, J. (1953) *Child Care and the Growth of Love*. Pelican, London.

Bowlby, J. (1969) *Attachment and Loss. Vol. 1: Attachment*. Hogarth, London.

Bowlby, J. (1988) *A Secure Base: Clinical Applications of Attachment Theory*. Routledge, London and Basic Books, New York.

Boyer, P. (1994) *The Naturalness of Religious Ideas: A Cognitive Theory of Religion*. University of California Press, California.

Breckenridge, J. N. and Zimbardo, P. G. (2007) The strategy of terrorism and the psychology of mediated fear. Ch. 9 in *Psychology of Terrorism*, Bongar, B., Brown, L. M., Beutler, L. E., Breckenridge, J. N., and Zimbardo, P. G. (eds.) Oxford University Press, Oxford.

Brewin, C. R., Furnham, A. and Howes, M. (1989) Demographic and psychological determinants of homesickness and confiding among students. *British Journal of Psychology* 80(4): 467–477.

Budd, T., Sharp, C. and Mayhew, P. (2005). *Offending in England and Wales: First Results from the 2003 Crime and Justice Survey*. Home Office Research Study No. 275. Home Office, London.

Bureau of Democracy, Human Rights, and Labor (2010) Human Rights Report: Rwanda. Bureau of Democracy, Human Rights, and Labor. US Department of State. http://www.state.gov/j/drl/rls/hrrpt/2010/af/154364.htm

Burns, J. M. (1978) *Leadership*. Harper & Row Publishers, New York.

Bush, K. (2000) *Stolen Childhood: The Impact of Militarised Violence on Children in Sri Lanka*. CIDA/SAP, Ottawa.

Buzan, B. (1982, 2nd ed. 1991) *People, States and Fear: An Agenda for International Security Studies in the Post-Cold War Era*. Harvester Wheatsheaf, New York, London, etc.

CAIN (Conflict Archive on the Internet) Web Service (2012a) 'Bloody Sunday', Derry 30 January 1972—Circumstances in Which People were Killed. http://cain.ulst.ac.uk/events/bsunday/circum.htm (Accessed 17th November 2012).

Cameron, D. (2011) Speech at Munich Security Conference. UK Government on 5th February. http://www.number10.gov.uk/news/pms-speech-at-munich-security-conference/ (Accessed 26th January 2013).

Carta, M. G., Bernal, M., Hardoy, M. C., and Haro-Abad, J. M. (2005) Migration and mental health in Europe (The state of mental health in Europe working group: appendix 1). *Clinical Practice and Epidemiology in Mental Health*, 1: 13.

Carver, C. S., Genellen, R. J., Froming, W. J. and Chambers, W. (1983) Modeling: An analysis in terms of category accessibility. *Journal of Experimental Social Psychology*, 19: 403–421.

Cassidy, J. and Shaver, P. R. (eds.) (1999) *Handbook of Attachment: Theory, Research and Clinical Applications*. Guilford, New York.

Chalk, F. (2007) Intervening to prevent genocidal violence: The role of the media. Ch. 30 in *The Media and the Rwandan Genocide*, Allan Thompson (ed.). Fountain Pub., Kampala.

Chaon, A. (2007) Who failed in Rwanda, journalists or the media? Ch. 13 in *The Media and the Rwandan Genocide*, Alan Thompson (ed.). Fountain Press, Kampala, Uganda.

Church, A. T., Katigbak, M. S., Del Prado, A. M., Ortiz, F. A., Mastor, K. A., Harumi, Y., Tanaka-Matsumi, J., De Jesus Vargas-Flores, J., Ibanez-Reyes, J., White, F. A., Miramontes, L. G., Reyes, J. A. S. and Cabrera, H. F. (2006) Implicit theories and self-perceptions of traitedness across cultures: Toward integration of cultural and trait psychology perspectives. *Journal of Cross-Cultural Psychology* 37(6): 604–716.

Clark, P. (2012) *How Rwanda Judged Its Genocide*. Counterpoints series. Africa Research Institute, ISBN 978-1-906329-18-1

CNN (Cable News Network) (2012) Underwear Bomber Moved to Supermax Prison. http://www.cbs19.tv/story/17463924/underwear-bomber-moved-to-supermax-prison (Accessed 26th January 2013).

CNRC (Clemens Nathan Research Centre) (2007) *Foreign Policy and Human Rights*. CN Research Publications Martinus Nijhoff, PO Box 9000, 2300 PA Leiden, The Netherlands.

CNRC (2008) *International Development and Foreign Policy*. CN Research Publications (v.s.).

CNRC (2009a) Reparations for Victims of Human Rights. CN Research Publications (v.s.).

CNRC (2009b) *Media and Human Rights*. CN Research Publications (v.s.).

Cockburn, T. (2007) 'Performing' racism: Engaging young supporters of the far right in England. *British Journal of Sociology of Education* 28(5): 547–560.

Communiqué issued at the end of regional summit meeting held in Dar es Salaam on 6th April (1994) The Situation Prevailing in Burundi and Rwanda. US State Department document # 1994DARES0214 6.

Connell, R. W. (1995) *Masculinities*. Berkeley: University of California Press.

Crenshaw, M. (1989) *Terrorism and International Cooperation*. Westview Press, New York.

Crenshaw, M. (1998) The logic of terrorism: Terrorist behaviour as a product of strategic choice. In *Origins of Terrorism: Psychologies, Ideologies, Theologies, States of Mind*, Reich, W. (ed.). The John Hopkins University Press, Baltimore, p. 10.

Critchley, M. and Critchley, E. A. (1998) *John Hughlings Jackson Father of English Neurology*. Oxford University Press, Oxford.

Cronin, A. (2009) *How Terrorism Ends: Understanding the Decline and Demise of Terrorist Campaigns*. Princeton University Press, Princeton NJ

Curran, S. and Miller, P. (2001) Psychiatric implications of chronic civilian strife or war: Northern Ireland. *Advances in Psychiatric Treatment*, APT January 7: 73–80; doi:10.1192/apt.7.1.73.

Dallaire, R. (2003) *Shake Hands with the Devil: The Failure of Humanity in Rwanda*. Carol & Graf, New York.

Daly, E. (2000) *Mister: Are You a Priest?* Fourcourts Press, Dublin.

Dar-Nimrod, I. and Heine, S. J. (2011) Genetic essentialism: On the deceptive determinism of DNA. *Psychological Bulletin* 137(5): 800–818.

Darwin, C. (1872/1998) *The Expression of Emotions in Man and Animals*, 3rd edition, P. Ekman. (ed.). Oxford University Press, New York.

Davidson, R. J., Scherer, K. R. and Goldsmith, H. H. (2009) (eds.) *Handbook of Affective Sciences*. Oxford University Press, Oxford.

Davies, L. (2008) *Educating Against Extremism*. Stoke on Trent, Trentham.

Dearing, R. (1997) The Dearing Report. National Committee of Inquiry into Higher Education. London. http://www.leeds.ac.uk/educol/ncihe/ (Accessed 26th January 2013)

Des Forges, A. (1999) *Leave None to Tell the Tale: Genocide in Rwanda*. Human Rights Watch, NY et Fédération internationale des droits de l'homme, Paris.

Dettmer, J. (2004) Supplying terrorists the "oxygen of publicity." In *Violence and Terrorism*, T. J. Bradley (ed.). McGraw-Hill/Duskin, Guilford, CT, pp. 136–137.

Devine, P. G. (1989) Stereotypes and prejudice: Their automatic and controlled components. *Journal of Personality and Social Psychology* 56: 680–690.

Dingley, J (2001) The Bombing of Omagh, 15 August 1998: The bombers, their tactics, strategy, and purpose behind the incident. *Studies in Conflict and Terrorism*, 24: 451–465.

Dixon, B. and Johns, L. (2001) *Gangs, Pagad and the State: Vigilantism and Revenge Violence in the Western Cape*. Cape Town: Violence and Transition Series 2, Centre for Studies in Violence and Reconciliation.

Dodd, V. (2010) Profile: Roshonara Dhoudry. *The Guardian* 2.11.2010. http://www.guardian.co.uk/uk/2010/nov/02/profile-roshonara-choudhry-stephen-timms (Accessed 26th January 2013).

Duffy, M., Gillespie, K. and Clark, D. M. (2007) Post-traumatic stress disorder in the context of terrorism and other civil conflict in Northern Ireland: randomised controlled trial. *British Medical Journal* 334: 1147–1150. (Full version published electronically at www.bmj.com. Ref: BMJ, doi:10.1136/bmj.39021.846852.BE.)

Dutton, D. G., and Hart, S. G. (1992) Evidence for long-term, specific effects of childhood abuse and neglect on criminal behavior in men. *International Journal of Offender Therapy and Comparative Criminology* 36: 129–137.

Edwards, R. D. (Circa 2007) Shed No Tears for this Roaring Bigot. Daily Mail Online, http://www.dailymail.co.uk/news/article-527351/Shed-tears-roaring-bigot-He-did-did-Ian-Paisley---peace.html#ixzz25tFQt9S2 (Accessed Jan 2013).

Edwards, R. D. (2009) *Aftermath: The Omagh Bombing*. Harvill Secker, London.

Eppel, A. (2009) *Sweet Sorrow: Love, Loss and Attachment in Human Life*. Karnac Books, London.

Evans, J. St. B. T. and Over, D. E. (1996) *Rationality and Reasoning*. Psychology Press, Hove.

Ey, H. (1962) Hughlings Jackson's principles and the organo-dynamic concept of psychiatry. *American Journal of Psychiatry*, 19(1): 673–682.

Fairbrother, N., Newth, S. J. and Rachman, S. (2005) Mental pollution: Feelings of dirtiness without physical contact. *Behaviour Research and Therapy* 43(1): 120–130.

Falk, A. (2004) *Fratricide in the Holy Land*. University of Wisconsin Press, Wisconsin.

Ferry, F., Bolton, D., Bunting, B., Devine, B., McCann, S. and Murphy, S. (2008) Trauma, Health and Conflict in Northern Ireland. The Northern Ireland Centre for Trauma and Transformation, University of Ulster. Online. Available http://www.nictt.org/downloads/Trauma%20health%20and%20conflict.pdf (Accessed Feb 2013).

Festinger, L. (1957) *A Theory of Cognitive Dissonance*. Stanford University Press, Stanford, CA.

Forgas, J. P. (2009) Affective influences on attitudes and judgement. In *Handbook of Affective Sciences,* Davidson, R. J., Scherer, K. R. and Goldsmith, H. H. (eds.) Oxford University Press, Oxford, pp. 596–618.

Fox, E. (2008) *Emotion Science*. Palgrave Macmillan, New York.

Freedman, L. (2005) Strategic terror and amateur psychology. *The Political Quarterly*, 76: 161–170.

Freeman, T. (1981) On the psychopathology of persecutory delusions. *British Journal of Psychiatry* 139: 529–532

Freud, S. (1921) Group psychology and the analysis of the ego. *Standard Edition* 18: 67–147. Hogarth Press, London.

Freud, A. (1946) *The Ego and Mechanisms of Defence*. International Universities Press, Madison, CT.

Fried, M. (1962) Grieving for a lost home. In *The Environment of the Metropolis*, L. J. Duhl (ed.). Basic Books, New York.

Frodi, A. (1975) The effect of exposure to weapons on aggressive behaviour from a cross-cultural perspective. *International Journal of Psychology*, 10: 282–292.

Fujii, L. A. (2009) *Killing Neighbours—Webs of Violence in Rwanda*. Cornell University Press, Ithaca.

Galinsky, A. D., Maddux, W. W., Gilin, D. and White, J. B. (2008) Why it pays to get inside the head of your opponent: The differential effects of perspective taking and empathy in negotiations. *Psychological Science* 19(4): 378–384.

Gallagher, T. and O'Connell, J. (1983) *Contemporary Irish Studies*. Manchester University Press, Manchester.

Gersons, B. P. R. and Olff, M. (2005) Coping with the aftermath of trauma. Editorial. *British Medical Journal* 7: 330(7499): 1038–1039.

Ghaemi, S. N. (2007) *The Concepts of Psychiatry: A Pluralistic Approach to the Mind and Mental Illness*. John Hopkins University Press, Maryland.

Ghanea, N. (2007) 'Phobias' and 'Isms': Recognition of difference or the slippery slope of particularisms. In *Does God Believe in Human Rights?: Essays on Religion and Human Rights*, Ghanea, N., Stephens, A. and Walden, R. (eds). Martinus Nijhoff Publishers, Leiden, pp. 211–232.

Gigerenzer, G. (2008) *Gut Feelings: Short Cuts to Better Decision Making*. Penguin Books, London:

Gillespie, K., Duffy, M., Hackmann, A. and Clark, D. M. (2002) Community-based cognitive therapy in the treatment of posttraumatic stress disorder following the Omagh bomb. *Behaviour Research and Therapy* 40: 345–357.

Gilligan, J. (1996) *Violence—Our Deadly Epidemic and Its Causes*. GP Putnam's Sons, New York.

Girard, R. (1977) *Violence and the Sacred*. The Johns Hopkins University Press, Baltimore.

Gladwell, M. (2005) *Blink: The Power of Thinking Without Thinking*. Penguin Books, London.

Glees, A. (2003) *The Stasi Files: The UK Operations of the East German Intelligence and Security Service*. Simon & Schuster. ISBN: 0-7432-3104X, p. 460. Paperback edition 2004: ISBN: 0-7432-3105-3.

Glees, A. (2009) Arab and Islamic Funding of Islamic Studies: a Question of Western Security. In *The National Observer*, No 81 December 2009–February 2010, 10 pp. http://www.nationalobserver.net/2009_81_glees.htm (Accessed 26th January 2013).

Glees, A. (2012) Universities: The Breeding Grounds of Terror. *The Telegraph* 6th June. http://www.telegraph.co.uk/education/universityeducation/8560409/Universities-The-breeding-grounds-of-terror.html (Accessed 26th January 2013)

Glenny, M. (2011) *Dark Market—CyberThieves, CyberCops and You*. The Bodley Head., London.

Food and Agricultural Organisation of the United Nations. (1997) Rwandan refugees' return home puts heavy strain on limited food resources. *Global Watch* http://www.fao.org/english/newsroom/global/GW9716-e.htm (Accessed 20 September 2013).

Goetz, J. L., Keltner, D. and Simon-Thomas, E. (2010) Compassion: An evolutionary analysis and empirical review. *Psychological Bulletin*, 136(3): 351–374.

Goldberg, D. P. and Williams, P. (1988) *A User's Guide to the General Health Questionnaire* NFER-Nelson, Windsor.

Goldhagen, D. J. (2009) *Worse than War: Genocide, Eliminationism, and the Ongoing Assault on Humanity*. PublicAffairs, New York.

Gopin, M. (2002) *Holy War, Holy Peace: How Religion can Bring Peace to the Middle East*. Oxford University Press, Oxford, 106; 243.

Gourevitch, P. (1998) *We Wish To Inform You That Tomorrow We Will Be Killed With Our Families: Stories from Rwanda*. Picador, London.

Granqvist, P., Ljungdahl, C., and Dickie, J. R. (2007) God is nowhere, God is now here: Attachment activation, security of attachment, and God's perceived closeness among 5–7 year old children from religious and non-religious homes. *Attachment and Human Development* 9(1): 55–72.

Grant, R. (2010) Paul Kagame: Rwanda's Redeemer or Ruthless Dictator? *The Telegraph* 22nd July.

Greenberg, J., Pyszcynski, T. and Solomon, S. (1986) The causes and consequences of a need for self-esteem: A terror management theory. In *Public Self and Private Self*, R. F. Baumeister (ed.). Springer Verlag, New York, pp. 189–212.

Greenberg, M. T. (1999) Attachment and psychopathology in childhood. Ch. 21 in *Handbook of Attachment: Theory, Research, and Clinical Applications*, Cassidy, J. and Shaver, P. (eds.). The Guilford Press, New York and London, pp. 369–496.

Guardian Newspaper (2012) Q and A: DR Congo Conflict. News leaked to Reuter's by UN Panel. *Guardian*, 17th November.

Gumbel, E. J. (1922) Four years of political murder. In *The Orientalist*, T. Reiss (ed.). Random House, 2006, p. 180.

Haidt, J. (2001). The emotional dog and its rational tail: A social intuitionist approach to moral judgment. *Psychological Review* 108: 814–834.

Haidt, J. (2012) *The Righteous Mind: Why Good People are Divided by Politics and Religion.* Allen Lane, London.

Hansard, 1 August 1972 quoted in Saville, Hoyt and Toohey (2010) Report of the Bloody Sunday Inquiry. *The National Archives* (Accessed 1 November 2012).

Harber, C. (2004) *Schooling as Violence.* RoutledgeFalmer, London.

Hart, J. (2011) Young people and conflict: The implications for education. In *Education and Reconciliation: Exploring Conflict and Post-Conflict Situations*, Paulson, J. (ed). Continuum Books, London, New York, Doha, Delhi and Sydney, pp. 11–31.

Hart, J., Shaver, P. R., and Goldenberg, J. L. (2005). Attachment, self-esteem, worldviews, and terror management: Evidence for a tripartite security system. *Journal of Personality and Social Psychology* 88: 999–1013.

Haslam, N. (2011) Genetic essentialism, neuroessentialism, and stigma: Commentary on Dar-Nimrod and Heine. *Psychological Bulletin* 137(5): 819–824.

Hassin, R. R., Uleman, J. S. and Bargh, J. A. (2005) (eds.) *The New Unconscious.* Oxford University Press, Oxford.

Hatzfeld, J. (2000) *Into the Quick of Life: The RWANDAN genocide, the Survivors Speak.* Farrar, Straus et Giroux, Paris. 2000 trs. L. Coverdale (2005) Serpent's Tail, London.

Hatzfeld, J. (2003) *A Time for Machetes: The Rwandan Genocide The Killers Speak.* Editions du Seul, Paris. 2003 trs. L. Coverdale (2005) Serpent's Tail, London.

Hatzfeld, J. (2007) *The Strategy of Antelopes: Rwanda after the Genocide.* Farrar, Straus et Giroux, Paris. English trs. (2009) G. Feehily, Serpent's Tail, London.

Henrich, J., Heine, S. J. and Norenzayan, A. (2010) The weirdest people in the world? *Behavioural and Brain Sciences* 33: 61–135.

Henriksen, C. A., Bolton, J. M., and Sareen, J. (2010) The psychological impact of terrorist attacks: Examining a dose-response relationship between exposure to 9/11 and Axis I mental disorders. *Depression and Anxiety* 27(11): 993–1000.

Heuler, H. (2013) Josef Kony's Bodyguard Killed in Car. *Voice of America.* January 21st. http://www.voanews.com/content/joseph-konys-bodyguard-killed-in-car/1587885.html (Accessed 12th February 2013).

Home Affairs Committee (2012) *Roots of Violent Radicalisation—Nineteenth Report of Proceedings of the Home Affairs Committee.* UK Government, London.

Horgan, J. (2003) The search for the terrorist personality. In *Terrorists, Victims and Society,* Silke, A. (ed.). John Wiley & Sons, West Sussex.

Howard, R. (2003) The media's role in war and peacebuilding. Report on Conference 'The Role of the Media in Public Scrutiny and Democratic Oversight of the Security Sector', Budapest. Working Group on Civil Society Centre, Geneva, Switzerland. Available at http://ics-www.leeds.ac.uk/papers/pmt/exhibits/2360/Howard.pdf (Accessed 5th January 2013).

Hughes, J. (2011) Are separate schools divisive? A case study from Northern Ireland. *British Educational Research Journal* 37(5): 829–850.

Human Rights Watch (2006) The Rwandan Genocide: How It Was Prepared. Briefing Paper, Human Rights Watch, http://matteodominioni.it/md/documenti_ruanda_files/rwanda0406.pdf (Accessed 15th November 2012).

Hunter, R. S., Kilstrom, N., Kraybill, E. N. & Loda, F. (1978) Antecedents of chid abuse and neglect in premature infants: A prospective study in a newborn intensive care unit. *Pediatrics,* 1, 197–2003.

International Committee of the Red Cross (ICRC) (2007) Report on the Treatment of Fourteen 'High Value' Detainees in CIA Custody. ICRC, Geneva.

International Work Group on Death, Dying and Bereavement (IWG) (1997–1998b.) Document on Violence and Grief. Violence and Grief Work Group (Chair Stevenson, R. G.). *Omega* 36(3): 259–272.

IWG (2005) Breaking cycles of violence. *Death Studies* 29(7): 585–600.

IWG (2011) Can individuals who are specialists in death, dying, and bereavement contribute to the prevention and/or mitigation of armed conflicts and cycles of violence? *Death Studies* 35(5): 455–466.

IWG (2013) Armed conflict: A model for understanding and intervention. *Death Studies* 37(1): 61–88. DOI:10.1080/07481187.2012.655647.

Jackson, H. (1884) Evolution and dissolution of the nervous system. Croonian lectures delivered at the Royal College of Physicians, March 1884. *Lancet* i: 739–744.

Jackson, H. (1887) Remarks on evolution and dissolution of the nervous system. *Journal of Mental Science* 23: 25–48.

James, D. V., Mullen, P. E., Meloy, J. R., Pathé, M. T., Farnham, F. R., Preston, L., Darnley, B. (2007) The role of mental disorders in attacks on European politicians 1990–2004. *Acta Psychiatr Scand* 116(5): 334–344.

Jensen, S. G., Neugebauer, R., Marner, T., George, S., Ndahiro, L., and Rurangwa, E. (1997) *The Rwandan Children and their Families: Understanding, Prevention and Healing of Traumatization: An Evaluation of the Government of Rwanda and UNICEF Trauma Recovery Program (1995–1997)*. The European University Center for Mental Health and Human Rights, Copenhagen & New York.

Jones, B. (2011) Understanding responses to postwar education reform in the multiethnic district of Brcko, Bosnia-Herzegovina. In *Education and Reconciliation: Exploring Conflict and Post-Conflict Situations*, Paulson, J. (ed.). Oxford Studies in Comparative Education, Oxford University Press, Oxford. pp. 81–102.

Kahneman, D. (2010) *Thinking, Fast and Slow*. Allen Lane, London.

Kahneman, D., Slovic, P. and Tversky, A. (1982) (eds.) *Judgement under Uncertainty: Heuristics and Biases*. Cambridge University Press, Cambridge.

Kamukama, D. (1993, 2nd ed. 1997) *Rwanda Conflict: Its Roots and Regional Implications*. Kampala, Uganda.

Kapur, R. (2002) Omagh the beginning of the Reparative Impulse. Ch. 19 in *Terrorism and War*, Covington, C., Williams, P., Arundale, J., and Knox. J. (eds.) Karnac, London.

Kass, L. R. (2002) *Life, Liberty and the Defence of Dignity: The Challenge for Bioethics*. Encounter Books, New York.

Katan, M. (1960) Dream and psychosis. *International Journal of Psychoanalysis*, 41: 341–351.

Kellner, M. (1999) *Must a Jew Believe Anything*. The Littman Library of Jewish Civilization, London.

Kerr, A. (1996) *Cultures in Conflict*. Guildhall Press, Derry.

Khan, S. M. and Robinson, M. (2001) *The Shallow Graves of Rwanda*. I.B. Tauris.

Kinzer, S. (2008) *A Thousand Hills: Rwanda's Rebirth and the Man Who Dreamed It*. John Wiley & Sons, Hoboken, New Jersey.

Kirkpatrick, L. A. (1999) Attachment and religious representations and behavior. Ch. 35 in *Handbook of Attachment: Theory, Research and Clinical Applications*, Cassidy, J. and Shaver, P. R. (eds.) Guilford, New York and London, pp. 803–822.

Kirkpatrick, L. A. and Shaver, P. R. (1990) Attachment theory and religion: Childhood attachments, religious beliefs and conversion. *Journal for the Scientific Study of Religions*, 29: 305–334.

Kruglanski, A. W. and Fishman, S. (2006) Terrorism between "syndrome" and "tool". *Current Directions in Psychological Science*, 15(1): 45–48.

Lehrer, J. (2009) *The Decisive Moment: How the Brain makes up its Mind*. Canongate Books, Edinburgh.

Lewin, D. (2011) Keeping Britain Safe: An Assessment of UK Homeland Security Strategy. All-Party Parliamentary Group on Homeland Security— http://www.henryjacksonsociety.org/cms/harriercollectionitems/APPG.pdf (Accessed 26th January 2013).

Lifton, R. J. (2003) *Superpower Syndrome: America's Apocalyptic Confrontation with the World*. Nation Books, New York.

Liotti, G. (1991) Insecure attachment and agoraphobia. In *Attachment Across the Life Cycle*. (eds.). C. M. Parkes, J. Stevenson-Hinde & P. Marris. Routledge, London & New York.

Little, G. (2009) Political therapy: An encounter with Dr John Alderdice, psychotherapist, political leader and peer of the realm. *International Journal of Applied Psychoanalytic Studies*. 6(2) 129–145.

Longman, T. (2010) Reevaluating Gacaca Courts in Post-Genocide Reconciliation. *Harvard Law Review*, August 1, p. 3.

Lorenz, K. (1966) *On Aggression*. Methuen, London.

Luscombe, B. (2011) Rwanda: 10 Questions for Paul Kagame. 6th January. VirungaNews. com http://www.time.com/time/magazine/article/0,9171,2072601,00.html

Lyons, H. A. and Harbinson, H. J. (1986) A comparison of political and non-political murderers in Northern Ireland, 1974–1984. *Medicine, Science and the Law*, 26, 193–197.

MacCulloch, D. (2009) *A History of Christianity*. London: Allen Lane.

Mamdani, M. (2001) *When Victims Become Killers: Colonialism, Nativism, and the Genocide in Rwanda*. Princeton University Press, Princeton, NJ.

Management Systems International (MSI) (2008) *Are Schools Safe Havens for Children? Examining School-Related Gender-Based Violence*. USAID, Washington, DC.

Mandel, D. R. (2005) Are risk assessments of a terrorist attack coherent? *Journal of Experimental Psychology: Applied* 11: 277–288.

Mandela, N. (1994) *The Long Walk to Freedom*. Abacus, London.

Marris, P. (1974) *Loss and Change*. Routledge and Kegan Paul, London.

McDoom, O. S. (2011) The Psychology of Security Threats in Ethnic Warfare: Evidence from Rwanda's Genocide. Political Science and Economy Working Paper. Department of Government, London School of Economics, London.

McKittrick, D. and McVea, D. (2001) *Making Sense of the Troubles*. Penguin Books, London

Melaugh, M. (2012) 'Bloody Sunday', Derry 30 January 1972—Circumstances in Which People were Killed. Conflict Archive on the Internet (CAIN) http://cain.ulst.ac.uk/events/bsunday/circum.htm (Accessed 1st November 2012).

Melnik, T. A., Baker, P. H., Adams, M. L., O'Dowd, K., Mokdad, A. H., Brown, D. W., Murphy, W., Giles, W. H., and Bales, V. S. (2002) Psychological and Emotional Effects of the September 11 Attacks on the World Trade Center—Connecticut, New Jersey, and New York, 2001. *Morbidity and Mortality Weekly Report,* Centers for Disease Control and Prevention Atlanta, GA.

Melvern, L. (2004) *Conspiracy to Murder: Rwanda Genocide*. Hbk Verso, Pbk, ISBN 1-84467-542-544.

Merari, A. (2010) *Driven to Death: Psychological and Social Aspects of Suicidal Terrorism*. Oxford University Press, Oxford

Milton, J. (1645) *Areopagitica*. MacMillan and Co. Limited, London 1915.

Mitchell, G. J. (1999) *Making Peace*. London: William Heinemann.

Miyamoto, Y. and Kitayama, S. (2002) Cultural variation in correspondence bias: The critical role in attitude diagnosticity of socially constrained behaviour. *Journal of Personality and Social Psychology* 83: 1239–1248.

Moghaddam (2007) The staircase to terrorism: A psychological exploration. Ch. 5 in *Psychology of Terrorism*, B. Bongar, L. M. Brown, L. E. Beutler, J. N. Breckenridge and P. G. Zimbardo (eds.) Oxford University Press.

Moore, H. (1994) The problem of explaining violence in the social sciences. In *Sex and Violence: Issues in Representation and Experience*, P. Harvey and P. Gow (eds). London: Routledge.

Morris, S. (2012) Newspaper report of Scott Anthony's discovery of documents drawn up by British Intelligence in 1942. *Guardian* 4th May.

Moscovici, S. (1976). *La psychanalyse son image et son public*. Presses Universitaires de France, Paris, 175. National Institute for Clinical Excellence (NICE) (2005) Post-Traumatic Stress Disorder: The management of PTSD in adults and children in primary and secondary care. Clinical Guideline 26, www.nice.org.uk, 3rd March 2005.

Nemeroff, C. and Rozin, P. (1992) Sympathetic magical beliefs and kosher dietary practices: The interaction of rules and feelings. *Ethos*, 20: 96–115.

Neusner, J. and Chilton, B. (2008) *The Golden Rule: The Ethics of Reciprocity in World Religions*. Continuum International Publishing Group, London.

Nijdam, M. J., Olff, M., de Vries, M., Martens, W. J. and Gersons, B. P. R. (2008) *Psychosocial Effects of Threat and Protection*. National Coordinator for Counterterrorism, The Hague, Netherlands, www.english.nctb.nl/

Nijdam, M. J., Olff, M. and Gersons, B. P. R. (2010) Dutch politicians' coping with terrorist threat. *British Journal of Psychiatry* 197(4): 328–329.

Norenzayan, A., Choi, I. and Nisbett, R. E. (2002) Cultural similarities and differences in social inference: Evidence from behavioural predictions and lay theories of behaviour. *Personality and Social Psychology Bulletin*, 28(1): 109–120.

Norenzayan, A. and Heine, S. J. (2005) Psychological universals: What are they and how can we know? *Psychological Bulletin*, 131: 763–784.

Norwegian Refugee Council (2005) Ensuring Durable Solutions for Rwanda's Displaced People: A Chapter Closed Too Early. Global IDP Project. www.idpproject.org 8th July.

Novelli, M. and Smith, A. (2011) The Role of Education for Peacebuilding: A Synthesis of Findings from Lebanon, Sierra Leone and Nepal. UNICEF, New York. http://www.educationandtransition.org/wp-content/uploads/2012/01/EEPCT_Peacebuilding SynthesisReport.pdf (Accessed 5th March 2012).

Olff, M., Langeland, W. and Gersons, B. P. R. (2005), Effects of appraisal and coping on the neuroendocrine response to extreme stress. *Neuroscience and Biobehavioral Reviews* 29(3): 457–467.

Omagh Support and Self-Help Group (OSSHG) (1998) http://www.omaghbomb.co.uk/index.html—Support & Self Help Group (OSSHG) home page (Accessed 26th September 2013).

Organisation of African Unity (OAU) (2006) Report on the Rwandan Genocide, para ES 26.

Owen, D. (2012) *The Hubris Syndrome*. Methuen & Co, York, UK.

Park, M. (2011) Small Choices, Saved Lives: Near Misses of 9/11. CNN U.S. 9.03.2011. Available online at: <http://artcles/cnn.com/2011-09-03/us/near.death.decisions>.

Parkes, C. M. (1998) Bereavement: Understanding grief across cultures. *Psychiatry in Practice* 17(4): 5–8.

Parkes, C. M. (2006) *Love and Loss: The Roots of Grief and its Complications*. Routledge, London & New York.

Parkes, C. M. & Prigerson, H. G. (2010) *Bereavement: Studies of Grief in Adult Life*. 4th edition. Routledge, London & New York.

Parkes, C. M., Stevenson-Hinde, J., and Marris, P. (1997) *Death and Bereavement across Cultures*. Routledge, London and New York, pp. 216–233.

Parkes, J. (2007) The multiple meanings of violence: Children's talk about life in a South African neighbourhood. *Childhood* 14(4): 401–414.

Parkes, J. and Conolly, A. (2011) Risky positions? Shifting representations of urban youth in the talk of professionals and young people. *Children's Geographies* 9(3–4): 411–423.

Parkes, J. and Conolly, A. (2013) 'Dangerous Encounters? "Boys" peer dynamics and neighbourhood risk.' *Discourse: Studies in the Cultural Politics of Education* 34(1), 94–106.

Parkes, J. and Heslop, J. (2011) *Stop Violence against Girls in School: A Cross-Country Analysis of Baseline Research from Ghana, Kenya and Mozambique*. Cross-Country Review, Action Aid International. Kenya and London.

Paulson, J. (2011) Reconciliation through educational reform? Recommendations and realities in Peru. In *Education and Reconciliation: Exploring Conflict and Post-Conflict Situations*, Paulson, J. (ed.). Continuum, London & New York. pp. 126–150.

Paxman, J. (2002) *The Political Animal*. Penguin Books, London.

Pearse, P. (1915) Speech at the graveside of O'Donovan Rossa. Script in Pearse Museum. Dublin, Ireland.

Perry, M. (2010) *Talking to Terrorists*. Basic Books, New York.

Peterson, S. (2001). *Me against My Brother: At War in Somalia, Sudan and Rwanda*. Routledge, London & New York.

Pfefferbaum, B., Call, J. A., Lewegraf, S. J. et al. (2001) Traumatic grief in a convenience sample of victims seeking support services after a terrorist incident. *Annals of Clinical Psychiatry* 13: 19–24.

Physicians for Human Rights (1994) *Rwanda: A Report of the Genocide*. Physicians for Human Rights, University Department of Forensic Medicine, Dundee, DD1 9ND.

Pinker, S. (2011) *The Better Angels of Our Nature: The Decline of Violence in History and its Causes*. London: Penguin Books, p. 369.

Police Service of Northern Ireland (2012) Security Statistics 1968–2011. http://www.psni.police.uk/deaths_cy.pdf (Accessed 18th December 2012).

Power, M. and Dalgleish, T. (1997) *Cognition and Emotion: From Order to Disorder*. Psychology Press, Hove.

Rachman, S. (2006) *Fear of Contamination: Assessment and Treatment*. Oxford University Press, Oxford.

Rashid, A. (2001) *Taliban: The Story of Afghan Warlords*. Pan MacMillan, Basingstoke & Oxford.

Rassin, E. (2005) *Thought Suppression*. Elsevier Ltd., Oxford.

Read, P. (1996) *Returning to Nothing. The Meaning of Lost Places*. Cambridge University Press, Cambridge and Melbourne.

246

Robinson, A. (2001) *Bin Laden—Behind the Mask of the Terrorist*. Mainstream Publishing, Edinburgh.

Rogers, M. B., Loewenthal, K. M., Lewis, C. A., Amlot, R., Cinnirella, M. and Ansari, H. (2007). The role of religious fundamentalism in terrorist violence: A social psychological analysis. *International Review of Psychiatry* 19(3): 253–262.

Rojas Arangoitia, V. (2011) 'I'd Rather be Hit with a Stick … Grades are Sacred': Students' Perceptions of Discipline and Authority in a Public High School in Peru. Working paper 70, Young Lives, Oxford.

Rothfuss, J. (1997) *'Willie Doherty', No Place (Like Home,)*, exhibition catalogue, Walker Art Center, Minneapolis, p. 42. Online available http://www.tate.org.uk/art/artworks/doherty-remote-control-p78747/text-summary (Accessed 1st November 2012).

Rothschild, M. L. (2001) Terrorism and you: The real odds. *AEI Brookings Joint Center: Policy Matters* 1(31): 1–2.

Rowan, B. (2008) *How the Peace Was Won*. Gill & Macmillan, Dublin.

Ruane, J. and Todd, J. (1996) *The Dynamics of Conflict in Northern Ireland*. Cambridge University Press, Cambridge.

Rucker, P. M. (2002). *This Troubled Land*. Ballantine Books, New York.

Sadler, M. S., Lineberger, M., Correll, J. and Park, B. (2005) Emotions, attributions, and policy endorsement in response to the September 11th terrorist attacks. *Basic and Applied Social Psychology* 27(3): 249–258.

Sageman, M. (2004) *Understanding Terror Networks*. University of Pennsylvania Press, Philadelphia.

Sageman, M. (2005) Global Salafi Jihad: Empirical assessment and social network analysis (*Conference Presentation to the World Federation of Scientists Permanent Monitoring Panel on Terrorism*, Erice, Sicily).

Salkovskis, P. M. (1996) Cognitive-behavioural approaches to the understanding of obsessional problems. In *Current Controversies in the Anxiety Disorders*, Rapee, R. M. (ed.). New York: Guilford Press.

Saville, The Lord, Hoyt, W. and Toohey, J. (2010) Report of the Bloody Sunday Inquiry. The National Archives. http://webarchive.nationalarchives.gov.uk/20101103103930/http://report.bloody-sunday-inquiry.org/ (Accessed 20th October 2012).

Schaal, S., Dusingizemungu, J.-P., Jacob, N., Neuner, F. and Elbert, T. (2012) Association between prolonged grief disorder, depression, post-traumatic stress disorder and anxiety in rwandan genocide survivors. *Death Studies* 36(2): 97–117.

Schofield, H. (2012) Rwanda Genocide: Kagame Cleared of Habyarimana Crash. *BBC News*, 10th January. http://www.bbc.co.uk/news/world-africa-16472013 (Accessed 7th September 2012).

Sebba, J. and Robinson, C. (2010) Evaluation of UNICEF UK's Rights Respecting Schools Award. Universities of Sussex and Brighton. http://www.unicef.org.uk/Education/Impact-Evidence/External-evaluation/ (Accessed 5th March 2012)

Sen, A. (2006a) *Identity and Violence—The Illusion of Destiny*. Allen Lane, London.

Sen, A. (2006b) Reflecting on resistance: Hindu women 'soldiers' and the birth of female militancy. *Indian Journal of Gender Studies* 13(1): 1–36.

Shear, M. K., Frank, E., Houck, P. R., and Reynolds, C. F. (2005) Treatment of complicated grief: A randomized controlled trial. *Journal of the American Medical Association* 293(21): 2601–2607.

Shear, K. M., Jackson, C. T., Essock, S. M., Donahue, S. A. and Felton, C. J. (2006) Screening for complicated grief among project liberty service recipients 18 months after

247

September 11, 2001 *Psychiatric Services* 57: 1291–1297, September 2006 doi: 10.1176/appi.ps.57.9.1291.

Silke, A. (1998) Cheshire-cat logic: The recurring theme of terrorist abnormality in psychological research. *Psychology, Crime and Law* 4: 51–69.

Simcox, R., Stuart, H. and Ahmed, H. (2010) *Islamist Terrorism: The British Connections.* Centre for Social Cohesion, Henry Jackson Society, London.

Sloman, S. A. (2002) Two systems of reasoning. In *Heuristics and Biases: The Psychology of Intuitive Judgement*, Gilovich, T., Griffin, D. and Kahneman, D. (eds.) Cambridge University Press, Cambridge, pp. 379–380.

Slone, D. J. (2007) *Theological Incorrectness: Why Religious People Believe What They Shouldn't.* Oxford University Press, Oxford.

Smith, V. (2008) *Clean: A History of Personal Hygiene and Purity.* Oxford University Press, Oxford.

Snyder, T. (2011) *Bloodlands: Europe between Hitler and Stalin.* Vintage Books, London.

Solomon, N. (2012) *Torah from Heaven: The Reconstruction of Faith.* The Littman Library of Jewish Civilisation, London, p. 13.

Sroufe, L. A. (2005) Attachment and development: A prospective, longitudinal study from birth to adulthood. *Attachment and Human Development* 7(4): 349–368.

Staub, E., Pearlman, L. A., Gubin, A. and Hagengimana, A. (2005). Healing, reconciliation, forgiving and the prevention of violence after genocide or mass killing: An intervention and its experimental evaluation in Rwanda. *Journal of Social and Clinical Psychology* 24(3): 297–334.

Stein, R. (2003) Evil as love and as liberation: The mind of a suicidal terrorist. Ch. 11 in *Hating in the First Person Plural: Psychoanalytic Perspectives on Racism, Sexism, Homophobia, and Terror* (Hardcover), Donald Moss (ed.). The Other Press, New York.

Stein, R. (2010) *For Love of the Father: A Psychoanalytic Study of Religious Terrorism.* Stanford University Press, Stanford, California.

Stern, J. (2003) *Terror in the Name of God: Why Religious Militants Kill.* Harper Collins Publishers, New York.

Stroebe, M., van Vliet, T., Hewstone, M., and Willis, H. (2002) Homesickness among students in two cultures: Antecedents and consequences. *British Journal of Psychology* 93(2): 147–168.

Sultan, W. (2010) Interview. Hudson, New York. May 19th.

Sunstein, C. R. (2005) Moral heuristics. *Behavioural and Brain Sciences* 28: 531–573.

Symonds, M. (1980) Victim responses to terror. *Annals of the New York Academy of Science* 347: 129–136.

Taft, C. T., Schumm, J. A., Marshall, A. D., Panuzio, J., and Holtzworth-Munroe, A. (2008) Family-of-origin maltreatment, posttraumatic stress disorder symptoms, social information processing deficits, and relationship abuse perpetration. *Journal of Abnormal Psychology* 117: 637–646.

Tallis, R. (2011) *Aping Mankind: Neuromania, Darwinitis and the Misrepresentation of Humanity.* Acumen Publishing, Durham.

Tamimi, A. S. (2001) *Rachid Ghannouchi: A Democrat within Islamism.* Oxford University Press, Oxford.

Teasdale, D. and Barnard, P. J. (1993) *Affect Cognition and Change: Re-modelling Depressive Thought.* Lawrence Erlbaum Associates, Hove.

Tedeschi, R. G. and Calhoun, L. G. (2004) Posttraumatic growth: Conceptual foundations and empirical evidence. *Psychological Inquiry,* 15(1): 1–18.

Tetlock, P. E. (2002) Theory-driven reasoning about plausible pasts and probable futures in world politics. In *Heuristics and Biases: The Psychology of Intuitive Judgement*, Gilovich, T., Griffin, D. and Kahneman, D. (eds). Cambridge University Press, Cambridge, pp. 752–753.

Thompson, A. (2007) The responsibility to report: A new journalistic paradigm. Ch. 35 in *The Media and the Rwanda Genocide*, Alan Thompson (ed.). Pluto, London and Fountain, Kampala.

Thorne, J. and Stuart, H. (2008) *Islam on Campus: A Survey of UK Student Opinions*. The Centre for Social Cohesion. London.

Todorov, A. and Bargh, J. A. (2002) Automatic sources of aggression. *Aggression and Violent Behaviour* 7: 53–68.

Trakakis, N. (2008) Theodicy: The solution to the problem of evil, or part of the problem? *Sophia*, 47: 161–192.

Trull, T. J., Tragesser, S. L., Solhan, M. and Schwartz-Mette, R. (2007) Dimensional models of personality disorder: Diagnostic and statistical manual of mental disorders, 5th edn. and beyond. *Current Opinion in Psychiatry* 20(1): 52–56.

Tversky, A. and Koehler, D. J. (1994) Support theory: A nonextensional representation of subjective probability. *Psychological Review* 101: 547–567.

United Nations Children's Fund (UNICEF) (1995) Children of Rwanda. A UNICEF Update on Children in Especially Difficult Circumstances—Report #1. 21 February.

United Nations Children's Fund (UNICEF) (1997) Report on Trauma Recovery Program in Rwanda. UNICEFTRP 94–96.pdf.

United Nations Educational Social and Cultural Organisation (UNESCO) (2011) Education for All Global Monitoring Report: The Hidden Crisis: Armed Conflict and Education. UNESCO, Paris.

United Nations Organisation (1999) Report of the Independent Inquiry into the Actions of the United Nations during the 1994 Genocide in Rwanda. S/1999/1257. United Nations Organisation, New York.

Vanderwerker, L. C., Jacobs, S. C., Parkes, C. M. and Prigerson, H. G. (2006) An exploration of associations between separation anxiety in childhood and complicated grief in later life. *Journal of Nervous and Mental Disease* 194(2): 121–123.

Volkan, V. D. (1979) *Cyprus—War and Adaptation*. University Press of Virginia, Charlottesville.

Volkan, V. D. (2004) *Blind Trust*. Pitchstone Press, Charlottesville, Virginia.

Volkan, V. D. (2006) *Killing in the Name of Identity*. Pitchstone Publishing, Virginia.

Volkan, V. D. (2013) *Enemies on the Couch*. Pitchstone Publishing, Durham, North Carolina (in press).

Volkan, V. D. and Itzkowitz, N. (1984) *The Immortal Ataturk: A Psychobiography*. University of Chicago Press, Chicago.

Wagner, W., Duveen, G., Verma, J. and Themel, M. (2000). 'I have some faith and at the same time I don't believe in it'—Cognitive polyphasia and culture change. *Journal of Community and Applied Social Psychology* 10: 301–314.

Wallsten, T. S. (1981) Physician and medical student bias in evaluating clinical information. *Medical Decision Making* 1: 145–164.

Walsh, D. (2012) Bias Conflict Archive on the Internet (CAIN). http://cain.ulst.ac.uk/events/bsunday/walsh3.htm#bias (Accessed March 2012).

Walsh, S. D. and Tartakovsky, E. (2012) The mother and motherland: Their internal representations among immigrant and non-immigrant adolescents. *Attachment and Human Development* 14(2): 185–204.

249

Weber, M. (1946) Science as a vocation. In *Essays in Sociology*. Oxford University Press, Oxford and New York.

Wegner, D. M. (1989) *White Bears and Other Unwanted thoughts: Suppression, Obsessions and the Psychology of Mental Control*. Viking, New York.

Whyte, J. (1991) *Interpreting Northern Ireland*. Clarendon Press, Oxford.

Widgery, The Lord (1972) Report of the Tribunal Appointed to Inquire into The events on Sunday, 30th January, 1972 which Led to Loss of Life in Connection with the Procession in Londonderry on that Day. HI 101 & HC 220. HMSO and CAIN web service. http://cain.ulst.ac.uk/hmso/widgery.htm (Accessed 25th February 2013).

Widom, C. S. (1989) Child abuse, neglect and violent criminal behaviour. *Criminology* 27, 251–271.

Williams, J. M. G., Watts, F. N., MacLeod, C. and Matthews, A. (1997) *Cognitive Psychology and Emotional Disorders*. John Wiley & Sons, Chichester.

Woods, J. (2011) Framing terror: An experimental framing effects study of the perceived threat of terrorism. *Critical Studies on Terrorism* 4(2): 199–217.

Woolf, H. K. (2011) The Woolf Inquiry: An Inquiry into the London School of 'Economics' links with Libya and Lessons to be Learned. Council of the LSE. http://www.woolflse.com/dl/woolf-lse-report.pdf (Accessed 1st June 2013).

Wright, L. (2006) *The Looming Tower: Al-Qaeda and the Road to 9/11*. Knopf, New York.

Yuksel, S. and Olgun-Özpolot, T. (2004) Psychological problems associated with traumatic loss in Turkey. *Bereavement Care* 23(1): 5–7.

INDEX

11th September 2001 (9/11) 53; influence of media 85; mood and responses 35, 87, 96; perceptions 35, 85; policy recommendations 35–6; reactions 35, 89; studies 169; terrorists 10, 17

abuse 102, 208, 228; in childhood 16; of power 80, 115–6; punishment for 228; reduction in prevalence 225; of 'sacred' causes 45; of suspects 58, 61, of self 106; *see also* human rights
acceptance 27, 191 challenging 142; of recovery 223
accountability 40–1, 140; *see also* law, punishment
actors: devoted 178, 233–4; rational 178, 233
adolescents and young adults 12; and insecure attachments 80; attachment to leaders 17, 164; attachment to peers 17, 164; recruitment 12, 17; in Rwanda; 71–2; violent crime 137; *see also* gender differences, interahamwe
affect *see* emotion
affiliation 12
Afghanistan 95, 97–9, 138, 155, 170
aggression 19, 32, 54; feeding 81; group myths and 81, and hunting 128; imitative 16, 54; macho 137; perception of 138; priming for 33; social pressures 22 and survival 88; *see also* anger, conflict, submission
agoraphobia 20–1
AIDS 216
Ainsworth, M. 11, 14, 19, 236
akazu 69–70, 120–1, 123; *see also* MRND
alcohol/alcoholism *see* drugs
Alderdice, J.T. ix, xiii, 4–5, 17, 42–55, 73, 106, 113, 128–9, 151, 164–180, 191, 193–6, 199, 201, 207, 233, 235–6

Alliance Party of Northern Ireland (NI) 166; 178–9
Al-Qaeda 10, 51; recruitment from British universities 144–5, 148; and WMDs 8
ambivalence 12–14, 51, 168; *see also* Oedipus complex
Amnesty International 69, 73, 225, 236
anger 19, cycles of 90; and grief 90, 92, 214; displaced 20; evolution of 88; management 216; neural pathways 88; in Northern Ireland 50; primary emotion 34–5; response to intervention 25; in Rwanda 88; *see also* aggression, appraisal
anxiety 25; and attachment 17; defences against 48; disorders 43, 89, 198, 205, 216; globalisation and 51; influence of learning 80; manipulation by media 85; influence on perception 85; *see also* fear, separation anxiety
anxious ambivalence; see clinging
apocalypse: danger of 10, 15; myth of 82–3; *see also* weapons of mass destruction
appraisal 34, 232; automatic 35; propositions 35; schematic 35
Arab 51; Awakening 171; royal families 52
armaments 72, 99, 124; force of 232
armed forcers, *see* military
Arusha Peace Accords 71, 73, 118
assassinations 4; of Archduke Ferdinand 84; of politicians 181
Association des Etudiants Et Éleves Rescapés Du Genocide, (AEERG) 216–7
Association for Widows of the Rwandan Genocide (AVEGA) 217
assumptive world 231–3 changing 26–7, 35, 90, 166–7, 232 core assumptions 26

251

narratives 176; mass 58, modern 85; obstacle to 97; prerequisites for 27, social under threat 90; through action 175
communism: in universities 145
community xiii; commitment to change 140; division of 63; international 122; leaders 165, 168; loss of 21; religious 27; regression 48; response to terrorist attacks 53; 60; target 42; terrorist's view of 44; violent 135
compromise: openness to 168, 206
conflict: in adolescents 80; asymmetrical 24, 42; ethnic, 24–5; family 26; marital 26; resolution 141, 194; taking sides 154; territorial (in non-humans 19), territorial (in human beings 19); *see also* Northern Ireland, Rwanda, splitting
consciousness 29, 40; terrorist's dissolution of the field of 47; *see also* automatic processing
conservatives *see* moral foundation theory
conspiracy 51, 148
containment: need for 55; *see also* boundary: setting
contamination 35–6; *see also* disgust, ethnic cleansing, purification
contempt 34–6, 119; *see also* disgust, denigration
control 12; assertive/aggressive 16; boundary 18; central 69; cortical 88; dissolution of 47; governmental 68; impulse outside conscious 40, 87; self- 13; the uncontrollable 39; of WMDs 83; *see also* freedom
conversion: to terrorism 46
coping strategies 5, 12–13 moral imperatives 13, with traumatic memories 216; with violence 204, 207
counselling 234–5; bereavement 215; rejection of 163, 198; trauma 215
counter-terrorism: 230; protection of leaders 181–9
courts: gacaca 222–3; *see also* International Criminal Tribunal for Rwanda
criminality 42, 44–5, 52
Cronin, A.K. 1, 27, 87, 97–8, 169, 170, 239
cruelty 67, 219; desensitisation to 131
cults 12, 25
cultural: boundaries 54; differences 23–4; identity 13; *see also* rules
cultures: 54; Asian v. USA 41; state-centred 24, theocentric 24, family-centred 24; *see also* attachments

cyber-security 44
cycles of violence 3, 4, 83; after terrorist attack 83–100, 231; breaking the cycle in NI 191–207; breaking the cycle in Rwanda 209–226; *see also* violence

deaths counts 163, 203, 226; denial 10, responses to 84–5; by terrorism 58; threats 181; witnessed 163; *see also* bereavement, grief
decommissioning 5, 176–7, 194 of mind-sets 194, 233
defence: against anxiety 48; against modernity 54; inhumanity 53; self-defence 72; *see also* identification with the aggressor
dehumanisation 53, 128, 152
democracy 94–5, 135, 145, 150; challenges 146; culture of 171; interruptive 142; leading to authoritarian leadership 171; leading to intolerant, populist leadership 171; liberal 171; obstacles to 232; without violence (Mitchell Principle) 195
Democratic Republic of the Congo (DRC) 61, 131, 209, 226; *see also* Great War of Africa
Democratic Unionist Party (DUP) 62, 200–1
demonisation 152
denial 22, 53, 183, 204
denigration 10, 25, 65, 73, 142; of terrorists 142/6; by terrorists 96, 128; by use of word 'terrorist' 152
depolarisation, *see* polarisation
depression, major: after genocide 216; and homesickness 20; with long-term threat 204; in mothers of martyrs 81; in politicians under threat 188; response to therapies 206, 216; roots of 34–6; after terrorist attacks 89, 198, 205
destabilisation of state: by terrorist activity 170
detention without trial: in NI 58–60, 113, 190; in Rwanda 225, 236; demonstrations 60, 103; effect on recruitment of militants 60, effect on death rate 60; *see also* 'Free Derry', Bloody Sunday
detribalisation 220; and grief 99
Derry (or Londonderry) 58–66; 'Free Derry' 60; *see also* Bloody Sunday

identification 54; with the aggressor 16, 52; with cause 175; imitation 54; with role 175

immigrants: mental illness in 21; *see also* relocation, territory: homelands

impurity 36; attributions of 73; myths of 82, 231

independence: attachment avoidance 12; financial 222; *see also* avoidance, conflicts, territory

Independent Monitoring Commission (IMC) 176–7, 179–80, 201, 233; *see also* decommissioning

individuation 54

indoctrination of terrorists: 138; re-education 27; secret 17, 74

informers 165; *see also* security services

inhibition 12, relinquishing 128

injustice; see justice

insecurity 14, of both sides in conflict 231; clinging under stress 65–6, insecure countries 93, 190–2; insecure attachments 3; feeding 25; and oppression 17; reduction of 26; and repression of feelings 215; and resistance to change 71; sparking vigilantes 114; *see also* adolescence, attachment insecurity

Institute for Research and Dialogue for Peace (IRDP) Rwanda 215

intelligence: 150, 156–7; 'fire prevention' 146–7; in Netherlands 181–2; role of counter-terrorist police 147–8, 150; 161 problems of secrecy 157–8, 160–1; and torture 225; *see also* MI5, secrecy

Interahamwe (hutu militia) 70–1, 126; in DP camps 211; groups 126; immunity from prosecution 71; plan for insurrection 71, 74; recruitment to 12; spearhead and organise genocide 121, 123, 129, 131; sharing loot 125, rape 126

internal model of the world, 80; *see also* assumptive world

International Attachment Network 11

International Campaign to End Genocide 226

International Criminal Court 94, 228; for East Timor 227; for Rwanda 119, 222–3, 226

internet (The Web) 86; recruitment to terrorism 138; 'self-radicalisation' 125; threats to politicians 182; virtual community 44; *see also* Breivik

internment, *see* detention without trial

interrogation: 'abusive and degrading' 58, 157; *see also* torture

intervention 25–8; moral 55; traditional 25; *see also* prevention, postvention

intolerance 15, 94, 142; divisionism 221, 225; of intolerance 221; *see also* tolerance

Irish Free State, *see* Republic of Ireland

Irish Republican Army (IRA) 178–9; on Bloody Sunday 105; changing 'sacred' values 196; 'decrimilisation' of 155; recognition of failure of terrorism 53, 191; triggering recruitment into 59–60, 115–6; secret talks with 174; Stake-knife 157–8; 'tit-for-tat' conflict 190; war of words 112; *see also* assassination, ceasefires, decommissioning, McGuiness. Omagh bomb, Sinn Fein, stalemate

Islam 14, 52, 135; binary thinking 138; Islamophobia 35; on campus 147–9; reciprocity in 38; Shiite 51; Sunni 51; theocentric 24; *see also* deprivation, disrespect, fatwa, injustice, jihad, humiliation, Muslim

Islamism 51, 53–4, 144; Al Qaeda 145, 148; David Cameron on 150; group equivalent of psychosis 55; and terrorism 144–5; versus democracy 146; *see also* universities

Israel 52; homeland 23; punitive operations 49; 'rational self-interest' 49

Jew 13; anti-Semitism 34; *see also* Israel

jihad 45–6, 51; rewards 46

Joint Terrorism Analysis Centre (JTAC) UK 147

journalists: attachments 153; code of ethics 86, 161; coping with trauma 158; cost of involvement 155, 158–9; counselling dilemma 163; decoding disinformation 158, detachment 155; ethics 161; fear 162–3; labelling 156; roles 157; partiality (taking sides) 86, 154; 'permissible lies' 158, 160; pressures 152, 156, 161; respect 206; responsibilities 152, 154, 156; search for the hidden 157; protecting sources 160–1; talking to 'terrorists' 156; trust 161; value judgements 156; *see also* Bloody Sunday: perceptions of, no-go areas, news, Northern Ireland, Omagh bomb: perceptions, secrecy

81, 90, 98, 155; hardening 131,
mistakes 88, 90, 103, 107, 113;
over-reaction 61, 71–2; response to
attack 88, 116; yellow card 102; *see
also* assassination, Bloody Sunday,
heroes, insurrection, massacres,
military, overkill
South Africa 52; recovery 54
Soviet Union: collapse of 51
support to leaders; by civil servants 172,
security awareness 172, by
psychological services 181–9;
psychological consequences 181;
protection 172–3, 182; safety measures
182–3; *see also* legitimising authorities,
protection
splitting 48–50, 128; assumptive world 26;
good and bad 48–9, 128; and
internecine violence 167
stalemate 103, opportunity for negotiation
165, in NI 191; in Rwanda 220
state 24; -centred 24; weak or failed 42,
171; *see also* societal breakdown
stress, *see* traumatic stress
submission 19–20, as objective 87; to
God's will 10, 13, 86
subwars; escalation of terrorism into 77;
successful 98
suicidal terrorists: conceal plan from
families 26; differences from non-
suicidal 16; impact on victims 42;
Kamikaze xi; as martyrs 26, 77, 81;
perception by terrorists of their history
46; perception by victims of 42–3;
personality of 16; religious
extremism 9
support: building trust 195; emotional 25,
195; for leaders 181–9, 195; for
terrorism 26; settings 25; *see also*
places: safe
suppression: of thoughts 39; *see also*
obsessive compulsive disorder
survival skills 129–30
symbols 23, 176

Tamil Tigers (Sri Lanka) 9, 171
territory 3, 19–25; changing 174;
homelands 3, 21, 223; partition 174;
sharing 174; *see also* homes
terror 42; 'terror management theory' 184;
see also post-traumatic growth

terrorist attacks: aims and outcome 87,
101–5; nature of 4, 105–7, 118;
perception of 85–6, 101, 107–10,
118–20; predisposing to cycle of
violence 83–5, 117; *see also* Omagh
bomb, responses to terrorism
terrorism: anarchist 170; context of 78–83;
definitions xi, 1–2, 24, 42, 152;
escalation 77, 113–5, 123–30; global
42; group identity as cause 42–58; how
it ends (outcomes) 27, 40, 169–70 (*see
also* leaders: decapitation of,
destabilisation, negotiation, repression,
success); with new narratives 176;
monitoring 177–8; perception of 'noble
cause' 138; and primary relationships
54; priming by word 'terrorism' 33,
152; roots of 3, 42–58, 145–6; religious
17; success 98; preconditions for 43–4,
73, 232; by state 42; staircase to 71;
support for 61, targets of 40;
transgenerational transmission of 46;
triangular tactic 42 understanding 43,
152 ; *see also* freedom fighters, mental
illness, responses to terrorism
terrorist: changing mind-sets 206 (*and see*
Omagh bomb); communities of 43;
comparison with other criminals 45;
context of 3, 167; conversion to 46;
'decriminalising' the 155; election to
government of former terrorists and
supporters 201; dissolution of field of
consciousness 47; family influences on
43; gender 43, groups 46; guilt suicide
162; 'higher cause' 42; holding leaders
to account 177; ideals 46; identification
(imitation) 47; immigrants 46;
informers 165; leadership 169, 200–2;
perception of being shamed or
humiliated 46, 49; psychiatric
symptoms in 43; protecting others 43;
punishment of 77; recruitment 59, 80,
144–50; regression 46–8; revenge 43;
Stake-knife 159; traumatic experiences
influencing 43, 158; virtual
communities of 44; war weariness 191;
see also leaders of attacked side, leaders
of terrorism, martyrs, myths, suicidal
terrorists, post-traumatic stress disorder
theocentric societies 24; *see also*
attachment to God, Islamism

warfare: 219; asymmetric 42, 95;
    psychological 99
warlords 95
weapons: of mass destruction (WMD) 10,
    33, 82–3, 95, 171; *see also* apocalypse
Widgery Inquiry 112–3
World Bank 218, 222, 228

World War I: 54, 68, 85, 170
World War II: 58, 171

Yellow Card 102–3
youth clubs: places/safe 25

Zulu Wars 98